DAVID HUME'S HUMANITY

RECOVERING POLITICAL PHILOSOPHY

SERIES EDITORS: THOMAS L. PANGLE AND TIMOTHY BURNS

PUBLISHED BY PALGRAVE MACMILLAN:

Lucretius as Theorist of Political Life
By John Colman

Shakespeare's Political Wisdom
By Timothy Burns

Political Philosophy Cross-Examined: Perennial Challenges to the Philosophic Life
Edited by Thomas L. Pangle and J. Harvey Lomax

Eros and Socratic Political Philosophy
By David Levy

Xenophon the Socratic Prince: The Argument of the Anabasis of Cyrus
By Eric Buzzetti

Reorientation: Leo Strauss in the 1930s
Edited by Martin D. Yaffe and Richard S. Ruderman

Sexuality and Globalization: An Introduction to a Phenomenology of Sexualities
By Laurent Bibard and translated by Christopher Edwards

Modern Democracy and the Theological-Political Problem in Spinoza, Rousseau, and Jefferson
By Lee Ward

Prudential Public Leadership: Promoting Ethics in Public Policy and Administration
By John Uhr

The Companion to Raymond Aron
Edited by José Colen and Elisabeth Dutartre-Michaut

Montesquieu's Political Economy
By Andrew Scott Bibby

David Hume's Humanity: The Philosophy of Common Life and Its Limits
By Scott Yenor

DAVID HUME'S HUMANITY

THE PHILOSOPHY OF COMMON LIFE AND ITS LIMITS

Scott Yenor

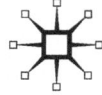

DAVID HUME'S HUMANITY
Copyright © Scott Yenor 2016
Softcover reprint of the hardcover 1st edition 2016 978-1-137-53958-8

All rights reserved. No reproduction, copy or transmission of this publication may be made without written permission. No portion of this publication may be reproduced, copied or transmitted save with written permission. In accordance with the provisions of the Copyright, Designs and Patents Act 1988, or under the terms of any licence permitting limited copying issued by the Copyright Licensing Agency, Saffron House, 6-10 Kirby Street, London EC1N 8TS.

Any person who does any unauthorized act in relation to this publication may be liable to criminal prosecution and civil claims for damages.

First published 2016 by
PALGRAVE MACMILLAN

The author has asserted their right to be identified as the author of this work in accordance with the Copyright, Designs and Patents Act 1988.

Palgrave Macmillan in the UK is an imprint of Macmillan Publishers Limited, registered in England, company number 785998, of Houndmills, Basingstoke, Hampshire, RG21 6XS.

Palgrave Macmillan in the US is a division of Nature America, Inc., One New York Plaza, Suite 4500, New York, NY 10004-1562.

Palgrave Macmillan is the global academic imprint of the above companies and has companies and representatives throughout the world.

ISBN 978-1-349-71193-2
E-PDF ISBN: 978–1–137–53959–5
DOI: 10.1057/9781137539595

Library of Congress Cataloging-in-Publication Data
Names: Yenor, Scott, 1970– author.
Title: David Hume's humanity : the philosophy of common life
   and its limits / by Scott Yenor.
Description: New York, NY : Palgrave Macmillan, 2016. | Series: Recovering
   political philosophy | Includes bibliographical references and index.
Identifiers: LCCN 2015030186 |
Subjects: LCSH: Hume, David, 1711–1776. | Virtues. | Skepticism. | Political
   science—Philosophy—History—18th century. | BISAC: PHILOSOPHY /
   Metaphysics. | PHILOSOPHY / Political. | POLITICAL SCIENCE / General. |
   POLITICAL SCIENCE / History & Theory.
Classification: LCC B1498 .Y46 2016 | DDC 192—dc23 LC record
   available at http://lccn.loc.gov/2015030186
A catalogue record for the book is available from the British Library.

I dedicate the book to Bruce and Jackie Yenor

CONTENTS

Series Editors' Foreword — ix
Preface and Acknowledgments — xi
List of Abbreviations — xv

1. David Hume's Philosophy of Common Life — 1
2. "Nothing but Sophistry and Illusion": Metaphysical Speculation before Hume — 13
3. Active Sovereignty in Natural and Moral Philosophy — 29
4. "Mitigated Scepticism" and Our "Mixed Kind of Life": The Philosophic Modesty of Hume's Science of Common Life — 51
5. The Liberal Imagination and the Problem of Abstract Speculative Principles in Politics — 75
6. Humanity and Commerce — 97
7. Religious Revolution and England's Humane Political Constitution — 123
8. Religious Belief and Hume's Philosophy of Common Life — 155
9. Humanity and Theology in Hume's Religious Dialogues — 175
10. Toward a More Philosophical Philosophy of Common Life — 199

Notes — 211
Index — 245

SERIES EDITORS' FOREWORD

Palgrave's *Recovering Political Philosophy* series was founded with an eye to postmodernism's challenge to the possibility of a rational foundation for and guidance of our political lives. This invigorating challenge has provoked a searching re-examination of classic texts, not only of political philosophers but also of poets, artists, theologians, scientists, and other thinkers who may not be regarded conventionally as political theorists. The series publishes studies that endeavor to take up this re-examination and thereby help to recover the classical grounding for civic reason, as well as studies that clarify the strengths and the weaknesses of modern philosophic rationalism. The interpretative studies in the series are particularly attentive to historical context and language, and to the ways in which both censorial persecution and didactic concerns have impelled prudent thinkers, in widely diverse cultural conditions, to employ manifold strategies of writing—strategies that allowed them to aim at different audiences with various degrees of openness to unconventional thinking. The series offers close readings of ancient, medieval, early modern and late modern works that illuminate the human condition by attempting to answer its deepest, enduring questions, and that have (in the modern periods) laid the foundations for contemporary political, social, and economic life.

Scott Yenor sets out to understand, critique, and rehabilitate David Hume's "philosophy of common life," which he understands to be part of the long-standing debate within modernity between the spirit of geometry and the spirit of finesse. Hume is famous for his critique—in the *Treatise of Human Nature* and the *Enquiry concerning Human Understanding*—of scientific concepts that earlier modern philosophers thought would help order our political life. Yenor attempts to connect that critique to Hume's broader philosophic vision, and to show that while Hume was an Enlightenment thinker, he is most suited to our postmodern age: He "knew of the postmodern temptation" against science, Yenor argues, "but thought that human beings have the resources to resist it." Yenor accordingly begins with Hume's case that we are unable to explain why one thing causes another, but then shows that Hume builds his humane political philosophy on the assumption that in our political life we can bypass tension-laden, irresolvable ontological, metaphysical, and philosophic disputes by means of a "philosophy of common life." Hume himself offered criteria by which reliable "natural assumptions" of common life—assumptions he presented as permanent, irresistible, and universal—can be distinguished from flights of fancy. Following these assumptions, he endorsed the political, economic, and social arrangements that we today associate with enlightenment modernity—commerce, free trade, progress in the arts. Yenor shows that Hume saw these as essential to the erosion of superstition and religious enthusiasm, and therefore as the key means for the removal of the cultural governance of religion. He considered this removal to be the best bulwark against excessive partisanship and priestly power, and therefore the best guarantor of the moderate, common sense modernity that was developing in Europe and especially in England.

Yenor also argues, however, that Hume's rendering of his philosophy of common life sometimes founders on the embarrassing issue of what should count as genuine "natural assumptions" of common life. He focuses on two of Hume's alleged "natural assumptions." The first concerns history: can one derive from common sense alone the view that historical change is driven, as Hume claims, mostly by accident and chance? The second concerns Hume's understanding of religious faith: is such faith really born, as Hume holds, of ignorance, fear, and terror about economic and political matters, so that it can be eliminated by a political regime that relieves these? Might it not also be "that religion arises from a human thirst for justice and righteousness"? Yenor proposes that Hume's philosophy of common life can be redeemed from the partisanship Yenor sees as having informed these two allegedly natural assumptions of Hume—that it can entertain alternative, but still reasonable accounts of what drives historical change and gives rise to religious faith. By thus "pluralizing" Hume's philosophy of common life, Yenor argues, it can be rescued. In short, Yenor not only takes seriously and presents persuasively Hume's teaching but also plumbs its limits and suggests how they might be overcome by a refashioned yet still Humean philosophy of common life.

PREFACE AND ACKNOWLEDGMENTS

Few things are as interesting or as complex as reasoning about political life. Such reasoning involves overcoming partisanship, gaining a storehouse of knowledge about the nature of political life, establishing a solid ground for evaluating the health of a political community, and recognizing the place of politics in the human condition itself. It is the work of a lifetime, especially as the world has, in some measure, given up such reasoning and replaced it with a sterile scientism that neither knows itself nor aspires to genuine knowledge of the whole. Too many of those taken with the life of the mind have abandoned themselves to a thinly disguised partisanship, dropped the idea that there might be something above politics or replaced reasoning with method. This is a great crisis, with implications for the health of our civilization and for the future of philosophy.

These issues inspire many worthy studies of ancient, modern, and "postmodern" thinkers. These studies offer diagnoses of this crisis and look for a way out of it through the thoughtful discipline of thinkers who, it is hoped, have thought through the issues more deeply than we have. As I began to understand the great crisis during my graduate studies at Loyola University Chicago, I was first introduced to David Hume, a seminal thinker of the Scottish Enlightenment. Hume was skeptical of the way early modern thinkers, especially John Locke, justified and accounted for modern political life. He put forward profound criticisms of social contract theory, natural rights, the right to property, the right to revolution, and other staples of the classical liberal political teaching. He rarely talked about the principle of religious toleration. Hume's criticisms of liberal political teachings were but examples of his criticisms of the approach of modern philosophy as such. Its methods were reductive. Its aspirations toward clarity were inhumane. It seemed oblivious to its own partisanship. Its ideology secretly elevated the place of politics in a good life. Hume appeared to offer a way out of the crisis of modern philosophy.

There were other reasons to be attracted to Hume's philosophy and his immense, humble learning. He endorsed, with seemingly few qualifications, the broad contours of modern political life, including modern commerce, the virtues of humanity, republican government, the separation of powers, dampened religious enthusiasm and superstition, the rule of law, and intellectual freedom. His system of thinking seemed far from dogmatic, while his conclusions were friendly to much that was familiar and well functioning. He proposed a way of thinking that led to an endorsement of our way of life. He was genuinely philosophic—engaged enough in political life to understand it and abstracted enough from political life to have sufficient perspective on the stakes. What is more, Hume's thought reflects an understanding of the various complexities, mysteries, obscurities, and competing goods that define the human condition, so Hume appeared to provide a modern version of very ancient insights into the tensions in our situation. I have never stopped believing that this is true, and hence that Hume's basic perspective provides one way of thinking us through our thicket of intellectual problems and of providing real humane learning in an age of excessive dedication to technology and scientism.

At the same time, I must confess that greater reading and what I hope is deeper thinking about these issues led me to see that Hume could sometimes be a clumsy or somewhat partisan practitioner of his own philosophic perspective. On issues of great importance to him, he manifests a partisanship or dogmatism at odds with his own approach. So after giving an account of Hume's approach, I hope this book points the way to more fruitful ways to apply his approach. Hume's is a philosophy of common life, as several prominent scholars have shown, but there is a more philosophic philosophy of common life to be found on the other side of Hume's thought. These problems are manifest most obviously in Hume's writings on religion—an aspect of Hume's thought that has always been the most controversial.

Completing this book brings to a conclusion what I regard as the first part of my career, though the second part of my career began years ago, too. I am happy to thank teachers, mentors, family, friends, and colleagues for the support that has been necessary to complete this manuscript. My interest in Hume and the crisis of the West was kindled in graduate school under two great thinkers and even better men, John W. Danford and Thomas S. Engeman, both of whom encouraged me to think for myself and to respond to their arguments. I chose better than I knew when I went to Loyola to study with them, in part because Peter C. Myers, my undergraduate teacher, pointed me in the right direction. Mrs. Karen Danford once told me, as I was choosing dissertation topics, that those who study Hume either go crazy or become sane. I wonder, "Which was it for me?"

Perhaps it is another testament to Hume's idea that a "great mixture of accident" plays a large role in human affairs that a National Endowment for the Humanities seminar on how medieval thinkers in the three major religions integrated classical political philosophy gave rise to the publication of this book on David Hume. Fruitful conversations during hot Spokane evenings with Tim Burns, Greg McBrayer, Charles Butterworth, Doug Kries, Khalil Habib, and others began as a means of understanding how philosophy had adapted to the presence of major revealed religions and ended, for me, with a much better understanding of how modern philosophers generally, and Hume in particular, conceived of religious belief. Tim Burns, co-editor of this indispensable series on Recovering Political Philosophy, encouraged me to revise and extend my thoughts on Hume into a completed manuscript. This meant dusting off my Hume and clarifying my thinking, and I thank Tim for the opportunity to do that. The anonymous reviewers of my initial draft offered great suggestions on how to improve several specific chapters and they provided me the space to improve more chapters on the same principles. While my thinking has, I think, moved further away from Dr. Danford's conclusions about Hume, I hope that I deviate from Hume and from Dr. Danford in the non-partisan spirit of Hume and Dr. Danford.

Further evidence of the role accident and chance play in the production of even this most imperfect book is the accumulation of interested, interesting colleagues at Loyola when I first encountered Hume. Conversations with Will Jordan (a great Hume scholar in his own right), Travis Cook, Steven Engel, and Nick Lantinga about the problems in modern thinking and the various ways out of it led me to see the importance of Hume's political thought—and to begin to understand its limits. Support from William Voegeli and the Olin Foundation's fellowship program early in my career helped me put Hume in a much broader intellectual context, and support from Les Alm and Elizabeth Frederickson, chairs during my early years at Boise State, gained me time to deepen my understanding of the alternatives that Hume was, subtly, rejecting. This was the time I identified some of epigrams for the book chapters and sections, in order to show that other thinkers often would take thoughts similar to Hume's in different directions than Hume did; other epigrams point to the main point of the chapter or section. I also thank Brian Wampler, chair as I finished this work, for adapting my schedule to allow for its completion. All the defects in this book are my responsibility, but those defects would be more numerous without the helpful conversations with my graduate school teachers and colleagues and the time afforded by my Boise State colleagues.

As careers go through stages, so does life. My wife and family have been a constant sources of joy and perspective throughout the years as I brought this book to a conclusion. My oldest son, Jackson, was an infant when I completed my first paper on Hume; now he is a fine young man out on his own. My next oldest son, Travis, came along as I was finishing my dissertation proposal, and soon he too will leave the house for a life on his own. Sarah and Paul (aka Lumpy) were born as I finished my dissertation on Locke and Hume and published my first articles on Hume. Mark (aka Biscuit) was born just when I thought I had moved on from Hume, but it turns out that I had one more confrontation with Hume left. Amy, my beloved wife, and I still have several years with these three younger ones, but, alas, she will not hear much more about this book. Amy has always understood my need to think through these issues and has forgiven me the times that it was necessary to put family and other matters aside to get things done. I could sit there amidst the chaos of family life with my nose in a book, and she would try to quell the chaos and give me the space to finish. There is much cause for reflection as I have the pleasure to consider all that I am grateful for—a wonderful education at a time when it was increasingly difficult to get one, a loving wife and family, and a productive and fulfilling career at Boise State. I am tempted to think that there may be much more to it than "a great mixture of accident."

ABBREVIATIONS

Unless otherwise noted, all works are cited by page number

D   David Hume, *Dialogues Concerning Natural Religion*, edited by Richard H. Popkin (Indianapolis: Hackett, 1980).
E   David Hume, *Essays, Moral, Political, and Literary*, edited by Eugene F. Miller (Indianapolis: Liberty, 1985).
EHU and EPM David Hume, *Enquiries Concerning Human Understanding (EHU) and Concerning the Principles of Morals (EPM)*, edited by L. A. Selby-Bigge. 3d ed. rev. P. H. Nidditch (Oxford: Clarendon, 1975).
ECHU   John Locke, *An Essay Concerning Human Understanding*, collated and annotated by Alexander Campbell Fraser (New York: Dover Publications, 1959). (Cited by book, chapter, and paragraph.)
H   David Hume, *History of England*, 6 volumes (Indianapolis: Liberty Fund, 1983). (Cited by volume and page number.)
Letters   David Hume, *The Letters of David Hume*, 2 volumes, edited J. Y. T Greig (London: Garland Press, 1983). (Cited by volume and page number.)
NHR   David Hume, *The Natural History of Religion*, edited by H. E. Root (Stanford: Stanford University Press, 1957).
PHK   George Berkeley, *A Treatise Concerning the Principles of Human Knowledge*, edited by Colin M. Turbayne (Indianapolis: Bobbs-Merrill, 1957).
T   David Hume, *A Treatise of Human Nature*, edited by L. A. Selby-Bigge, second edition with text revised and variant readings by P. H. Nidditch (Oxford: Clarendon, 1978).

CHAPTER 1

DAVID HUME'S PHILOSOPHY OF COMMON LIFE

There is a crisis in the scientific study of politics. This crisis manifests itself in the increasing specialization and focus on quasi-mathematical reductive research methods and in the irrelevance of political science to the actual practice of politics in America and in the modern world. Political scientists are, more and more, trained in a particular subfield and those trained in political science share only a commitment to methods of study; research design seems to be what holds the profession together. There are depressingly few books or bodies of knowledge that one would have to master in order to be considered an educated political scientist today: the idea that there is a body of knowledge that defines the profession seems quite quaint or naïve. This constitutes a victory of method or skills over content and substance. What is true of political science is true of university life as such, where the split between science and humanism grows larger every year. Today the "spirit of geometry," to use Pascal's phrase, triumphs over the "spirit of *finesse*," just as it seemed to be doing in the early seventeenth century.[1] The currency of the scientific spirit is ascendant relatively and absolutely, while the prestige of humanities has rarely, if ever, been lower. "Humanists" in philosophy and history, for instance, seem to have turned to science as a model for how to conduct their studies.

At the same time the problem of science and ideology is ever more evident to those with eyes to see—superficially in scandals suggesting that science has devolved into a body of conclusions and in the willful ignorance of those who ignore scientific results that contradict their political wishes. Science provides the standard of knowledge in today's world, but its status as an *objective* standard is shaky. More important for political science as such, its results seem obscure and irrelevant to political life. The study of politics is increasingly removed from the practice of politics, much less the speeches and words of politicians and statesmen. Political scientists do not think that mere practitioners are properly trained to study politics; practitioners see political scientists are useless number-crunchers or obscurantists. It is as difficult to imagine a responsible senate majority leader sitting down to read the American Political Science Review cover to cover as it is imagining a political scientist publishing peer-reviewed articles for an audience of senators. The estrangement of one from the other impoverishes politics but that perfectly understandable impoverishment of politics stems from the poverty of political science as such.

Doubts about the genuinely scientific character of science, one discovers upon reflection, however, are coeval with science itself. The reference to Pascal's "spirit of *finesse*" provides needed perspective on today's doldrums, which are no different in principle from the situation that Pascal faced as he reacted to the influence of Cartesian philosophy. Today does seem worse, of course. The "scientists" of the early Enlightenment appear to be quite learned and "humanistic" when compared with the specialist political scientists of today. The early modern political science had a greater effect on the world than anything political scientists could aspire to today. Nevertheless, Pascal's important distinction calls into question whether early modern thinkers gave us a scientific or scientistic ideology instead of genuine knowledge. It causes us to ask whether the way in which modern political science informed politics was scandalous or partisan at the creation. In any event, there are good reasons to worry that the effects of early modern political science on political practice and human life have not been altogether salutary.

This issue manifests itself through the relation between scientific knowledge and common sense. The scientific spirit of Descartes called for a methods-based detachment from the world around him and a skepticism about the messy, contradictory conclusions entertained about things in everyday life. From that point of estrangement from pre-scientific experience, Descartes sought to discover (or invent) the simplest elements that constituted nature and the human world and, following the spirit of geometry, to reconstruct that world from those most basic elements. These clear, distinct starting points, the discovery of which the new philosophy supported, for Descartes, allowed human beings to become "Lords and Possessors of Nature" through this creative reconstruction and the assertion of human will. This science, shunning the world of common sense and ancient philosophy, is precise, reductionist, reconstructive, and transformational.

Against this spirit, Pascal, a famous geometer himself, offered a "spirit of *finesse*" that alone could make good use of the spirit of science or geometry. The spirit of finesse is humane, grounded in the un-thought attachments and loves of common life, aimed at understanding the truth about, and beauty of, the whole. The whole is not thereby made or constructed, much less reconstructed: it is immediate, felt, grasped and discovered; it exists independent of human making and it absorbs the inquirer but not completely. The spirit of science or geometry has a place in human inquiry, Pascal implies, and that place is as a subordinate inquiry that sheds light on *parts* of the whole and can measure the lower, constant elements of human nature with some accuracy. The scientific spirit remains important, though the humane or humanistic knowledge within which science finds meaning is even more important (though more elusive and less certain).

These attachments and loves provided the focus for political science over the course of millennia, during which political scientists have been concerned to promote political health, mixed regimes, or a sustainable liberal democracy. As these "attachments" and "loves" came to be seen as prejudices, pre-rational commitments, political science has intentionally, gradually, but eventually with gusto stripped such public-spirited concerns from inquiry so that today political science is focused on establishing quantifiable, measurable relationships between variables; predictive value, not regime maintenance, is, ostensibly, at least, the goal of today's political science profession. The result is behaviorists and rational choice theorists who cannot give an account of why they study what they study and studies based on narrow or partial conceptions of human nature and partial concepts of the human good.[2] Political science as it is practiced today becomes ever more divorced from the perspective of the statesman or of common sense and ever more politicized to serve the often unstated "preferences" of the scientist.

Pascal's embrace of an orthodox view of the whole—that is, his intense Christian faith—may especially have inclined him to worry about a "spirit of geometry" unmoored from humane knowledge; the love at the heart of Pascal's "spirit of finesse" is part of a ladder of love reaching to the Lord of the universe. Either in light of this or despite this, Pascal offers sober and sobering first thoughts about the scientific spirit near the birth of modern thinking. His broader concern about the sufficiency and wisdom of scientific reductionism and ideological science dogs modern thinking at every turn. Many of these thoughts appeared to be sober and sobering second thoughts after the first wave of modern thinkers established the principles of this new science. In France, the initial quarrel between the ancients and the modern proceeded toward the work of Rousseau (1750), who called into question passionately both the status of modern "knowledge" and its contributions to human thriving. In England, the "battle of the books" brought to the fore humane essays from Alexander Pope (1734) and hilarious criticisms from Jonathan Swift (1725). Germany, as represented by Goethe, Schiller, Herder, and Schlegel, among others, had a national consciousness founded more on a seemingly humane critique of science and scientific culture in the later half of the 1700s.

The quarrel between those who sought to defend or revivify humane learning and those who propagated scientific progress reveals a second, more paradoxical issue within modern thought. As modern thinkers put forward advances in thinking or "new concepts," scientific concepts seep into common life, the "spirit of *finesse*" itself changes, and humane knowledge appears less distinct from social science. New doubts arise about modern theory's transformation of the world. Pascal, like many who came after him, saw that this embrace of "knowledge" was headed for falsehood and an obscuring of our most human features; he sought to upset the certainty and pride in the modern scientific method so that it could find its proper, subordinate sphere. The "spirit of *finesse*" and humanism never again gained the upper hand against the "spirit of geometry" and social science and they were soon eclipsed in the scientific transformation of the world of common sense. Perhaps this is because humanists did not think through the problems as deeply as they needed to or in the direction that they needed to; perhaps because there were no longer ears to hear; perhaps because science had itself provided a truthful enough, or at least an appealing, account of the whole.

In this dialogue between social science and humanism I find the importance of David Hume's philosophy of common life and his defense of humane learning. Common life philosophy as Hume practices it begins with a critique of scientific concepts that earlier modern philosophers seemed to think would bring order to our experience and political life. Born in opposition to what he took to be the excessively hopeful rationalism of early Enlightenment thinkers such as John Locke, Hume's specific rendering of common life philosophy is humane, path-breaking and promising. Hume writes an essay "That Politics May be Reduced to a Science," for instance—something that seems akin to the scientific spirit. That essay, however, proves to be a classic example of Hume's humane learning, with conclusions about what arrangements are generally good for a particular country, with the aim of reducing the influence of simplifying theoretical parties, and with the hopes of promoting political moderation in a world of extremes. His science is neither mathematical nor reductionist: it aims to orient practitioners of the political art toward a vision of political health. Hume's promise to "reduce" politics to a science appears to be a joke in light of today's political science: Hume's political science is a Cro-Magnon version of "modern" political science compared to our fully evolved species or, perhaps, it is a different species altogether. Certainly Hume is attached to the English Constitution: his researches aim to understand and preserve it. Hume called this humane approach to learning the "philosophy of common life." This philosophy of common life is the product of thinking through the aspirations and inadequacies in early modern rationalism, which Hume exposes especially in his technically philosophic writings in the *Treatise of Human Nature* and the *Enquiry concerning Human Understanding* and in his essays against social contract theory and its associated doctrines. The logic-chopping and technical sufficiency of these arguments continues to draw scholarly attention and Hume's technical moral theory has especially been of concern in our postmodern age.[3] Much of recent scholarship concerned with technical issues misses Hume's broader philosophic vision or, insofar as scholarship identifies some of his broader intentions, it fails to connect Hume's intentions to his profound interest in the nature of human knowledge. The destructive technical side of his thought is for the most part preparatory and the "technical" moral theory should be seen within the broader political vision.

On a general level, Hume's philosophy of common life alternates between vexation and agnosticism about the most difficult philosophic questions on one side and natural suppositions of common sense on the other. His agnosticism proceeds from an acknowledgement of our fundamental ignorance about the world around us, as seen in Hume's famous observation that we are unable to explain why one thing causes another. Hume builds his humane philosophic enterprise on the assumption that we can bypass tension-laden, irresolvable ontological, metaphysical, and philosophic disputes while assuming the "common sense" of the matter. We may not be able to explain why one thing causes another (this marks his agnosticism), but we can presume *that* one thing causes another and such knowledge suffices for our purposes (this is his natural supposition). I may not be able to explain why I have a continued existence and identity from one day to the next, but I assume *that* I am the same person I was yesterday. Though we cannot explain the ultimate grounds of the difference, we must presume that there is the difference between virtue and vice in order to conduct moral philosophy.

Each of these moments—the initial agnosticism and the subsequent entertaining of natural suppositions—integrates powerful insights into human being. Philosophic agnosticism itself consists in two distinct moments. Initially agnosticism manifests itself in skepticism and questioning, with the effect of laying bare the basis of our lack of knowledge. In metaphysics, Hume's moment of skepticism and questioning leads him to argue that we cannot explain causation, cannot fathom the nature of human perception, and cannot discover why matter holds together. Philosophic agnosticism demands that Hume subject previous philosophic systems, both ancient and modern, to devastating critique. In politics, Hume's moment of skepticism and questioning demands a thoroughgoing critique of political systems such as the divine right of kings and social contract theory. After this almost postmodern clearing away of debris from counter-productive philosophic systems, Hume must maintain a non-dogmatic attitude of suspense and quietism about underlying issues that gave rise to philosophic debate in the first place. If we cannot know the foundations of unity, or the mechanism of human perception, or the universal basis for political legitimacy, Hume counsels that we pass over these issues without resolving them and instead pursue the insights that follow from the fact that we cannot resolve them.

Inquiry can still proceed after this agnosticism if we can identify uncontroversial natural assumptions that ground all thinking. This is the second moment in Hume's philosophy of common life, and it is a devilishly tricky and controversial one. Are there uncontroversial, common sense assumptions? If so, how can we identify them? Without natural assumptions, Hume's philosophy of common life is a mere castle in the air; it is a castle suspended perhaps just as our judgment must remain, but without anything to say to or about the real world. Hume lays forth criteria by which reliable deliverances of common life are distinguished from flights of fancy in an effort to ground common life philosophy. Reliable natural assumptions are "permanent, irresistible, and universal" and "the foundation of all our thoughts and actions, so that upon their removal human nature must immediately perish and go to ruin" (T 225). These criteria are relatively easy to apply to technically philosophic issues such as causation, perception, and identity, while they are much more controversial and heated in politics, religion and history.

Hume's common life philosophy grounds and is grounded in a conception of human nature and the human condition, for we identify reliable natural assumptions by reference to human nature. As people think about themselves and their world, puzzles come to their minds. As philosophers pursue answers to these common questions, Hume thinks the human condition manifests contradictions, obscurities, and mysteries that philosophy can adumbrate but not relieve; this should cultivate a spirit of modesty and moderation in all enquirers. Human life, for Hume, is a "mixed kind of life," by which he means that human beings are mixed creatures—partly selfish and partly social; partly reasonable, partly imaginative, and partly sentimental; partly body and partly thinking substance; and partly knowing and partly ignorant. This account of our condition has important implications for morality and politics. The moderate, humane virtues characteristic of the modern commercial republic reflect the proper social reaction to the contradictions and mysteries that define our existence; the humane, gentle virtues are scientific modesty refracted into social life. Above all, Hume warns against the blinding effects of philosophic and political partisanship and excessive relativism, all of which result from a failure to appreciate human limits. Hume endorses the political, economic, and social arrangements associated with modernity as those most inimical to excessive partisanship. His opposition to priestly power, enthusiastic religion, and absolute, arbitrary rule, when combined with his endorsement of free trade, commercial arrangements, progress in arts and learning, and, generally, the humane virtues, place him inside Enlightened politics. To borrow a phrase, he stands athwart the tracks of Enlightenment yelling "Stop" to its dogmatic scientific self-understanding and "Go" to (most of) its humane, sociopolitical project.

So we see in Hume's philosophy of common life echoes of much that is characteristic of today's skepticism and the modern approach to knowing, of what I loosely call our postmodernism and our rationalism [4] Steering clear of excesses in each of these perspectives, common life philosophy promises nevertheless to integrate each of their most powerful insights. We also see in Hume a defense of soft and humane virtues and of the modern commercial republic—of our virtues and our civilization broadly conceived. His thought promises that we can have a lot, if not everything, that we could hope for. Because Hume appreciates "the wretched condition, weakness, and disorder" (T 267) of human faculties but nevertheless thinks political philosophy and science are both possible and desirable, he is a useful guide in our skeptical, somewhat postmodern maze. Because he endorses the outlines of Western commercial republics while standing outside Enlightenment certainty and postmodern doubts, he is a useful guide as we try to understand and justify liberal society. Because Hume articulates the structure of our "not-knowing" and defends our ability to explain why we do not know, he is a guide to human knowledge even as he exposes the limits of human understanding. Hume is an Enlightenment thinker suited to our age because he knew of the postmodern temptation but thought that human beings have the resources to resist it. He may not promise deliverance from this situation, but he promises a way of thinking that helps us orient ourselves amidst our all-too-human uncertainty.

Hume's philosophy of common life represents a humanist reaction against the imperial spirit in the scientific view, and, when applied today, this puts him in opposition to the social scientific view as well. Despite its promise, common life philosophy, as Hume practices it, is not sweeping the nation, nor is it sweeping philosophy or political science departments. This probably tells us something about our age. This contemporary rejection of or indifference to common life philosophy also forces us to wonder about why Hume's common life approach is not viable or why this road has not been taken. Skepticism about Hume, as we shall see, has a venerable tradition, dating at least from Hume's role in awakening Immanuel Kant from his dogmatic slumber. This tradition is too dismissive of Hume's accomplishments in decisive respects, but its implicit conclusion that Hume's "common sense" approach is naïve and implausible is not easily dismissed. Some of the common sense assumptions or natural suppositions (the phrases are interchangeable) assimilated into Hume's philosophy of common life are more controversial than Hume seems willing to concede. Philosophers must often penetrate into the controversies Hume seeks to bypass if they are to choose and identify natural assumptions. Entertaining natural assumptions sometimes, at least, means that one must take sides in the underlying, apparently irresolvable controversy, and taking sides in an irresolvable controversy violates the philosophic agnosticism that is a crucial moment in Hume's philosophy of common life. Hume's rendering of common life philosophy founders, sometimes, on the embarrassing issue of what counts as a deliverance of common life. The question of what counts as a natural assumption reveals what I take to be the inescapable difficulties human beings face as they attempt to ascend from common experience to scientific knowledge.

Consider as an illustration of this problem Hume's philosophy of history (a topic to which I turn in chapter 7). It is not from history or common sense alone that Hume derives his view that historical change is driven mostly by accident and chance. This assumption about the character of history is controversial even within the purview of common sense. The problem is that common life philosophy demands that Hume entertain other reasonable, alternative accounts of what drives history or historical change. He assumes it is accident and chance, but it could just as easily be the "cunning of reason" or it could be that historical change is less fundamental than he assumes. This problem also arises in Hume's treatment of religion. Hume's understanding of religious faith and revealed knowledge arises from untested and, perhaps, untestable assumptions about the psychology of religion. He assumes that religious faith is borne of fear and terror about economic and political discontents and that religious passions can be satisfied by a political regime relieving the fear and terror following from war, penury, and scientific ignorance. He assumes miracles cannot happen because he assumes that God does not actively intervene in nature and human affairs (at the least). These assumptions are reasonably and rightly controversial, and therefore cannot constitute the *only* natural supposition within a system of common life. It might also be that religion arises from a human thirst for justice and righteousness, not just from fear and want. When Hume treats topics such as history and religion, then, he entertains assumptions that violate his philosophic agnosticism. His non-partisan philosophy of common life becomes an instrument of partisanship on behalf of a particular view of history or a particular understanding of what religion is and thus he seems to repeat the errors of the science that he rightly criticizes.

Hume persuasively shows that all thought must find its humble beginnings in common life, but there seem sometimes to be fundamental, inescapable problems in ascending from common life and in defining the assumptions of common life. Sometimes more than one assumption is validated by common life; sometimes, at least, reason and sentiment cannot ascertain what the proper assumption should be. This dilemma can be solved or at least managed, and the philosophy of common life can be rescued from Hume's occasional misapplication of it, if we students of philosophy diversify the assumptions assimilated into a philosophy of common life. A more pluralized common life philosophy than the one Hume presents promises to be more philosophic and more accommodating, more humane and more open to the outside, freer while also truer. In this manner, Hume's own errors point to a way in which we might be able to have it all, if a bit more uncertainly than we and he would like. Thus the promise of Hume's philosophy of common life can be redeemed if we take a skeptical and revisionist approach to his own justification for, development of, and application of his philosophy.

Toward the end of understanding this, this book proceeds in three sections. In chapters 2–4, I develop Hume's conception of common life philosophy and his defense of philosophic modesty through his critical confrontation with previous philosophers. Hume's treatment of metaphysics and morals shows that metaphysical systems reveal the strange contradictions endemic to common sense. Hume uses these strange contradictions as lodestars for his insights into the mysteries and obscurities of human condition. In chapter 4 I define Hume's philosophic project as oriented by his understanding of the "mixed kind of life" to which nature has confined human beings.

The book's second section, chapters 5–7, treats how Hume's account of our "mixed kind of life" orients his understanding of politics and history. Chapter 5 serves as a bridge between the opening section on metaphysical issues and this second section on politics and history. It concerns Hume's account of how the "spirit of geometry" has come to infect modern politics and how this trend threatens to undermine the moderate modernity that Hume sees developing in Europe and especially in England. For Hume, England's political constitution works well because its public opinion is ruled by humane, common sense impulses instead of "abstract speculative principles" (as Hume calls them) and because vestiges from its pre-modern constitution remained to restrain parliamentary rule. Those turning Lockean principles into Whig dogma threaten this settlement because they try to ground political legitimacy directly in universal principles of right and to disregard historical circumstances. These political problems are traceable to the embrace of the sovereign imagination, which arrives at conclusions and gives orders divorced from common life. As against this kind of modern republicanism, Hume would have us conceive of modern arrangements in light of the virtues of moderation and humanity they produce, for these virtues embody the proper reaction to our mixed condition (as we will see in chapter 6). Chapter 7—another bridge—outlines Hume's account of how the commercial republic arose in England. It describes the erosion of superstition and enthusiasm as a means of showing how the engine of humanity thrives only after the cultural governance of religion is removed. Together these sections present the most persuasive case I can for Hume's philosophic enterprise and its alignment with commerce and modern republicanism. These sections take seriously the way in which Hume's philosophic tone informs his more "certain" political teaching.

Only after presenting the best case for Hume's orientation and its implications for politics will I plumb the limits of Hume's project. These limits appear in Hume's political and religious writings, though they have profound implications for Hume's philosophic enterprise as a whole. The third section is somewhat more speculative than the previous sections, in that it leaves the firmer ground of interpretation and moves toward the realm of philosophical criticism. I try to show that Hume assimilates controversial assumptions about the nature of history and religion into his treatment of those topics and that this undermines the aspirations of his philosophy of common life, but perhaps not of philosophies of common life as such. I do not mean to play "gotcha" with Hume in this respect, but rather to provide an entrée into the great difficulties involved in a philosophy of common life and to point a path forward.

Only by pluralizing common life philosophy can it be redeemed from Hume's occasional dogmatic misuse of it. I sketch such a pluralized common life philosophy in the conclusion, with the aim of showing, perhaps, the problem with humanism as such. Humanism, like Hume's philosophy as he understands it, presumes the sufficiency of the human and does not, as Hume practices it, seek to show the human place within the whole. Foreclosed to the idea that there is something above the human in the light of which one can understand the human, humanism seems powerless against those who would understand the human in light of that which is below the human. Humanism without something above tends to devolve into social science, which understands the human in a reductionist way. A rediscovery of humanism requires an advance beyond the Enlightenment approach to the whole, which Hume, unwittingly, perhaps, adopts.

Several chapters and sections are preceded by epigrams. While sometimes these epigrams capture the main point of the section or chapter, often my purpose is to show that other philosophers from quite different perspectives have shared Hume's insight. This is designed to show that the philosophy of common life, informed by a profound universe of meaning, can be assimilated in more directions than the one Hume takes it—and especially to show that Hume's philosophy of common life can be open to religious belief.

CHAPTER 2

"NOTHING BUT SOPHISTRY AND ILLUSION": METAPHYSICAL SPECULATION BEFORE HUME

> *If we take in our hand any volume of... a school of metaphysics...; let us ask, Does it contain any abstract reasoning concerning quantity or number? No. Does it contain any experimental reasoning concerning matter of fact and existence? No. Commit it then to the flames; for it can contain nothing but sophistry and illusion.*
>
> —Hume, *Enquiries concerning Human Understanding* (1748)

Hume's situates his philosophy of common life in the broad context of ancient and modern treatments of human capacities. The *Treatise* contains an explicit discussion "Of the Antient Philosophy" and "Of the Modern Philosophy" (Book 1; Part IV; Sections III and IV, respectively), though his views on both permeate this Part and Book. The elements that concern Hume include how previous philosophers have accounted for the nature of matter, the intelligibility of nature, and explaining how or if people reliably sense matter. The most telling question concerns the reliability of the senses and the tendency of previous philosophers to entertain "skepticism with regard to the senses" (1.IV.II) because that is where human capacities intersect with the broader world. Previous thinkers provided an account of nature that allowed people to depend upon the accuracy of the senses or perhaps not to rely upon them. The previous accounts of first things require a penetration into the hidden recesses of nature and a showing of how people fit into that stream of nature (or do not). These are questions of metaphysics, a word of opprobrium for Hume (see, e.g., EHU 165, T 268). Hume criticizes these previous treatments to reveal the true sphere of human knowledge. He continues the work of "some late philosophers in England, who have begun to put the science of man on a new footing" (T xvii), yet he furthers and radicalizes this work to reveal a footing both less and more sure. Francis Bacon and John Locke, Hume mentions, have helped to destroy the figments of ancient and scholastic metaphysics, but they reproduced previous errors at another remove. A truer, more thorough critique is what Hume promises, one culminating in his philosophy of common life.

This chapter presents the "metaphysical" tradition mostly as Hume saw it, relying on Hume's hints to point to the most basic concepts of ancient and modern metaphysics. By metaphysics Hume seems to mean the investigation of how human reason grasps the nature of being, and it includes implications for what the human is, what nature ultimately is, and what the divine is. While Hume's understanding of the ancient and modern approaches is my focus, this chapter also goes back to the original authors (especially Aristotle and Locke) to understand their views on the ultimate stuff of reality. Simplifying as a prelude to the Hume's account, differences between ancient and modern philosophy concern the intelligibility of common sense. Aristotle, at least, sees common opinion and language as windows to an intelligible, ordered world, while modern philosophers generally see in common opinion and language a confused jumble of error and prejudice. Ancient philosophy begins by confronting common opinion sympathetically as if it contained insights into the way the world operates, while modern philosophy proceeds by doubting the reliability of common opinion in an effort to reconstruct the world scientifically.

Ancient Metaphysics and Common Sense

Hume's discussion of ancient and peripatetic philosophy concentrates on what he calls the "fictions" concerning *"substances, and substantial forms"* (T 219). As Hume relates it, substance is the matter, the coming and going of which explains the gradual revolutions and changes in each thing. A duck is made "of the very same substance" as a rock. Ducks differ from rocks in form, which ancient philosophers suppose "to be the source of all those different qualities [things] possess, and to be a new foundation for simplicity and identity to each particular species" (T 221). Hume considers this explanation to be "entirely incomprehensible" (T 222), and we do well to understand it—the reasons why ancient thinkers entertained such a system and whether it is plausible.

Aristotle's *Metaphysics* is the *locus classicus* for the distinction to which Hume draws attention. Let a sketch of Aristotle's treatment suffice. The "greatest" and "most necessary" question Aristotle concerns himself with is this: "If there is nothing apart from concrete individuals...how is a science of infinite individuals possible?" (999a24–6). Before Aristotle, many philosophers denied the existence of anything beyond or apart from particular, material things. This philosophy of matter in motion emphasizes how all the knowledge that we have of nature—"and indeed all things that are"—"must be sensible" (1010a4). Only particular things or the appearance of particular things present themselves to the senses. Human beings perceive the world as a series of snapshots, on this view, wherein particles of matter are flying in and out of those bundles; even the things we think are stable are in reality not. The metaphor for all things, from Heraclitus, but adverted to by Aristotle, is a river. It is impossible to step in the same river twice, just as it is impossible to see the same duck twice; no material being is ever the same one it was a moment ago. By the continual addition of new matter and the continual loss of old, matter lacks the stability, permanence, and coherence on which steady, scientific judgments could be based. As Aristotle characterizes it, "as [these philosophers] saw this whole world of nature changing, and as nothing true had been said about what changes, they concluded that nothing could possibly be said truly about what is always and everywhere changing" (1010a7–9).[1]

This view errs in several ways, according to Aristotle. The most important objection is that it is inconsistent with science, knowledge, and common sense: "If there is nothing apart from concrete individuals, then nothing would be conceived; all things would be perceived, and there would be no science of anything" (999b1–3). Objects of science presume that something unchangeable and permanent exists amidst the apparent flux of matter. The view that everything is matter in motion undermines (or is inconsistent with) our use of language, by which we subsume particulars under general or specific categories (987b8). From the "conviction" that all is matter in motion proceeds "the most extreme" doctrines, such as that of Cratylus, a follower of Heraclitus, "who finally thought one ought not to speak at all" (1010a10–5). Something could be offensive to common sense and yet true (and Aristotle offers philosophic arguments to confute the Heraclitean position[2]), but its offensiveness to human practice, sensory experience and action is illustrative.

Others before Aristotle, including Plato, noticed the poverty of the Heraclitean position. As Aristotle presents it, Plato, following Socrates, began looking for permanence in morals, turning away from the apparently insolvable problems posed by Heraclitean metaphysics. Eventually Plato returned to metaphysics, seeking to explain the permanence in all things seen and unseen. On Aristotle's account, Plato never abandoned the conviction that sensible things are always changing and unstable and that no common intelligible or sensible structure could be found in anything.[3] Universal definitions for things could exist only if there was something else in things besides matter, only if individual things "participate in" something objective and eternal, something immune from the vicissitudes of matter in motion. These universal verities Plato called Ideas or Forms, and his so-called doctrine of Ideas holds that "all the objects of perception...are defined by and in terms of ideas" (987b9). A duck is composed of two principles—a specific principle or the Idea of a duck and an individuating principle or that which distinguishes one duck from another: a hunter shoots at an individual duck, but the Idea of a duck allows the hunter to speak steadily about ducks. Aristotle thinks such a teaching is incoherent and implausible. Plato seemed to argue that Ideas were outside of common sensory experience (they "do not belong inherently to the things which participate in them") in order to explain their permanence.[4] If Ideas are altogether different from sensible things, Aristotle asks in what he takes to be his most important objection to Plato on this matter, of what use can they be in furthering our knowledge of sensible things? Human beings know things by knowing each particular thing, its matter and substance, not by knowing that which is separate from the thing. Precisely how Ideas give rise to particular things or the extent to which Ideas can explain the movement of things is also unclear from the doctrine of Ideas; in sum, the doctrine of Ideas explains neither being nor becoming nor passing away.[5] Aristotle concludes, "To say that the ideas are patterns and that other things participate in them is to use empty words and poetical metaphors" (991a9–21). In the ancient struggle between philosophy and poetry, Plato, insofar as he adopted the Ideas, sided with poetry. He invented conventions that are the noble lies needed to sustain the normal functioning of language and hence political life against the corrosive influence of the pernicious (but arguably true) Heraclitean position.

There is, from Aristotle's perspective, a promising aspect to the Platonic turn to Ideas, for the need to explain the coexistence of permanence and change is real and necessary. If Heraclitean arguments with respect to natural things were to win the day, political and ethical inquiry would be fruitless. Naturally occurring objects seem to exist with greater permanence and to be more readily sensible than ethical codes or political constitutions. Moral codes and political constitutions, on the other hand, fluctuate to a greater degree and require fleshing out in order for people to know how to live. With the natural world reduced to an unintelligible rubble what hope could there be for any inquiry, least of all ethics? People constructing a conventional world amidst an unintelligible natural world could not talk intelligibly about justice or virtue or truth; political life would be reduced to a fight of sorts, wherein the stronger or most cunningly persuasive would be unrestrained by any moral reservations. Heraclitean metaphysics leads to Alcibiades, a versatile power-monger willing to serve whatever side honors him, or to a Melian slaughter, where an imperial power self-consciously reduces all calculations to imperial interest.[6] Plato's metaphysics, no matter what its philosophic shortcomings, is an expression of his love for justice as much as his love of philosophy.

Like Plato, Aristotle thought it was necessary for metaphysics to provide an account of permanence amidst change as a means of resisting the radical skepticism inherent in the Heraclitean cum sophistic position. Aristotle distinguished matter from form. Matter is that out of which everything is made, but it is indeterminate and without boundaries or limits. Natural philosophers, while interested in matter, must be more interested in the part of each thing that makes it intelligible and specific; substantial form is that stable thing (1037a16). Substantial form is composed of the essential characteristics that make substances what they are; the principle according to which a thing is generated is the form or nature of the thing generated (1032a22–3). We can know forms only to the extent that essential characteristics are observed in particular things. Against Plato, then, Aristotle holds that "nothing that is general [*universale*]" exists "separated and removed from concrete individuals" (1040b27; see also especially 1033b19–29).

The fact that all knowledge begins with sensing and all sense perception is grounded in particulars causes a serious problem for this view: How can human beings distinguish between the accidental and essential characteristics of things?[7] This question forces us to ask how human beings come to know substantial form, one of the most perplexing and mysterious questions in Aristotle. This issue can be stated in the following way. All knowledge of external things originates in sense perception that proceeds from bodies outside the human being. Such sensory knowledge is particular and inseparable from material bodies. In contrast to corporeal faculties of sense, the intellect [*nous*] is an incorporeal or immaterial faculty that apprehends universals or substantial forms. Our ability to move from the particular, sensitive knowledge to universal, intellectual knowledge is predicated on the ability of corporal things (the senses) to make an impression on an incorporeal thing (the intellect). This move is as impossible as it is ridiculous because, as Aristotle explains, an immaterial mind is not disabled by unusually loud music or bright light the way that our sensitive ears and eyes may be. Aristotle posits the existence of a rational activity that translates, in effect, the particular and material into the universal and immaterial. Imagination [*phantasia*] is that impossible, translating faculty that takes a picture, in effect, of what the senses perceive.[8] The ability to move from the material to the immaterial via imagination is a necessary, but not a sufficient basis for our capacity to grasp universal forms. The mind must be able to sort out the essential from the accidental in these images as well.[9] The intellect [*nous*] discerns "fundamental principle[s] or starting point[s]" that cannot themselves be objects of science (*Nic. Ethics* 1140b34; see also *Posterior Analytics* 100b5–14). When studying an eye, for instance, the active intellect abstracts from the accidental characteristics of an eye's blue color in order to arrive at its universal or essential characteristics. It is almost as if human beings see things in two different ways: the sight sees something that exists outside of the body, while the intellect sees a likeness or image of that thing (i.e., its intelligible species or form).[10]

It has been necessary to sketch these somewhat abstruse matters so that we can understand the underlying purpose behind Aristotle's metaphysics. These distinctions—between essential characteristics and accidental ones and between fluctuating matter and intelligible form—are part of ordinary experience and language.[11] We say that eyes are blue or near-sighted and we notice that things wear away or age or grow. Noticing these realities, Aristotle defends common experience from the excessive skepticism of the senses as reflected in Heraclitean assumptions (which elevated accident and matter) and the excessive idealism of those who take Platonic forms very seriously (which emphasized essence and Ideas or form). What Fr. Copleston writes of St. Thomas Aquinas applies equally to Aristotle: "What the philosopher does is not to invent a gratuitous theory or even to make a discovery of which the ordinary man has no inkling, but rather to express explicitly and in abstract terms a distinction which is implicitly recognized by the ordinary man in concrete instances."[12] Aristotle questions and questions until he reaches fundamental unsolvable mysteriousness. Far from being dogmatic in the traditional sense, his approach bespeaks an account of what might (or must) be true about human nature if it is to confront nature's incomprehensibility and our ignorance of ourselves.

Far from engendering "skepticism of the senses," as Hume implies,[13] scholastic philosophy, insofar as it is true to its Aristotelian roots, illumines the harmony between the senses and the mind, and between both the senses and mind and nature and, more generally, shows that the world is intelligible. That Hume never seems to understand scholastic philosophy in this way is a tribute, perhaps, to the success of the modern critique of scholastic philosophy, which Hume seems to accept without reservation.[14]

Modern Metaphysics and the "Skepticism with regard to the Senses"

Modern philosophers criticized the ancient system of metaphysics for asserting an essential harmony between human faculties and nature and hence failing to do justice to human freedom and ingenuity. A metaphysic emphasizing matter and form does not contribute to the psychological and scientific unsettling necessary for the advancement of learning, nor does it make any contribution to a scientist's quest for testable hypotheses. Scholastic assumptions were, in Locke's words,[15] "wholly useless and unserviceable to any part of our knowledge" (ECHU 3.3.17).[16] Ancient metaphysics and common experience share a commitment to the basic intelligibility of things, while modern scientists find this natural intelligibility (on some level) inimical to scientific progress. Perhaps because he initiated the break with previous thinking, Descartes rejects the harmony between sense and intellect and between human mind and nature most decisively:

> We must take care not to assume—as our [scholastic] philosophers commonly do—that in order to have sensory awareness the soul must contemplate certain images transmitted by objects to the brain; or at any rate we must conceive the nature of these images in an entirely different manner from that of the philosophers. For since their conception of images is confined to the requirement that they should resemble the objects they represent, the philosophers cannot possibly show us how the images can be formed by the objects, or how they can be received by the external sense and transmitted by the nerves to the brain. Their sole reason for positing such images was that they saw how easily a picture can stimulate our mind to conceive the objects depicted in it, and so it seemed to them that the mind must be stimulated to conceive the objects that affect our senses in the same way—that is, by little pictures formed in our head.[17]

Explaining the congruence between our perception of objects and the objects themselves is the hallmark of ancient metaphysics. Descartes and his philosophic successors find the pre-modern apology for trustworthiness of the senses linked to religious or superstitious credulousness[18] and lazy complacency. This is the scholastic's Luddite temptation: believing in the accuracy of the senses and the adequacy of a few observations, scholastic scientists are tempted to believe that words, in Locke's characterization, *"stand also for the reality of things"* (ECHU 3.2.5; see also 3.6.30).[19] Scholastics believe that the names of substances are somehow authorized by nature and they are not primarily interested in refining their definitions with careful observations and scientific tests. As a result, they advocate a science concerned with "verbal propositions" and "the bare contemplation of their abstract ideas" (4.8.11; 4.12.9), while ignoring investigations of nature. Modern "metaphysicians" before Hume faced a choice: either refine the scholastic system to show how it is consistent with the advancement of learning or jettison the entire system in an effort to found another, more congenial to their ends.

Modern philosophy followed the latter path, finding in ancient and scholastic philosophy insuperable obstacles to scientific progress. The modern metaphysic integrates features of Heraclitean hypothesis of matter in motion while emphasizing human constructive powers instead of natural species or form. Modern thinkers such as Locke explain the nature of perception or sensation in terms of the essential qualities of existing external bodies. In response to the question of "how bodies produce ideas in us," Locke's corpuscularian hypothesis answers "manifestly by impulse, the only way which we can conceive bodies operate in" (ECHU 2.8.11). A "more rational opinion" than that of substantial form, the corpuscularian hypothesis owns that "natural things...have a real, but unknown constitution in their insensible parts; from which flow those sensible qualities which serve us to distinguish them one from another" (3.3.17). When we perceive objects, "it is evident some single imperceptible bodies must come from [external objects] to the eyes, and thereby convey to the brain some motion; which produces these ideas which we have in us" (2.8.12). Different perceptions are caused "by the impulse of such insensible particles of matter, of peculiar figures and bulks, and in different degrees and modifications of their motions" (2.13.8). This account of the origin of sense perception mirrors the account in *Leviathan*, where Hobbes writes that all sensible qualities are "in the object that causeth them, but so many several motions of the matter, by which it presseth our organs diversely."[20]

Locke elaborates on the corpuscularian hypothesis with the distinction between primary and secondary qualities, which Hume later labels the "fundamental principle of modern philosophy" (T 226). Imperceptible bodies or "insensible corpuscles," as Locke also calls them, are "the active parts of matter, and the great instruments of nature, on which depend not only all their secondary qualities, but also most of their natural operations" (ECHU 4.3.25). The primary qualities of bodies, which precede and produce secondary qualities, are "utterly inseparable from the body, in what estate soever it be." Material things cannot exist without the attributes of "solidity, extension, figure, motion or rest, and number." To put this differently, primary material bodies give rise to the active parts of matter which human beings sense as secondary qualities. These secondary or *"sensible qualities"* include our "different ideas of several colours, sounds, smells, tastes, &c." An apple's color or taste, for example, is not in the apple; an apple only has the power to produce these sensations in us. Secondary qualities "in truth are nothing in the objects themselves but powers to produce various sensations in us by their primary qualities." In contrast to secondary qualities, the "real, original, or primary qualities...are in the things themselves, whether they are perceived or not: and upon their modifications it is that the secondary qualities depend" (2.8.9, 10, 23).[21]

The corpuscularian hypothesis is connected with, but analytically distinct from, Locke's account of the origin and kinds of ideas. Locke distinguishes between qualities and ideas: "Whatsoever the mind perceives *in itself*, or is the immediate object of perception, thought, or understanding, that I call *idea;* and the power to produce any idea in our mind, I call *quality* of the subject wherein the power is" (ECHU 2.8.8). Qualities or "powers which are in things...excite certain sensations in us" (2.31.2). An apple has some power to produce ideas of green and tart in us; the perceptions of green and tart are only ideas in us. This leads to the distinction between simple and complex ideas. Simple ideas are what Locke calls "the materials of all our knowledge" (2.2.2). We combine simple ideas to make complex ideas. Continuing with our example, the simple ideas of green and tart are a couple of the simple ideas that constitute our complex idea of apple. Simple ideas form the limit of human understanding and human power—we cannot imagine a complex idea that is not reducible to simples and we cannot make or destroy a simple idea (2.12.1).

The corpuscularian system undermines the scholastic system by providing a theoretical justification for the contention that substantial form does not exist. Locke writes, "The like ignorance as I have of the real essence of this particular substance, I have also of the real essence of all other natural ones: of which essences I confess I have no distinct ideas at all" (ECHU 2.31.6). Our inability to form clear and distinct ideas about "substantial form" is, in Locke's view, suggestive evidence against those who maintain the existence of form in the world. Ideas of things in reality are clear and distinct (2.29.2; 2.30.5), not obscure and confused like the schoolmen's ideas of substantial form.[22] Thomas Hobbes is typically more forceful in denying that form is in the world: "The World...is Corporeall, that is to say, Body...and consequently every part of the Universe, is Body, and that which is not Body, is no part of the Universe: and because the Universe is All, that which is no part of it, is *Nothing,* and consequently *nowhere.*"[23] In other words, the corpuscularian hypothesis reflects a neo-Heracliteanism by reducing everything, even faculties of sense, to matter in motion (2.8.12–13).

Form had been the linchpin of pre-modern attempts to explain the intelligibility of the world; Locke and the other modern thinkers replace form and natural species with a more empowering understanding of where order comes from. As a preliminary matter, Locke realizes that his hypothesis that "the mind, in all its thoughts and reasonings, hath no other immediate object but its own ideas" (ECHU 4.1.1) runs counter to the common understanding of things. Men generally think that warmth or cold, for example, are in the water itself or that the apple is tart (2.8.17–21, 24). By attacking the common understanding of mankind, Locke's corpuscularian hypothesis would seem to be more radical and destructive than the old philosophy he seeks to replace. Whereas Locke contends that the old philosophy could prove that snow is black, his own system holds that snow is void of color altogether and that our idea of snow (e.g., white, cold, etc.) exists only in the mind.[24] Nor is this the most significant objection. From the perspective of Aristotelean thought and common sense,[25] Locke's most unsettling claim is that we do not immediately apprehend objects (or form). Just as our simple ideas are said to exist only in the mind, for Locke, sorts or species ("nominal essences," in Locke's language) exist only in the mind and are assembled actively by human beings. "Our ranking and distinguishing natural substances into species consists in the nominal essence the mind makes" (3.6.11; see also 3.3.13). "Nominal essences" are definitions or abstract ideas we make of something. That which is essential to a nominal essence is determined by human choice. "Essential and not essential relate only to our abstract ideas, and the names annexed to them; which amounts to no more than this, That whatever particular thing has not in it those qualities which are contained in the abstract idea which any general term stands for, cannot be ranked under that species, nor be called by that name; since that abstract idea is the very essence of that species" (3.6.4). Against the common sense view that posits a natural harmony between intelligence and the natural world, Locke holds that human beings assemble or make the intelligible order that seems to characterize our experience. Ancient advocates of form had found the permanent concepts of science and language in nature, while modern thinkers construct a "nominal essence" grounding the possibility of science in human creativity and ingenuity.

Locke's approach appears quite radical. The qualities essential to the species of humanity appear to be chosen by mankind itself. To use Locke's example, "if several men were to be asked concerning some oddly shaped *fetus*, as soon as born, whether it were a *man* or no, it is past doubt one should meet with different answers" (ECHU 3.6.27). More generally,

> If it be asked, whether it be essential to me or any other particular corporeal being, to have reason? I say, no; no more than it is essential to this white thing I write on to have words in it. But if that particular being be to be counted of that sort *man*, and to have the name *man* given it, then reason is essential to it, supposing reason to be part of the complex idea the name man stands for: as it is essential to this thing to write on to contain words, if I will give it the name *treatise*, and rank it under that species. (3.6.4; see also 3.6.39; 3.3.12)

The political implications of fluid species boundaries are quite important. With the power to define who is and who is not a human being, a government also decides whose lives are worth protecting and whose liberties are worth respecting; decisions about the allocation of resources among citizens depend first on deciding who is capable of citizenship. Based on these considerations, Eugene Miller "can find no basis in Locke's account of substances for criticizing someone who chooses to define the essence of man in such a way as to exclude Negroes or any other racial group." Generalizing from this specific example, Miller charges that as a consequence of Locke's principles, "the human essence or species itself is variable" and "there can be no natural or experimental basis for settling...disagreements as to what a true man actually is."[26] G. W. F. Hegel makes virtually the same point, arguing that Locke's empiricism lacks "all criteria for drawing the boundary between the accidental and the necessary; that is, for determining what in the chaos of the state of nature or in the abstraction of man must remain and what must be discarded."[27] In the *Lectures*, Hegel writes: "the basis for this [empirical] philosophy is merely to be found in the transference of the determinate to the form of universality."[28] This unjustified "transference" leads to errors in the making of nominal essences, where non-necessary or accidental features are wrongly thought to be necessary. Denying that nature makes species or that standards in nature decide where species end and begin, Locke, on this reading, authorizes men to define the boundaries of species arbitrarily.

Following Descartes, Bacon, and Hobbes, Locke holds that the world or "real essence" of things is in principle unknowable. A "real essence" is "the real constitution of substances, upon which depends [the] nominal essence" (ECHU 3.6.2). Locke repeatedly contends that we can have "no particular idea of" the real constitution of substances (3.3.18; see also 2.23.2–6, 32; 3.6.6). While our inability to know the nature of natural things may be a cause for worry, the scientific construction of "nominal essences" can proceed without knowing nature in the strict sense. In fact, for Locke and other advocates of modern science, our ability to conquer nature is premised on our inability to know nature.[29] Since "we know not the real essences of things; all we can do is, to collect such a number of simple ideas as, by examination, we find to be united together in things existing, and thereof to make one complex idea" (3.6.21). Nominal essences are human constructions, are made "by the mind" (3.6.26).

Although complex ideas of substances are made by the mind, they are not made "arbitrarily." In "making its complex ideas of substances," the mind "only follows nature; and puts none together which are not supposed to have a union in nature" (ECHU 3.6.28). Locke thus endorses the Baconian suggestion that "we cannot command nature except by obeying her."[30] Since science no longer aims at knowledge of nature and is even predicated on our inability to know natural things, scientific knowledge for Locke and for modern science in general is "fundamentally hypothetical,"[31] or "Conditionall,"[32] or, as Locke would have it, "experimental" (4.3.29); we can observe that X follows Y, but cannot know why this is so or what this relation means. This conditional knowledge suffices to secure a predictive science, which is all we need to command nature.

The paradox that this modern free (and, somehow, at the same time, not entirely free) construction of concepts raises is this: as it calls into question the intelligibility of nature and holds that our perceptions are merely in our mind without any relationship to the objects whence they came, how can it know that it is obeying nature? If effective obedience depends on some knowledge of the thing obeyed (as when our obedience to law depends on our knowledge of law), does not the modern approach as seen in Locke presume some kind of knowledge about nature? Modern skepticism assumes that human beings are estranged from nature, but one wonders if it can consistently maintain that estrangement and still conduct *natural* science. Does Locke think nature guides efforts to grasp intelligibility in the natural world?[33] Can Locke *on his own principles* accept the guidance of nature?

The Modern See-Saw: Estrangement and Harmony

Locke's thorough accounting of these questions shows him to be perhaps, the first modern thinker to diagnose the problems in the modern scientific self-understanding. He steps outside modern skepticism regarding the senses in order to address anew the issue of how human sensibilities come to confront nature and to acknowledge the limits of the modern experimental method. He does not call those principles into question, and he does not render those principles coherent, but his thought embodies the moment when the self-confidence in the modern philosophic edifice began to fracture.

That nature guides Locke's scientific enterprise concerning natural or external things cannot be gainsaid. Only through study of the "things themselves" (ECHU 3.11.5), study guided by experience and observation, does Locke's natural science proceed. Study of natural things could not proceed without the assumption that the "nominal essence" reflects, or has some ontological foundation in, the "real essence"; scientists cannot conduct experiments unless they also know that there is a stability in the objects under investigation; scientists repeat experiments because they assume individual objects belong to some stable, natural sort. Though he relates tales of monstrous births in an effort to undermine belief in the naturalness of species, Locke also supposes that nature produces things in kinds or species. He writes, "Nature, in the constant production of particular things, makes them not always new and various, but very much alike and of kin one to another" (3.6.37; also 2.8.15; 2.31.3; 3.3.13; 3.6.28 and 30; 3.9.11; and 4.4.12). Such observed likenesses, Locke infers, probably reflect a similarity in the unknowable "internal frame and constitution" (3.6.36).

Science can proceed only if nature presents its kinds to human senses in a stable way. This has several implications for issues treated in the preceding section. Something stable must almost certainly exist in each natural thing if it is to prompt stable perceptions in observers. Human senses must also operate with sufficient reliability to apprehend the stable, continually existing objects. From these inferences it follows that the stability perceived by observers must have some stable and necessary relationship to things observed. This is not necessarily to argue that the green we observe in an apple is in the apple (though it is not to deny such a possibility). Locke's concessions lead to the conclusion that for science to proceed, all human observations must (somehow) have a foundation in nature, or, to put this differently, that there is a natural, if inexplicable, harmony between the senses and nature.

Could it be that Locke gives back with one hand what he took with the other? Could Locke rely on observation and experience when he has subjected these concepts to such a thorough philosophic critique? Does the great criticism of ancient and scholastic metaphysics elaborated upon by modern thinkers culminate in a confirmation of ancient and scholastic metaphysics?

From Hume's perspective, Locke's thought on this score runs in opposite directions. The contradiction is not merely that Locke holds that human beings make the boundaries that separate species even as nature makes things in stable species, for such a contradiction might be in the nature of things, if we are only *partly* estranged from nature. It is not merely that Locke denies that we have access to the "real essence" of things while sometimes assuming that we can have probable knowledge of what amounts to the "real essence" of things, for such a contradiction might be in the nature of things, if we are only *partly* estranged from nature. The ultimate contradiction lies in this. The estrangement from nature in Locke's distinction between primary and secondary qualities cannot be sustained if science is to learn about the world. Realizing this, Locke supplements the *total* estrangement from nature inherent in the modern principle with a contention that we are only *partially* estranged from nature. Science ultimately must rest assured that nature is stable and that our senses and perceptions are reliable guides to the world, though modern philosophy is founded in radical opposition to those assumptions. Locke's thought embodies a radical skepticism of the senses and, unwittingly, perhaps, presumes the reliability of the senses. Moreover, *given the premises of modern skepticism*, it is not at all clear that Locke's formulation of the modern scientific method can yield *partial* knowledge of nature (as one Locke commentator has held[34]). Modern skeptical premises rule out reliance on nature from the very start. The modern principles turn science into an assertion of human constructivism. Science proceeding without reference to nature ends up, like scholastic science, with the contemplation of abstract ideas compounded by the problems of assertiveness, willfulness, and inventiveness. On this view, Nietzsche and post-moderns are moderns in the truest sense, in that they adhere to the creative and constructivist premises of modern philosophy without blinking (Locke, from this perspective, blinks when he burdens science's creativity with assumptions about a reliable nature). Modern skepticism on which modern philosophers sought to ground science contradicts itself, undermines itself, or culminates in a hypothetical, abstract, potentially dangerous variety of language game.

    Locke realized that science could not proceed while consistently relying on modern skeptical principles, so he surreptitiously brought non-skeptical premises about natural order, intelligibility, and reliable senses into his scientific project. Good sense demands more of Locke than he gave, however. Locke's thought embodies the problems in the modern premises, but, unlike Hume, Locke does not subject those premises to searching and ultimately devastating philosophic examination. Only by mitigating modern skeptical principles at the onset and by *starting with* a (somewhat) sympathetic account of human faculties could a science aiming at partial knowledge of nature achieve partial knowledge of nature. Only by showing that science proceeds (and must proceed) with a skeptical trust in the reliability of the senses can philosophy consistently proceed with the confidence that nature shines through human senses sufficiently for our purposes.

Metaphysicians after Locke faced the problems Locke began to notice. Perhaps the crisis of modern philosophy could have led to a return to ancient explanations for intelligibility and order. Hume tried to tack away from metaphysics altogether.

CHAPTER 3

ACTIVE SOVEREIGNTY IN NATURAL AND
MORAL PHILOSOPHY

> *Those who have a lively imagination are a great deal more pleased with themselves than the prudent can reasonably be. They look down upon their fellow men; they argue boldly and confidently where others do so with fear and diffidence; and their cheerful look often gives them advantage in the minds of an audience, such esteem do those who imagine themselves wise command before judges of a like nature. Imagination cannot make fools wise, but she makes them happy, to the regret of reason.*
>
> —Pascal, *Pensees* 81

Hume accepts the "realistic" critique of ancient philosophy offered by modern thinkers. Hume's first, most obvious, and seemingly greatest philosophic accomplishment lies in subjecting the principles of modern philosophy to a searching skeptical criticism. The second, deeper goal is to illuminate our obscure condition and contradictory faculties and hence to distinguish the natural difficulties involved in philosophizing from artificial difficulties that modern thinkers have involved themselves in. Articulating the inconsistencies and mysteries, Hume provides a philosophy of common life and establishes grounds for philosophic modesty and political moderation.

Philosophers had undermined modesty and moderation by asserting what I call an active sovereignty of the imagination. Observing contradictions between common experience and reason, previous philosophers constructed principles on a clarified plane that seemed to be immune from the ambiguities of common life. Philosophic concepts such as the distinction between primary and secondary qualities seemed to be autonomous from problems inherent in pre-scientific sensibilities. Philosophic "reason first appears in possession of the throne, prescribing laws, and imposing maxims with an absolute sway and authority" (T 186). This sovereign clarity came at a price. Clarifying principles are products of imagination invented in an attempt to escape the mortifying limits of human understanding. Reason's throne is compromised because it must operate within the givens of our messy condition, which limits the active, assembling, poetic power of human reason.

Descartes and Locke are, for Hume, among the philosophers bringing the actively sovereign imagination to the modern sensibility. Their presumption is a constant temptation in our liberal order, where the human environment appears to be open to re-making by assertions of power; this aspiration to clarity brings utopianism to politics. Political utopianism comes from the modern theoretical stance and is characterized by an actively sovereign imagination aspiring for autonomy from common life. Hume hopes to reconfigure the relationship between theory and practice by offering a change in how to think about each. He grounds the unsettling active sovereignty and excessively theoretical politics while arguing against the autonomy of reason.

This is not the traditional view of Hume's relationship to previous philosophers or of Hume's purpose. The traditional view, suggested by Kant and Thomas Reid, saw a Hume aware of the self-defeating implications of modern rationalism, but unable to escape its strictures. On this view, Hume followed the logic of the skepticism suggested by Descartes and developed by Locke, which resulted in Hume's denying that we could explain existence of the world. In so doing, Hume undid the material and the spiritual world and left "nothing in nature but ideas and impressions, without any subject on which they may be impressed." Reid contends that Descartes, Locke, and Hume embraced the same system, and that Hume "wantonly sapped the foundation of this partition, and drowned all in one universal deluge" of skepticism.[1] In his "Dedicatory" introduction to the *Inquiry into the Human Mind*, Reid draws out the radical implications. "The ingenious author of that treatise upon the principles of Locke...hath built a system of scepticism, which leaves no ground to believe any one thing rather than its contrary."[2]

Several twentieth century scholars sought to rescue Hume from these critics. Norman Kemp Smith (1941) showed how Hume's "naturalism" prevented his thought from slipping into the universal skepticism Reid imputed to him. Hume's skeptical arguments showed that natural, non-rational features such as instinct and feeling determine belief. By "naturalism" Kemp Smith and his followers meant that human nature has the non-intellectual resources to perceive and analyze experience in ways that philosophers such as Locke did not account for. For Hume, it is "not reason but feeling—in Hume's terminology, the passions, inclusive of belief—which is in supreme control."[3]

Where Locke emphasizes the active construction of complex ideas about the natural world in our making of nominal essences, Hume's reliance on "natural belief" involves a critique of such "conventionalism" and of the imagination's role in the making of species. Hume emerges from this revision as a thinker whose reliance on nature leads to a more passive, trusting, and circumscribed account of our faculties and perhaps as a thinker more open to accepting the existence of natural species.

Extending the "naturalistic" reading of Hume, recent commentators draw connections between Hume's critique of modern rationalism and his political essays and histories. These scholars worry that naturalistic reading emphasizing the non-rational in Hume's account creates the impression of a Hume "for whom all thought is determined by feeling" or a Hume that is a "preromantic espouser of giving in to feeling in the face of skeptical triumphs."[4] This amended reading sees Hume endorsing a "mitigated naturalism,"[5] against the subordination of reason to the passions Kemp Smith saw. Hume's essays and histories are products of critical reasoning and insight. "The usual reading," John W. Danford writes, "is not wrong, it simply does not go far enough, because it does not bring out the connection to the positive side of [Hume's] philosophic program."[6] Danford, Donald Livingston, and others see this "positive side" in Hume's *Essays, History of England,* and *Dialogues Concerning Natural Religion.* His balanced, dual-faceted "mitigated skepticism" and "mitigated naturalism" orient Hume's moral inquiry. This interpretation sees a formidable Hume, whose naturalism is mitigated by a distrust of natural beliefs and a refining critical reason.

These different schools emphasize different moments of Hume's thought and see different purposes in Hume's "negative" philosophy. My aim is to provide a new account of Hume's philosophic vision, emphasizing how Hume establishes and charts the complex mix of faculties that constitute human nature. This involves traversing some well-traveled scholarly roads, on which we see that Hume exposes pretensions of the actively sovereign imagination in modern conception of perception, identity, and causation. I travel these roads to prepare for a deeper treatment of Hume's positive orientation.

The "Fundamental Principle" of Modern Philosophy

Like Locke, Decartes and other modern thinkers, Hume rejects the ancient-scholastic metaphysics as frustrating and inventive. Ancient philosophers conducted a "search for the qualities, in which [the] agency [of stability] consists," but it yielded only "incomprehensible," unnatural results. Even more problematic is their inventiveness. The "lamentable condition" in which philosophers found themselves as they tried to penetrate the way of being is akin to how the poets describe the "punishment of *Sisyphus* and *Tantalus*." As Hume asks, "what can be imagin'd more tormenting, than to seek with eagerness, what for ever flies us; and to seek it in a place, where 'tis impossible it can ever exist?" (T 222–3). For Hume, that ancients were defending common experience with their abstruse metaphysics is of no matter—he was not as concerned as the other moderns to upset the reliability of common experience; however, he sought to provide a metaphysics-free account of common experience.

"*Modern Philosophy,*" he continues, "pretends to be entirely free from" from the defect of inventing fictitious principles, "and to arise only from the solid permanent, and consistent principles of the imagination." Hume identifies the grounds of this modern pretension as the "fundamental principle" of modern philosophy, namely the distinction between primary and secondary qualities (T 226).[7] Like Locke, Hume opposes the modern system of natural philosophy to the normal opinion of mankind. Hume describes the common understanding of perception in the first *Enquiry*:

> When men follow this blind and powerful instinct of nature, they always suppose the very images, presented by the senses, to be the external objects, and never entertain any suspicion, that the one are nothing but representations of the other. This very table, which we see white, and which we feel hard, is believed to exist, independent of our perception, and to be something external to our mind, which perceives it.

"This universal and primary of opinion of all men," Hume continues,

> is soon destroyed by the slightest philosophy, which teaches us, that nothing can ever be present to the mind but an image or perception, and that the senses are only the inlets, through which these images are conveyed, without being able to produce any immediate intercourse between the mind and the object. The table, which we see, seems to diminish, as we remove farther from it: but the real table, which exists independent of us, suffers no alteration: it was, therefore, nothing but its image, which was present to the mind. (EHU 151–2)[8]

Modern philosophy thereby subverts our ability to make steady or penetrating comments about nature. Only appearances or impressions present themselves to the human mind and senses.

Neither ancient nor modern philosophers are tempted to argue that our impressions come from nowhere, for such a conclusion would defy common sense too much. In attempting to accommodate the common sense view (that our impressions have a foundation in the world) and the philosophical skepticism introduced by reason (that we only apprehend impressions), philosophers "contrive a new hypothesis, which seems to comprehend both these principles of reason and imagination." Whether it is the ancient-scholastic distinction between form and substance or Locke's distinction between primary and secondary qualities, "this hypothesis is the philosophical one of the double existence of perceptions and objects; which pleases our reason, in allowing, that our dependent perceptions are interrupted and different; and at the same time is agreeable to the imagination, in attributing a continu'd existence to something else, which we call *objects*" (T 215).[9] Modern philosophy's "fundamental principle" is the latest example of the penchant of philosophers to treat perceptions as appearances and underlying objects as realities.[10] The modern approach may improve on the ancient approach in holding that the underlying reality is inscrutable,[11] but it still partakes of the error of positing a "double existence of perception and objects."

Hume contends that "many objections might be made to this [modern] system," but he limits himself to a "very decisive" one (T 227). Following Bishop Berkeley, Hume thinks the distinction between primary and secondary qualities is untenable. Recall that secondary qualities do not exist in the objects themselves, but are merely perceptions of the mind.

> If this be allowed, with regard to secondary qualities, it must also follow, with regard to the supposed primary qualities of extension and solidity; nor can the latter be any more entitled to that denomination than the former. The idea of extension is entirely acquired from the senses of sight and feeling; and if all the qualities, perceived by the senses, be in the mind, not in the object, the same conclusion must reach the idea of extension, which is wholly dependent on the sensible ideas or the ideas of secondary qualities. (EHU 154)

This criticism constitutes what an astute Locke scholar considers "the central difficulty of Locke's theory of knowledge."[12] If sensible qualities are in the mind and not in the object and we can know of qualities only through the senses, then "we utterly annihilate all these objects, and reduce ourselves to the most extravagant scepticism concerning them" (T 228).[13] The logic of Hume's criticism is inescapable, given the premise of deriving all ideas from experience.[14] If perceptions do not exist in the world, modern grounds lead us to deny the existence of the world.

Insofar as modern philosophers, such as Locke, notice the difficulty of justifying the existence of the outside world, they simply presume the external world to exist (ECHU 2.23.2, 4, 5). This presumption cannot be justified on modern grounds, which demand skepticism of all deliverances of common sense. "Philosophers deny our resembling perceptions to be identically the same [as the objects from which they come], and uninterrupted; and yet have so great a propensity to believe them such, that they arbitrarily invent a new set of perceptions, to which they attribute these qualities."[15] This presumption is based on common sense, not philosophic rigor or argument; the vulgar *believe* and the philosophic *presume* that the world outside exists and that our perceptions necessarily reflect bodies in the world. The modern attempt to found a science free from the defects of common sense "is over-and-above loaded with this absurdity, that it at once denies and establishes the vulgar supposition" (T 218).[16] The hope of replacing the vague, defective, haphazard ways of previous science and common sense with a more precise, thorough approach to knowing nature is the modern see-saw of estrangement and harmony that we saw in the last section of chapter 2.

Nor is this the only example of the modern approach's surreptitious reliance on common opinion when it comes to explaining human perception. Modern metaphysics fails to explain itself and falls back on prescientific, common sense presumptions at every step. First, granting the existence of the external world, the modern system cannot explain the means by which objects convey perceptions to the human mind. "By what argument can it be proved," Hume asks, "that the perceptions of the mind must be caused by external objects, entirely different from them, though resembling them (if that be possible) and could not arise either from the energy of the mind itself, or from the suggestion of some invisible and unknown spirit, or from some other cause still more unknown to us?" (EHU 152–3).[17] Second, modern philosophy cannot explain why one event succeeds another or why a perception is necessarily connected to other perceptions (EHU 74). A pool ball struck by another, in Hume's example, will move. Reason cannot explain the tie between these two events, though we observe one following another. Third, the modern system cannot explain why solid matter coheres or supports the existence of perceptions with regularity (T 232–4, EHU 152). These aspects of perception—the regularity of delivery, necessary connection, the coherence of matter—are matters of common sense that philosophic accounts presume. Modern philosophy's skepticism of common sense presumptions makes each of those assumptions absurd.

Hume agrees with the premise that leads philosophers to posit the "double existence of perceptions and objects."

> There is a direct and total opposition betwixt our reason and our senses; or more properly speaking betwixt those conclusions we form from cause

and effect, and those that persuade us of the continu'd and independent existence of body. When we reason from cause and effect, we conclude, that neither colour, sound, taste, nor smell have a continu'd and independent existence. When we exclude these sensible qualities there remains nothing in the universe, which has such an existence. (T 231)[18]

The opposition between reason and the senses is permanent. "Sceptical doubt, both with respect to reason and the senses, is a malady, which can never be radically cur'd, but must return upon us every moment, however we may chace it away, and sometimes may seem entirely free from it." More pointedly, Hume denies we can know how objects in the world are perceived: "'Tis impossible upon any system to defend either our understanding or senses" (T 218). Philosophic modesty demands an acceptance of our limits and a common sense submission to the fact *that* we perceive the world. The order of our experience arises (with qualification) spontaneously and is available to people regardless of philosophic training.

This is the pattern of Hume's skepticism. He criticizes philosophic categories and constructs to show that there is a "total opposition" between reason and the senses or between reason and imagination. Hume boasts of the ingenuity he displays in presenting his "destructive" side (and today's philosophers still love him for it). His greatest philosophic accomplishment lies in articulating the complexities of human nature and showing how philosophy should proceed in light of them and in exposing errors in philosophy so she can find her proper domain. Let us canvas other cases of modern philosophy's attempt to overcome contradictions between reason and imagination as a means of showing how pervasive this destructive side of Hume's philosophy is and of presenting the complex ballast for his positive orientation.

Personal Identity. "There are some philosophers," Hume begins his account of personal identity, "who imagine we are every moment intimately conscious of what we call our SELF; that we feel its existence and its continuance in existence; and are certain, beyond the evidence of demonstration, both of its perfect identity and simplicity" (T 251).[19] Philosophers imagine a simple, persistent idea of personal identity when defending "the strongest sensation" and "most violent passion" of common experience—that our identities are stable through time. This belief is a "bias of the imagination" (T 254). Reason teaches a different lesson. In response to the question "From what impression cou'd this idea [of self] be deriv'd?" Hume answers, "'tis impossible to answer without a manifest contradiction and absurdity; and yet 'tis a question, which must necessarily be answer'd, if we wou'd have the idea of self pass for clear and intelligible" (T 251). Our imagination, which would see us as whole and single, contradicts our reason, which reveals that our impressions of self are variable, interrupted, and fleeting.

Philosophers have dealt with this opposition between imagination and reason by asserting "that these different related objects are in effect the same, however interrupted and variable." Philosophers side with imagination over reason and invent principles purporting to unify our disjointed experience. They feign "some new and unintelligible principle, that connects the objects together, and prevents their interruption." Examples of such constructs are "the notion of a *soul,* and *self,* and *substance*" (T 254). As with primary and secondary qualities, the inventive, sovereign imagination, masquerading as reason, constructs principles to explain our fleeting feelings of permanence.

The urge to imagine that human beings are persistent, unified creatures bespeaks an understandable pride in transcending the merely perceptional, particular elements of existence. Proud creatures want to see themselves as experiencing a continued existence over time or as having achieved unity through a self-conscious construction of self. Philosophers imagine that human beings have the capacity to achieve simplicity or identity above the "perpetual flux and movement" typical of the natural world. This singularity is founded on a self-conscious reflection about our perceptions. Hume criticizes the proud abstracting tendency of human imagination. We only feel one idea at a time. "Identity is nothing really belonging to these different perceptions, and uniting them together; but is merely a quality, which we attribute to them, because of the union of their ideas in the imagination, when we reflect upon them" (T 259–60). Nor does Hume think human beings are capable of abstracting from particular perceptions. "For my part," Hume writes, "when I enter most intimately into what I call *myself,* I always stumble on some particular perception or other, of heat or cold, light or shade, love or hatred, pain or pleasure. I never can catch *myself* at any time without a perception, and never can observe any thing but the perception" (T 252). Skeptical reason humiliates, frustrates, and embarrasses the imagination. The faculty that justifies human pride destroys it; this fact paradoxically establishes and vindicates human pride, for only an elevated creature can discover its humiliating limitations. This paradoxical destruction lays bare the "intermediate situation of the mind" (T 216).

In neither the *Treatise* nor the first *Enquiry,* where Hume discusses the "Reason of Animals," does he think that a clear line can be drawn between human beings and lesser animate creatures (EHU 104–8). Nowhere is our ignorance about fundamental things more apparent than in his discussion "Of the Immateriality of the Soul" (T Book I, Part IV, Section V). Hume takes up the subject of the soul after "having found such contradictions and difficulties in every system concerning external objects, and in the idea of matter" (T 232). Since we have no idea what substance is or how we perceive it, the "dispute concerning the materiality and immateriality of the soul" is absurd; Hume "condemn[s]...the question itself" (T 234). This condemnation appears near the outset of the section, and yet Hume continues for 17 pages. Much space is dedicated to a condemned question.

Hume devotes these pages to a discussion of opinions on how thought could mingle with body or soul with matter (T 235ff.). The point is to show that neither "materialists" nor "their antagonists" speak intelligibly. Materialists "affirm that plants, animals, men, &c. are nothing but particular actions of one simple universal substance, which exerts itself from a blind and absolute necessity." Hume does not say, as Aristotle did, that this opinion offends common sense or makes science impossible. For Hume, it is "unintelligible and contradictory," because a world governed by natural necessity cannot explain how and whether sensed perceptions are united to material objects (T 238).[20] The doctrine of immateriality holds that all things "are modifications of one simple, uncompounded, and indivisible substance" (T 242). This hypothesis is "unintelligible" too, in that it denies the existence of images or perceptions or motion (T 246, 239ff.). Hume thinks that believers in a simple immaterial soul embrace a "dangerous and irrevocable atheism" (T 244). Both schools of thought are unintelligible in the same way (T 243),[21] for both reduce human perceptions to a simple formula.

Hume's deconstruction of these dogmas reveals the priority of obscurity over contradiction in his teaching on the soul and personal identity. Hume sees people as mixtures of body and something even more obscure. These mutually repulsive principles define human nature. Any attempt to explain these obscurities is unintelligible, is mere words. We cannot understand a world conceived either as body or as thought, and we cannot comprehend how thought could embody itself in a human being. The unsatisfactory principles of philosophy seek to relieve our real situation of obscurity, and they serve to obscure the obscurity. Were it not for these fundamental obscurities, such contradictions would not arise. Philosophic principles are useful perhaps when we are forced to confront their insufficiency, though they can reduce our researches into verbal disputes. Hume's attempt to show that personal identity is not coherent or that body and thought comingle in mysterious ways reveals the limits of our self-knowledge. Philosophy may in some cases be necessary to lead us there, but it leads us to mysteries and obscurities from which all answers can be sought. Our obscure condition leads us to know ourselves, insofar as we can be said to know ourselves.

Causation. The problem of causation combines all the contradictions of perception with all the obscurities surrounding personal identity. "Of all the paradoxes" Hume discovers our idea of necessary connection is the "most violent" and the "most sublime" (T 166, 156). There is no shortage of deep, penetrating studies of Hume's treatment of causation, and I will not reproduce those treatments.[22] For my purposes, Hume's account of causation should be seen in light of his criticisms of previous philosophers.[23] Previous philosophic ideas of causation arise from the conflict between our senses and imagination on the one hand and our reason on the other. Our imagination and senses want to infer a general notion of causation from many particular instances of one body following another. With the application of sufficient heat, wax changes from a solid to a fluid; from this we not only want to infer that heat is the cause of the effected change in the condition of wax, but also to form our general notions of cause and effect.[24] From this inference derives the idea of power.

Reason destroys this imaginative inference from the senses. Hume's two claims against what he takes to be the traditional approach to explaining causation are mutually reinforcing. First, since we cannot know why one object changes another, we cannot conceive of particular instances of cause in the world. Second, since we cannot abstract from particulars in the formation of general ideas, we cannot have ideas about that which we do not have particular ideas. In Hume's judgment, Locke constructed an abstract notion of causation or power to please his senses and imagination, while at the same time accepting the conclusion of his reason that human beings cannot know the manner in which causes lead to effects. Locke's idea of power, in Hume's treatment, is yet another instance of an invented "notion of some spiritual and refin'd perception[]" used by philosophers to "cover their absurdities" without submitting their ideas to clear-sighted, sobering, somewhat mortifying analysis (T 72).

Attempts to justify human faculties with systematic explanations of natural conundrums lead to even greater problems. We "expose [our understanding and senses] farther when we endeavor to justify them in that manner" (T 218). As Hume writes in the first paragraph of his first work, "principles taken upon trust, consequences lamely deduced from them, want of coherence in the parts, and of evidence in the whole, these are every where to be met with in the systems of the most eminent philosophers, and seem to have drawn disgrace upon philosophy itself" (T xiii). Criticisms of human faculties are destructive enough, but philosophic attempts at justifying faculties obscure the real contradictions in human faculties and create new, artificial conundrums (such as the distinction between primary and secondary qualities). The manifest contradictions into which "intemperate" philosophical inquiry leads pose serious problems for philosophy and civil life. "The understanding, when it acts alone, and according to its most general principles, entirely subverts itself, and leaves not the lowest degree of evidence in any proposition, either in philosophy or common life" (T 267–8). Modern philosophy flatters with hopes that philosophic refinement can "solve" the maladies of human understanding. It fails to orient reflection because it is so concerned to escape the natural, inescapable middling orientation of all reflection.

Common Life Assumptions and the Paradox of the Imagination

The problem of philosophical imagination pronouncing principles that purport to unify experience leads to the proper subordination of the imagination to the dictates of common life. The philosophy of common life means first of all that philosophic inquirers must accept several "vulgar" assumptions about the world; it saves the appearances by assuming the appearances because without assuming the appearances philosophic inquiry cannot proceed. This means that the first principles of inquiry are not the product of philosophical analysis; they are accepted antecedent to all critical thinking. Iris Murdoch articulates the Humean, common sense position against abstruse philosophy: "Language *just does* refer to the world, we *just do* possess the *essential* talent of knowing that something is the same again."[25] I begin this section by showing what assuming the appearances means for philosophic approaches to perception, identity, and causation that we looked at in the previous section.

After Hume destroys false philosophic concepts such as primary and secondary qualities, personal identity, and causation, he assumes the natural, common sense assumption about each subject. Identifying natural assumptions may, in the final analysis, be fraught with philosophic problems: I proceed first by locating Hume's suppositions or assumptions and will then try to understand why he considers those assumptions to be natural. With respect to the senses, "we must take for granted in all our reasonings" *that* there are extended bodies outside our mind though we "cannot pretend by any arguments of philosophy to maintain its veracity" (T 187). Philosophic investigations of perception must also presume that "the appearances of objects to our senses" are consistent and resemble the objects themselves. We provide continuity to our experience "by *supposing* that...interrupted perceptions are connected by a real existence" (T 199, emphasis supplied; see also T 198). Just as thinkers must presume the existence of substance and our ability to perceive substances consistently so that analysis can proceed, so also must philosophers take the continued existence, identity, and coherence of matter for granted: they "*suppose* the whole train of perceptions to be united by identity" (T 259, emphasis supplied; also T 401), though they cannot find a principle uniting that train of perceptions.[26] However radical Hume appears to be in discovering the incoherence in our ideas of causation, Hume does not deny that causes exist in nature. The best evidence that Hume continues to *suppose* the existence of causation is his use of these terms in the first *Enquiry* and his later political works.[27]

Hume refers to our assumption about "the continu'd existence of sensible objects" as a "fiction" or as an opinion that we know to be "false" (T 209, 213). Our ideas about identity are likewise "fictitious" (T 259).[28] Hume drops this language in the first *Enquiry*, where, when such issues arise, he refers to these concepts as "suppositions" rather than feigned or false "fictions," as he had in the *Treatise*.[29] The language of supposition is not absent from the *Treatise*.[30] Between his youthful *Treatise* and his later *Enquiry* Hume seems to have learned that the language of fiction is inconsistent with the language of supposition. Continued existence and identity are inexplicable, pre-reflective, and unjustifiable by philosophical argument. By calling these concepts "false," Hume suggested in the *Treatise* that things do not have a continued existence or identity. This is problematic because the label "fictitious" or "false" presumes a level of penetration into nature that Hume does not think we can have. It also risks leaving the impression that Hume did not think the world to be as ordered as he supposed it to be. This is one of the great differences between the temper and substance of Hume's thought as it developed beyond his earliest work.

Previous philosophic constructs sought to justify our capacity to engage nature. All were correct in concluding that our capacities for perceiving identity and causation were necessary parts of human apprehension of nature, but all were wrong in thinking that we could explain the human capacity or that naming principles equated with penetrating to the depths of nature. Aristotelian distinctions between form and substance, or Platonic Ideas, and Locke's modern reductive principles of perception presume that human beings have access to the way things are. Hume's philosophy of common life is grounded in the observation that we can *only suppose* as part of the common sense "givens" of reasoning. The building blocks of reasoning are the appearances of things to the mind, the phenomena as the mind apprehends and constructs them. While this may seem to mean that he embraces a conception of the mind as a subjective, solipsistic echo-chamber where human beings cling to the only rope promising deliverance, Hume *presumes* that the "operations of nature are independent of our thought and reasoning" (T 168). There is something out there—there must be something outside the human mind; the heat must actually cause the wax to melt. We cannot know how we know that. Spinning our wheels trying to explain those faculties only distracts thinkers from the proper realm of scientific reflection. Hume seeks to relieve philosophers of penetrating, but fruitless and confusing questions about human faculties and the nature of nature.

Hume completes Locke by leaving the principles of modern philosophy behind. Engaging the world with suppositions, Locke had still clung to the "fundamental principle" of modern skepticism. Hume destroyed modern skeptical principles by showing how they could not account for themselves while showing that philosophy cannot begin with skepticism antecedent to suppositional knowledge (EHU 149ff.). Only by submitting initially to such suppositions can philosophers and scientists gain the partial knowledge to which they can aspire and achieve knowledge on consistent terms.

Hume warns against the imagination's tendency to try to escape and explain necessary assumptions. Hume is familiar with and somewhat sympathetic toward the sovereign, radical desire to know characteristic of modern and ancient philosophy—it is a moment in philosophy that admirably demonstrates discontent with received opinion. "Nothing is more curiously enquir'd after by the mind of man, than the causes of every phenomenon; nor are we content with knowing the immediate causes, but push on our enquiries, till we arrive at the original and ultimate principle" (T 266). This radical desire to know is based on an erroneous, sovereign account of reason that pretends to penetrate the hidden recesses of nature, but merely imputes to the world principles derived from human imagination. This actively sovereign imagination imposes maxims on phenomena as a means of explaining things. However admirable this desire to know is, previous philosophers were wrong-headed in their pursuit. "Nothing is more requisite for a true philosopher," Hume contends, "than to restrain the intemperate desire of searching into causes, and having established any doctrine upon sufficient number of experiments, rest contented with that, when he sees a farther examination would lead him into obscure and uncertain speculations" (T 13).

Lest we be tempted to see Hume as condemning the imagination in total, it is necessary to follow his thinking beyond the conflict between reason on the one hand and the imagination and the senses on the other. Each faculty, especially within the imagination, manifests paradoxes; the imagination, while dangerous to sound philosophic analysis, is indispensable to it. Hume's rehabilitation of imagination is part of his effort to change philosophy's focus from a concern with explaining our apprehension of nature to articulating why human beings believe some things and not others.[31] How appearances come to our eyes we cannot know, but we can know how we feel when we believe something to be true. Here imagination is crucial.

We see the import of imagination by tracing the first *Enquiry's* discussion of our belief in causation.

> After a repetition of similar instances, the mind is carried by habit, upon the appearance of one event, to expect its usual attendant, and to believe that it will exist. The connexion, therefore, which we *feel* in the mind, this customary transition of the imagination from one object to its usual attendant, is the sentiment or impression from which we form the idea of power or necessary connexion. (EHU 75; also EHU 43)

Hence Hume's conclusion that custom "is the great guide of human life" (EHU 44). Human beings are ignorant of the secret workings of nature. We know only that our ideas are founded on impressions. When we observe the same impressions constantly occurring with other impressions, we suppose through a "customary transition" of the imagination that the object related to the first impression "causes" the object related to the second impression.[32] Though cause and effect relations are inexplicable by reason, the imagination's custom of supposing the existence of cause and effect carries great weight in common life. "Without this influence of custom, we should be entirely ignorant of every matter of fact beyond what is immediately present to the memory and senses" (EHU 45).

In concluding that custom is the principle of human nature on which our idea of causation rests, Hume does not pretend "to have given the ultimate reason for such a propensity." Hume goes beyond mere custom in Part II of the first *Enquiry's* fifth chapter, in which he describes "the nature of this *belief*, and of the *customary conjunction*, whence it is derived." Hume suggests that some may not want to read this section. It is written for those entertained "with speculations, which, however accurate, may still retain a degree of doubt and uncertainty." As to other readers, "the remaining part of this section is not calculated for them, and the following enquiries may well be understood though it be neglected" (EHU 47).

Explaining our ability to distinguish truth from fiction poses a difficulty. Since a person's beliefs are shaped by a distorting education, what appear to be true sentiments may really be false (T 116). Hume's introduction to Chapter 5, Part II reflects a paradox of imagination. "Nothing is more free than the imagination of man; and though it cannot exceed that original stock of ideas furnished by the internal and external senses, it has unlimited power of mixing, compounding, separating, and dividing these ideas, in all the varieties of fiction and vision." Given the great creativity of human imagination, Hume asks, wherein "consists the difference between such a fiction and belief?" (EHU 47). This is a problem that Aristotle faced directly and mysteriously, and modern thinkers constructively and inconsistently.

The difference between fiction and true belief cannot be known by reason. Since "the mind has authority over all its ideas, it could voluntarily annex this particular idea [of reality] to any fiction and consequently be able to believe whatever it pleases; contrary to what we find by daily experience" (EHU 47–8). Using Hume's example, a man can easily imagine that a human torso is joined to the body of a horse. This imaginative act does not lead people to conclude that centaurs exist. Since reason cannot explain our ability to discern fact from fiction, "it follows...that the difference between *fiction* and *belief* lies in some sentiment of feeling, which is annexed to the latter, not to the former, and which depends not on the will, nor can be commanded at pleasure" (EHU 48). A definition of this feeling cannot be provided; feelings we cannot define. Hume offers a "*description* of this sentiment." True belief is "a more vivid, lively, forcible, firm, steady, conception of an object, than what the imagination alone is ever able to attain" (EHU 49). The distinction between true and false is made by reason if we understand reason to be a sentiment or as founded on sentiment.[33]

Truth and falsehood are manifestly not distinguished by the presence of imagination for imagination is involved in constructing fictions and truth. There is an ineradicable tension within imagination. The tension within imagination appears in the conclusion to the first book of the *Treatise*. On the one hand, as I noted above, "nothing is more dangerous to reason than the flights of the imagination" (T 267). On the other hand, "the memory, senses, and understanding are...all of them founded on the imagination" (T 265) and the imagination allows "us to reason from causes and effects; and 'tis the same principle, which convinces us of the continu'd existence of external objects, when absent from the senses'" (T 266). The imagination produces for us, pre-consciously, the concepts that we presuppose as we engage the world (T 267).[34] Even as Hume is critical of the philosophic imagination, he concedes the imagination is "the ultimate judge of all systems of philosophy." Hume distinguishes truth from falsity within the imagination's range.

> I must distinguish in the imagination betwixt the principles which are permanent, irresistable, and universal; such as the customary transition from causes to effects, and from effects to causes: And the principles, which are changeable, weak, and irregular... The former are the foundation of all our thoughts and actions, so that upon their removal human nature must immediately perish and go to ruin. The latter are neither unavoidable to mankind, nor necessary, or so much as useful in the conduct of life; but on the contrary are observ'd only to take place in weak minds, and being opposite to the other principles of custom and reasoning, may easily be subverted by a due contrast and opposition. (T 225)

No reasoning occurs without imagination, yet imagination can undermine reason. Aware of the insuperable difficulties into which philosophers are led when they abstract from the effects of custom, true philosophers ground their reflections in customary assumptions.

Matters become yet more complicated when we consider the relationship between the imagination and judgment. In a passage near the end of the first *Enquiry*, Hume writes:

> The *imagination* of man is naturally sublime, delighted with whatever is remote and extraordinary, and running, without control, into the most distant parts of space and time in order to avoid the objects, which custom has rendered too familiar to it. A correct *Judgement* observes a contrary method, and avoiding all distant and high enquiries, confines itself to common life, and to such subjects as fall under daily practice and experience; leaving more sublime topics to the embellishments of poets and orators, or to the arts of priests and politicians. (EHU 162)

The imagination abstracted from custom leads to the "embellishments of poets" rather than to sound philosophy. Hume sees the ancient quarrel between poetry and philosophy as a family feud between different varieties of poets. This stark juxtaposition of the imagination and judgment is misleading, in that a properly moored imagination is an aspect of correct judgment because it is involved in all attempts to apprehend the world. One cannot judge properly without the imagination. This complexity reflects Hume's double-edged or mixed account of the imagination.

Paradoxes and Human Nature in Moral Philosophy

Previous thinkers did not sufficiently understand the paradoxes and contradictions that constitute the human mind. Hume departs from the ordering of others by showing that these paradoxes *define* human nature and the clashing principles explain how human beings think and act. A philosophy suitable to the clashing principles begins with fundamental assumptions. Moral philosophy proceeds in a similar way. Some inquirers, an "irksome" and stubborn lot, deny "the reality of moral distinctions." These disputants do not seek to explain the basis of moral distinctions or to argue about whether or not a particular action is virtuous; they raise the more fundamental issue of *whether* moral disputes are real. This question is akin to trying to justify the reality of our perceptions of the world, except that there is more at stake in moral philosophy. No argument can be used to convince such disputants that moral distinctions are real because reason cannot justify givens in this way. "The only way...of converting an antagonist of this kind, is to leave him to himself. For, finding that nobody keeps up the controversy with him, from mere weariness, it is probable that he will, at last, come over to the side of common sense and reason" (EPM 169–70).[35] Moral philosophy gains traction only with those who submit to the common life distinction between good and bad acts. Hume tacitly follows Aristotle, who argues in the *Metaphysics* that people should not "seek a reason for things which have no reason" (1011a12). Hume's limitation of moral inquiry to those who are morally serious also resembles Aristotle's limitation of moral philosophy to those well-schooled in morality, though Hume's moral teaching is not akin to Aristotle's in all respects.

Hume's second *Enquiry* is concerned with a different species of those who try to evade common experience. In fact, moral philosophy is one of the last strongholds for the systematizing tendencies of the actively sovereign imagination. "Men," Hume writes in the second *Enquiry*, "are now cured of their passion for hypotheses and systems in natural philosophy, and will hearken to no arguments but those which are derived from experience" (EPM 175). This is a remarkable statement. If my reading of the *Treatise* and the first *Enquiry* is correct, previous philosophy had been taken with a passion for system in natural philosophy. In the second Enquiry, Hume speaks of people being cured of this passion for system. Perhaps the *Treatise* and first *Enquiry* provided the remedy for the love of system. Hume points to the relative health of natural philosophy because, to paraphrase what Hume elsewhere writes (T 272), while errors in natural philosophy are harmless and ridiculous, they do not engage human passions overmuch; errors in moral and political philosophy and philosophy are dangerous because they can distort natural human sensibilities and lead to destructive human conflict. Reforming moral philosophy is of greater practical importance, and Hume's tone in the second *Enquiry* directs philosophers to this pressing matter. Hume draws attention to his effort, in the words of the *Treatise's* subtitle, to "introduce the experimental method of reasoning into MORAL SUBJECTS."

Where did modern moral philosophers go wrong? Hume relates two accounts of modern moral philosophy. "There has been an opinion very industriously propagated by certain philosophers," Hume writes, "that morality is susceptible of demonstration; and tho' no one has ever been able to advance a single step in those demonstrations; yet 'tis taken for granted, that this science may be brought to an equal certainty with geometry or algebra" (T 463; also EPM 170).[36] Much like constructs in natural philosophy, moral constructs follow a scientific method wherein "a general abstract principle is first established, and is afterwards branched out into a variety of inferences and conclusions, may be more perfect in itself, but suits less the imperfection of human nature, and is a common source of illusion and mistake" (EPM 174).

Neither Hobbes nor Locke produced a complete demonstrated moral code (perhaps Mandeville's *Fable of the Bees* is such a work). Hume understood their thought to contain an unelaborated moral teaching, which he calls a "selfish system of morals." Some philosophers constructed systems holding "that, whatever affection one may feel, or imagine he feels for others, no passion is, or can be disinterested; that the most generous friendship, however sincere, is a modification of self-love; and that, even unknown to ourselves, we seek only our own gratification, while we appear deeply engaged in schemes for the liberty and happiness of mankind" (EPM 296). Locke, Hobbes, and even several ancient authors explain away the apparent diversity of human motivation and concern as epiphenomena and reduce every human action to a variant of the single passion of self-interest or self-love.[37] "By a turn of imagination, by a refinement of reflection, by an enthusiasm of passion, we seem to take part in the interests of others, and imagine ourselves divested of all selfish considerations; but, at bottom, the most generous patriot and most niggardly miser, the bravest hero and most abject coward, have, in every action, an equal regard to their own happiness and welfare" (ibid.). The reduction of all moral distinctions to self-interest has a kind of intuitive validity to it. "The interest of each individual is, in general, so closely connected with that of the community, that those philosophers were excusable, who fancied, that all our concern for the public might be resolved into a concern for our own happiness and preservation." These thinkers found it "simpler" to understand apparently other-regarding virtues "as modifications of self-love; and they discovered a pretence, at least, for this unity of principle, in that close union of interest, which is so observable between the public and each individual" (EPM 218–9).

Reason chafes at the diversity in moral life and asks the question, "Which moral code is best?" Modern philosophers resort to imaginative reasoning to answer this question because they do not see a basis within messy, contradictory common life from which to analyze the matter. They are drawn to abstract principles "from that love of *simplicity* which has been the source of much false reasoning in philosophy" (EPM 298). Human nature is imperfect (EPM 174) or irreducibly complex, and requires complex explanations, while simple explanations are suitable to perfect beings. Systems that have attempted to "reduce all the various emotions of the human mind to a perfect simplicity," Hume argues, distort the "nature of the subject" and expect a degree of certitude that the nature of the subject does not admit (EPM 298-9).[38] Simple systems are products of a proud, philosophic imagination, of an actively sovereign mind taken with its ability to lay rules for the world. It may even proceed from a self-deluding love of cleverness and the love of system, which often are connected with the desire to see a perfected, beautiful edifice produced by human labor. Productions such as the selfish system reveal, once again, the conflict between reason and imagination.

Hume's objection to the selfish system of morals in the name of common sense bespeaks an objection to previous moral philosophy. In their attempts to construct systems of morality, Hume contends, these philosophers expected too much of reason; abstracting reason cannot of itself account for the nature of moral distinctions. According to Hume, reason is sufficient only "to instruct us in the pernicious or useful tendency of qualities and actions; it is not alone sufficient to produce any moral blame or approbation" (EPM 286). A look at one of Hume's examples, the vice of ingratitude, will clarify the nature of this objection. Purveyors of the selfish system allow us to define the concept perfectly. Ingratitude exists "wherever we observe good-will, expressed and known, together with good-offices performed, on the one side, and a return of ill-will or indifference, with ill-offices or neglect on the other side." If you "anatomize all these circumstances, and examine by your reason alone, in what consists the demerit or blame," Hume contends, "you never will come to any issue or conclusion." The demerit of ingratitude "arises from a complication of circumstances, which, being presented to the spectator, excites the sentiment of blame, by the particular structure and fabric of his mind" (EPM 287-8). Reason instructs about the tendency of our actions, but sentiment alone gives "a preference to the useful above the pernicious tendencies" (EPM 286).

Like previous modern philosophers, Hume holds that human beings are the source of moral distinctions, that objects are considered right or wrong only in relation to human beings; there is no moral order outside of human beings or common life to which moral distinctions correspond. But this is not to say that, for Hume, moral distinctions are subjective or arbitrary. Unlike those rejecting common moral experience as awash in confusion and contradiction, Hume sees moral distinctions as arising naturally and regularly from within common life. "Vice and virtue," Hume writes, "may be compar'd to sounds, colours, heat and cold, which, according to modern philosophy, are not qualities in objects, but perceptions in the mind" (T 469). Absent the direct analogy to modern natural philosophy, the same characterization appears in the appendix to the second *Enquiry* called "Concerning Moral Sentiment":

> The hypothesis which we embrace is plain. It maintains that morality is determined by sentiment. It defines virtue to be whatever mental action or quality gives to a spectator the pleasing sentiment of approbation; and vice the contrary. (EPM 289)

The object of moral inquiry is not to clean up common moral experience, but to "consider all the circumstances in which...actions agree, and thence endeavour to extract some general observations with regard to these sentiments" (ibid.). As with natural philosophy, the love of system, which grounds the hope to transform the moral universe with theory, gives way to a different approach moral thinking. The new account places ordinary experience within philosophic reflection.

The systematizing philosophic imagination causes a deeper problem, in this case, as it steers away from more fruitful avenues of inquiry. Finding selfishness in every human action often requires moral philosophers to perform extensive mental gymnastics as they seek to avoid the nature of human moral distinctions.

> The most obvious objection to the selfish hypothesis is, that, as it is contrary to common feeling and our most unprejudiced notions, there is required the highest stretch of philosophy to establish so extraordinary a paradox. To the most careless observer there appear to be such dispositions as benevolence and generosity; such affections as love, friendship, compassion, gratitude. These sentiments have their causes, effects, objects, and operations, marked by common language and observation, and plainly distinguished those from the selfish passions. (EPM 299)

Hume cites anguish at the death of a sickly child, romantic love, gratitude, and friendship as human experiences that cannot easily or plausibly be explained by self-love (EPM 300). "The hypothesis which allows of a disinterested benevolence, distinct from self-love, has really more *simplicity* in it" (EPM 301); the complex explanation is simpler. Selfish passions exist, and may even predominate, in human nature, but so do social or humane feelings. Abstracting reasoners ignore sentiment and mistake a part of human behavior for the whole. "The degrees of these sentiments may be the subject of controversy; but the reality of their existence, one should think, must be admitted in every theory or system" (EPM 226). These principles—the selfish and the social—exist side by side in human nature in a complex, ever changing proportion to one another. The selfish system dissolves one of the principles into the other, thus resolving by legerdemain a chief contradiction in human nature, one roughly equivalent to the distinction between private and public passions. Hume's purpose in criticizing the selfish system is to draw philosophy back to the complicated questions at the heart of the human condition and the contradictions that define human nature.

The challenge for Hume is showing how a contradictory and mysterious creature—a creature divorced from nature and unable to know itself—can give rise to a coherent philosophic perspective. Can a being so beset with difficulties and limitations proceed? How can this "leaky, weather-beaten vessel" (T 263) set sail?

CHAPTER 4

"MITIGATED SCEPTICISM" AND OUR "MIXED KIND OF LIFE": THE PHILOSOPHIC MODESTY OF HUME'S SCIENCE OF COMMON LIFE

> *Let us not then look for certainty and stability. Our reason is ever deceived by fickle shadows; nothing can establish the finite between the two infinities which both enclose and flee therefrom.*
>
> —Pascal, *Pensees* 390.

This chapter lays out the contradictory features of human nature that make up the equipment out of which human beings form judgments about the world. It culminates in Hume's most complete statement of what the human condition is, which then forms the touchstone for his treatment of morality, politics, history and religion.

Hume's acceptance of modern premises is provisional and preparatory. He accepts them provisionally to show the exhaustion of modern premises by exposing embarrassing lacunae and delineating inexplicable, reliable assumptions necessary for investigation. His acceptance prepares for a philosophy that knowingly assimilates unproven and un-provable suppositions into its confrontation with the world. This philosophy of common life subordinates the imagination to essential, un-provable suppositions; submits in an easy, relaxed way to the limits of human understanding; and turns to topics suitable to our capacities. Hume's philosophy of common life articulates the paradoxes or contradictions that *define* human capacities. These paradoxes, contradictions and obscurities are a foundation for common life philosophy and a subject of concern for common life philosophy. I began to chart these paradoxes in chapter 3: reason shows that the inferences philosophers have imaginatively drawn from the senses are without a foundation in reason and that the imagination, while dangerous to sound reasoning, is an essential part of sound reasoning. Questions remain. How can a philosophy that delineates the paradoxes of human faculties lead to a coherent account of knowledge? Can the imagination in its role as producer and assembler of ideas permit a distinction between fact and fiction or sound judgment and flights of fancy? What can Hume mean by truth when the human mind is the touchstone for judgment? What is the human mind for Hume anyway? Does Hume replace the actively sovereign imagination with an equally arbitrary and immoderate philosophy?

One of the curious features of Hume's thought is his claim that the capacity to discern truth from falsehood is a matter of lively feelings. The elevation of sentiment, the deprecation of reason, and Hume's complex treatment of judgment have led Reid to ridicule what he sees as Hume's excessive reliance on sentiment in moral evaluation and Hume's unnecessary attack on the common understanding of things. "Mankind," writes Reid, "have very absurdly called [the moral evaluator] a *judge*; he ought to be called a feeler."[1] Some of Hume's formulations make Reid's reading seem reasonable. In Appendix I of the second *Enquiry*, Hume argues that "the ultimate ends of human actions can *never, in any case*, be accounted for by *reason*, but recommend themselves *entirely* to the sentiments and affections of mankind, without *any* dependence on the intellectual faculties" (EPM 293, emphasis partly supplied).

If this reading is correct, what can be done when our feelings and imagination lead us to confuse accidental with essential circumstances? How do people correct prejudices? Noticing a number of foolish and passionate French men, to use Hume's example, we conclude "a *Frenchman* cannot have solidity" (T 146) and, perhaps, trace this lack of solidity to the French weather, French national character, Jerry Lewis movies, or French religion. This prejudice confuses an accidental characteristic (being from France) with an essential one (whatever it is that makes a man unreliable). In the *Treatise*, he laments the "opposition betwixt the judgment and imagination arising from the effects of custom" and hopes that the application of "general rules" will somehow allow for the correction of prejudicial judgments (T 148; also E 254). Whence general rules? Themselves the product of imagination and judgment acting (somehow) in concert, how can we be sure that general rules are products of sound analysis and not mere prejudice? The ability to distinguish truth from falsehood requires that people possess a capacity to correct sentiment; dependent on "prejudicial" sentiment, we also (somehow) need a sentimental corrective of sentiment. What is this corrective and what is its status?

We must side (somehow) with nature and our sentiments and imagination in the conflict between nature and reason. The emphasis on sentiment and imagination is the foundation for the "naturalist" reading of Hume, which holds, to repeat, that "it is not reason but feeling—in Hume's terminology, the passions, inclusive of belief—which is in supreme control."[2] Only with severe qualification is this true. Though he emphasizes that people rely on natural sentiments and belief for discerning truth, Hume does not and cannot banish reason and judgment from science. The emphasis on feeling and sentiment in the naturalist reading risks creating the impression that Hume promotes an immodest irrationalism.[3]

Hume has rhetorical reasons both for emphasizing the role of sentiment in correct judgment and for under-emphasizing the role of reason. Modern philosophers had over-emphasized the capacity of reason. By showing that sentiments and the imagination are a part of sound judgment, Hume hopes to reform the way modern philosophers think about the relationship between science and common life or theory and practice. The overestimation of an actively sovereign reason and the belief, propagated by Hume's modern predecessors, that reason is the foundation for moral distinctions (EPM 170–1) led Hume to emphasize the limits of reason more than the correction of sentiment. Hume's teaching on this matter is flexible and double-edged, in that it points the way to correcting excesses in each direction. Some have criticized him for relying too much on feelings or sentiment and others for relying too much on reason in his theory of moral judgment. His thought has resources necessary to show how the critical intervention of reason corrects sentiments and how judgment implicates sentiment and lively belief. He is neither a thoroughgoing naturalist nor a thoroughgoing skeptic.

The Unstable Psychology of Philosophy

The conflict between nature and reason is one of the great themes of Hume's works. "It seems evident, that men are carried, by a natural instinct or prepossession, to repose faith in their senses." By a "blind and powerful instinct of nature," people believe in "continued existence," namely that the observed white table exists "independent of our perception, and to be something external to our mind, which perceives it." Instincts of nature suggest that we perceive causes and effects in the world as well. Though this "universal and primary opinion of all men is soon destroyed by the slightest philosophy," philosophy "finds herself extremely embarrassed" when she attempts to justify our natural beliefs by reason (EHU 151–2). As we saw in chapter 3, philosophic attempts to provide a reasoned, systematic defense of natural suppositions are products of an inventive, actively sovereign imagination masquerading as reason. Philosophic criticisms of common opinion are profound, but they point to questions that cannot be answered. Philosophy returns to nature as a touchstone.

Some may see this as an abandonment of philosophy rightly understood, as simply dropping the metaphysical, theological, and epistemological questions with which philosophers have long concerned themselves.[4] At least, Hume counsels a quiet agnosticism about how nature and human imagination work. In this sense, his philosophy is, to borrow Charles L. Griswold's description, "not so much 'antifoundationalist'... as he is self-consciously nonfoundationalist."[5]

The dramatic context of the conclusion to Book I of the *Treatise* presents the three critical moments in Hume's philosophy of common life. First, modern philosophy's embrace of imaginative explanations leads to such difficulties. An awareness of such difficulties tempts Hume to quit the cause of reason. In the depths of "philosophical melancholy and delirium," Hume feels an "intense view of manifold contradictions and imperfections in human reason [that] has wrought upon [him], and heated [his] brain." He is "ready to reject all belief and reasoning, and can look upon no opinion even as more probable or likely than another." The cure for these ills, second, is "nature herself," who, "by relaxing this bend of mind" or "by some avocation," obliterates "all these chimeras." Hume's naturalism is evident: "I may, nay I must yield to the current of nature, in submitting to my senses and understanding." This "current of nature" is akin to the easy, sociable, merry mood of a friendly backgammon game or dinner party and brings with it an impatience with philosophical disputes and an "indolent belief in the general maxims of the world." Indolent submission to the general maxims of the world is, to say nothing more, not a genuinely philosophic perspective. In the third moment, this submission to nature and pleasure is neither satisfying nor efficacious. Hume gets "*tir'd* with amusement and company," and, upon the return of a "*serious* good-humor'd disposition" and hence a more philosophically defensible stance, he is "naturally *inclin'd* to carry [his] view into all those subjects, about which [he has] met with so many disputes in the course of [his] reading and conversation" (T 268–70, emphasis partly supplied). Hume's philosophy finds its origin in opposition to the moods of "philosophical melancholy" *and* natural "indolence"; he hopes both to "compose [his] temper from that spleen, *and* invigorate it from that indolence, which sometimes prevail upon [him]" (T 269, 273, emphasis supplied).[6] Hume practices philosophy in a "careless manner" or in a manner free of cares about that which exceeds human ken. It is this "easy disposition" of "application" (against natural indolence) and "good humor" (against the spleen of philosophy) which defines the philosophical manner of mitigated skepticism (T 273).[7] Hume's treatment of philosophy in this context concentrates on describing what might be called the psychology of philosophy. The previous chapter was concerned mostly with the insufficiency in the first, skeptical moment and how the turn to nature helps to correct it; more must be said about this. The great hopes of modern rationalism, when dashed, as they must be, risk careening philosophy toward an indolence born of despair. We must grasp the problems endemic to the second, natural moment and then the character of the third and final moment—the moment where the philosopher adopts the philosophy of common life.

On this second moment, Hume sometimes seems to claim that skeptical theorizing has little influence on common opinion and to endorse the sufficiency of nature. "Nature is always too strong for principle. And though a Pyrrhonian may throw himself or others into a momentary amazement and confusion by his profound reasonings; the first and most trivial event in life will put flight to all his doubts scruples" (EHU 160). Investigations into natural objects are not affected by our inability to understand what substance is. Abstruse metaphysics do not influence ethics. Quite the contrary. The persistence of superstition and destructive systems of philosophy forces the responsible and curious out of the lazy submission to nature. The curiosity that leads many to search for first causes and final ends leads to superstitious "scenes, and beings, and objects, which are altogether new" and to politically "bold" theoretical systems.[8] Peaceful political practice, ordinary virtues, and common life itself require prophylactic help. Philosophy offers "mild and moderate sentiments" as against bold and disturbing passions encouraged by superstition (T 271–2) and helps to destroy the reasoning and confidence mingled with an inordinate love of system. Proper theory is needed to combat dangerous theory; quarrels among superstitions fuel philosophy. Natural curiosity and skepticism would not sustain philosophy, he writes, "did we not enlarge our view, and opposing one species of superstition to another, set them a quarrelling; while we ourselves, during their fury and contention, happily make our escape into the calm, though obscure, regions of philosophy" (NHR 76). The naturalist position also does not do justice to human curiosity and the restless human mind, which takes human beings "into speculations without the sphere of common life" (T 271). One must exceed common life to appreciate why deliverances of common life are the proper sphere of human reflection and to be able to defend that sphere. One hears stories in common life and thoughtful people must derive a method of discerning truth from fiction or accounting for reliability of judgment. This forces us beyond common life plain and simple toward developing standards of judgment.

Where we arrive in the third moment is not where we were in either the first or second. A philosophically informed awareness of the "strange infirmities of human understanding" inspires inquirers to display "more modesty and reserve, and diminish their fond opinion of themselves, and their prejudice against antagonists." This recommendation of modesty is tailored to the self-styled learned, who are "inclined, from their natural temper, to haughtiness and obstinacy." Exposure to the limits of human understanding "might abate their pride, by showing them, that the few advantages, which they may have attained over their fellows, are but inconsiderable, if compared with the universal perplexity and confusion, which is inherent in human nature." Their reason is no purer than other's, and their insights are often fictions of imagination. This lesson in sobriety shows inquirers that there "is a degree of doubt, and caution, and modesty, which, in all kinds of scrutiny and decision, ought forever to accompany a just reasoner" (EHU 161–2). As we have seen, reason cannot sit in a throne "prescribing laws and imposing maxims" (T 186). Hume counsels a critical distance from all opinions, including especially one's own, as a means of emphasizing philosophic modesty (see T 273–4).

Hume confines philosophy but does not abandon it. He hopes that his account of human understanding may, as he writes in the *Treatise*, "contribute a little to the advancement of knowledge, by giving in some particulars a different turn to the speculations of philosophers, and pointing out to them more distinctly those subjects, where alone they can expect assurance and conviction."[9] He points philosophy to "Human Nature," which is "the only science of man" (T 273). Hume repeats his intention of re-directing philosophy in the first *Enquiry*. "Those who have a propensity to philosophy, will still continue their researches," Hume writes, "because they reflect, that, besides the immediate pleasure, attending such an occupation, philosophical decisions are nothing but the reflections of common life, methodized and corrected" (EHU 162).

What does Hume mean by "reflections of common life"? A philosophy of common life treats the matter of common life and the concerns of human beings as they arise in their daily lives. A philosophy of common life is more apt to be concerned about politics and morals (as Hume was after he fully developed the foundation for his philosophy) than natural philosophy. Showing what human beings cannot know, Hume directs scientific inquiry toward what human beings can know. Nature, Hume relates at the beginning of the first *Enquiry*, tells a philosopher of common life to "indulge your passion for science" but also insists that that "science be human, and such as may have a direct reference to action and society" (EHU 9). The philosophy of common life is concerned with "the principles of moral good and evil, the nature and foundation of government, and the cause of those several passions and inclinations which actuate and govern" human beings, among other things (T 271). A philosophy of common life uses the intellectual apparatus of human beings in common life; it is literally constituted by, or of a piece with, common sense. A philosopher of common life accepts the role natural suppositions play in our ideas and acknowledges the indispensable place of the imagination in science. He acknowledges the place of psychological customs, but (somehow) is not a slave of custom.

The common life to which Hume's philosophy turns is not simply the common life that was "destroyed by the slightest philosophy." Understanding the limits of human understanding, philosophy orients itself by *"appearances"* (T 638), which are the only intelligible sources for philosophic reflection. Hume's "nonfoundational" judgment to refrain from asking how these appearances come to be relayed to human beings points to the fields of inquiry without the baggage of classical metaphysical debates. There may be something classical about the realization that philosophy must be embedded in common life,[10] even as Hume—against the classics, it seems—refuses to speculate about how appearances may be part of an objective reality beyond human beings.

Betraying a quiet agnosticism about how perceptions of common life reflect nature and presuming they do, a philosopher of common life turns to the study of nature and human nature in particular. Given what we have seen heretofore, what can Hume mean by human "nature?" After raising this question, Hume relays three different conceptions of nature, two of which will detain us here. First, "nature" may be "opposed to rare and unusual; and in this sense of the word, which is the common one, there may often arise disputes concerning what is natural or unnatural; and one may in general affirm, that we are not possess'd of any very precise standard, by which these disputes can be decided." Nature in this sense refers to the historically constant or the frequent, to the traits shared by human beings of all times and places. Hume equates the "unnatural" with the rare or extraordinary. That this is the "common" use of the term probably recommends it to a philosophy of common life, though there may be some sense in which this definition can be corrected. There are two difficulties in distinguishing the natural from the unnatural so understood. As the number of observations increases or decreases, "t'will be *impossible* to fix any *exact boundaries* betwixt them" (T 474, emphasis supplied), though approximate boundaries can be drawn. A second difficulty lies in the possibility that "the human mind" might be corrupted by "disease or madness" (ibid.). Our capacity to distinguish between madness and sanity presupposes that we have a steady understanding of the natural and unnatural. Rough boundaries emerge from repeated confrontations and experiments. Boundaries cannot be imposed from the outside by some "objective reality" or Platonic Forms. Observation precedes the categories, and even the belief that there are categories. There may be something circular about Hume's approach to distinguishing the natural from the unnatural, but his circularity is, perhaps, in the nature of things (if I can speak in such a manner).

Hume's thought marks an important shift in how nature is studied and understood in that he emphasizes the scientific study of history, but it does not represent the abandonment of nature.

> Mankind are so much the same, in all times and places, that history informs us of nothing new or strange in this particular. Its chief use is only to discover the constant and universal principles of human nature, by showing men in all varieties of circumstances and situations, and furnishing us with materials from which we may form our observations and become acquainted with the regular springs of human action and behaviour. These records of wars, intrigues, factions, and revolutions, are so many collections of experiments, by which the politician or moral philosopher fixes the principles of his science, in the same manner as the physician or natural philosopher becomes acquainted with the nature of plants, minerals, and other external objects, by the experiments which he forms concerning them. (EHU 83–4)

As Frank D. Balog writes, history, for Hume, "is studied as a fund of empirical evidence about human nature and society from which to draw generalizations regarding the operation of natural laws in human affairs."[11] This is not to say that nature is defined by the historical moment or that "nature" is relative to historical epoch; that is, by placing the study of history within the study of nature, Hume does not intend to undermine the study of nature understood as the historically constant. We are (somehow) capable of a critical distance from any particular historical moment that is the foundation for thinking about nature.

In the second sense of nature, nature is akin to the given or innate; it is opposed to the artificial, conventional or man-made (T 474). The understanding of nature opposed to the artificial or man-made need not be different from the understanding of nature opposed to the rare. Nature understood as the frequent can correspond to nature understood as the given, if by artifice we mean something rarely done or something corrupt. It is clear that this cannot simply be the case because justice is an artificial virtue for Hume, though every society practices some form of justice. In any event, a thing can be natural in either or both of these senses for Hume.

The Construction of Nature and the Character of Judgment

I pause to discuss Hume's treatment of nature because it engenders paradoxes and confusion. The complexity of Hume's understanding of nature is reflected in the scholarly treatments of Hume. Many ignore Hume's repeated claims to study and apprehend nature altogether, presumably because Hume's epistemological skepticism makes the study of nature problematic. Applying the discussion of imagination from earlier to Hume's treatment of nature reveals the wisdom behind this omission. "Nature" does not present itself to the human mind; only *"appearances* of objects" do. The imagination assembles appearances or raw data, or, to be precise, it fashions and creates our ideas of external things (which we call "nature") out of the raw "givens" presented (somehow) to the mind. This is the import of Hume's claim that the "memory, senses, and understanding are...founded on the imagination" (T 265), that principles within imagination "are the foundation of all our thoughts and actions" (T 225), and that the imagination alone extends "custom and reasoning beyond the perceptions" (T 198). Not nature, but the imagination as it assembles "nature" is the "ultimate judge of all systems of philosophy" (T 225). The factors that shape the imagination affect what each individual considers to be natural to an extent. The difference between the natural and the artificial is untenable because the imagination, through human artifice, constructs our "natural" and "artificial" ideas.

Others call attention to the passages wherein Hume makes clear that he discusses nature (consider, for instance, EHU 83 and T 404–5). The best study putting Hume's treatment of nature as central does not, however, raise questions about how the imagination constructs nature.[12] This procedure, while apparently more credulous than other procedures, follows Hume's. Hume never connects the dots between the assembling, creative power of the imagination and the apparently constructivist account of nature. Apparently untroubled by the problems his philosophy seems to engender, Hume treats nature and human nature in his works. The logic of Hume's philosophy makes nature a troublesome concept, but Hume's political philosophy proceeds as if these problems are not decisive. This may be the most startling and philosophically formidable antinomy and contradiction in Hume's philosophy. How can Hume concentrate so on nature when his philosophy shows that the mind is estranged from it and our ideas of it are constructed?

Hume's answer depends on what we mean by "construct." Hume's philosophy proceeds on the basis of suppositions that nature exists and operates independent of the human mind (T 168), that there is a regularity or necessity in nature (T 171), and that there is a constancy in the senses and a coherence in matter. The imagination adopts "permanent, irresistible, and universal" principles, though "changeable, weak, and irregular" ones sometimes affect it (T 225). These assumptions suggest that nature can be constructed consistently and with some precision by human imagination. Nature can be studied because the appearances come to the mind consistently.

The same problematic applies to Hume's understanding of historical data and the historical process. Hume conceives of history as a support for reason and imagination as they construct nature. The principles of imagination I have discussed suggest that the historical data used to construct nature is constructed too. Historians sift through materials, construct data and stories, and infer criticisms by sympathetically and imaginatively transporting themselves to the past in (re)constructing it. If, for Hume, history has an objective reality, it is an objective reality mediated, given its meaning, and ordered by the historian's imagination. It is subjective objectivity. History is both a human actuality and a product of human imagination, *res gestae* and *historia rerum gestarum*. How can nature serve as a standard of judgment—a standard that is both natural and man-made—and how can it be achieved?

We cannot address this issue without first discussing the place of judgment in Hume's thought. Let us look at two examples of how judgment corrects our natural, untutored perceptions. We are liable to have a "more passionate regard" for a contemporary statesman than a past statesman because we feel the benefits of his actions. This does not mean that his accomplishments are more impressive than the other's. "We may own the merit to be equally great, though our sentiments are not raised to an equal height, in both cases. The judgment here corrects the inequalities of our internal emotions and perceptions; in like manner, as it preserves us from error, in the several variations of images, presented to our external senses." Hume continues, "Indeed, without such a correction of appearances, both in internal and external sentiment, men could never think or talk steadily on any subject; while their fluctuating situations produce a continual variation on objects, and throw them into such different and contrary lights and positions" (EPM 227–8). In this illustration the standard of judgment, if natural, is distinguishable from natural (i.e., pre-reflective), innate sentiments. The correcting of immediate sentiments or appearances or our natural, untutored feelings demands an outside agency within the judgment to tamp down today's feelings or to elevate the past's. Judgment appears as this less natural, but no less needed, corrective.

In the second example, Hume surveys the limits of judgment as a corrective. Hume imagines a case where we compare wealthy lottery winners and a hard-working middle class family. People cannot help but be drawn to the lottery winners as their luck affects how we evaluate their character and joy. Much the same can be said of beautiful women and handsome men, who we presume to have moral and intellectual virtues that they may not have. "The tendencies of actions and characters, not their real accidental consequences, are alone regarded in our moral determinations or general judgement; though in our real feeling or sentiment, we cannot help" but praise the successful in their endeavors. Our judgment tells us that a person's character is the object of praise or blame, but our sentiments focus on the person's station. Judgment "endeavours to correct the appearance: But is not able entirely to prevail over sentiment" (EPM 228n).[13] Though judgment is not a completely successful corrective, this rehabilitation of judgment as a mechanism for correcting the sentiments implies, in one scholar's view, "the abandonment of the principle that moral judgment is a matter of sentiment."[14]

This is not the case in a simple way. Our capacity for moral judgment "depends on some internal sense or feeling, which nature has made universal in the whole species." Judgment is a refined, cultivated, enlarged, even elevated sentiment. Cultivating correct judgment involves learning how to feel the proper feelings. Reid's reduction of judgment to feeling, adverted to earlier, is not ridiculous as long as we recognize that Hume conflates judging and feeling in a decisive way. That does not obviate the need "to employ much reasoning, in order to feel the proper sentiment; and a false relish may frequently be corrected by argument and reflection." To feel proper feelings, it is necessary "that much reasoning should precede, that nice distinctions be made, just conclusions drawn, distant comparisons formed, complicated relations examined, and general facts fixed and ascertained" (EPM 173). Judgment can create a conflict with the imagination by recalling past experiences or "general rules" that contradict present experience. General rules are themselves products of perception, sentiments, and imagination gained through imaginative observation. A general rule is "more extensive and constant" than the "capricious and uncertain" present imagination and custom (T 149). As is so often the case with Hume, there are no simple answers. Perception, feeling, sentiment, imagination, belief, passion, reflection, argument, and reason are all indispensable, constitutive parts of a "correct Judgement." Accounts of our capacity for moral evaluation that do not see such a complex mix of human faculties are partial and incomplete. Hume seems to reconcile previous accounts of moral judgment to his own.[15]

Double-edged, sound judgment must avoid being pulled too far toward the poles of sentiment and reason.

It is difficult to draw a line between any of these springs, even those that are most opposed to one another in common speech. Hume's account of judgment is riddled with riddles. Consider the following. Although Hume sometimes opposes judgment and the imagination (see, e.g., EHU 162; T 147–9, 629), the imagination is essential to judgment. Although judgment can correct sentiments, it does so on the basis of sentiments; good judges are guided by what feelings a human being or "spectator" in the proper disposition should feel (see, e.g., T 585). Although moral distinctions are founded on sentiments, human beings can improve sentiments through argument, reflection, feeling, and reasoning. The best judges survey themselves "as it were, in reflection" (EPM 276). Judgment corrects natural sentiments and mitigates skepticism. Judgment incorporates every capacity necessary to describe and evaluate incidents of common life. The proper mix of these elements—what Hume calls a "correct Judgement"—defines or "grounds" the philosophy of common life. Hume's "nonfoundational" faculty of judgment is the *sine qua non* in the philosophy of common life and summarizes the proper use of human capacities. The realization that judgment is a complex, mixed faculty should be cause for modesty in its use. Awareness of its mixed character causes people to "hesitate or balance" (EHU 161) in the exercise of judgment. Since we can have no philosophic account of these qualities of mind,[16] we must rest satisfied with this. How we judge is a question of foundations, and Hume, agnostic on foundations, passes by the question after he outlines the paradoxes the question engenders. *How* we judge is less important than the fact *that* we judge.

There is a similar account of judgment in James Madison's quite Humean discussion of epistemology in *Federalist 37*. The complexity of human equipment leads Madison to explain the grounds for political modesty though there is a great desire for citizens to have certainty on matters of political controversy. Madison's reflections arise in the context of discussing the difficulties that the Constitutional Convention faced in demarcating the lines between the national and state governments. The first problem lies in the mind. "The faculties of the mind itself have never yet been distinguished and defined with satisfactory precision." Madison continues, "Sense, perception, judgment, desire, volition, memory, imagination are found to be separated by such delicate shades and minute gradations that their boundaries have eluded the most subtle investigations, and remain a pregnant source of ingenious disquisition and controversy." Madison emphasizes other obscurities in our ability to apprehend nature and others that plague our ability to delineate the works of man. An awareness of what Hume had called the "strange infirmities" of human understanding leads human beings to perceive, in Madison's words, "the necessity of moderating still further our expectations and hopes from the efforts of human sagacity."[17] So far was Madison from operating on the hopeful assumption that politics was a science capable of demonstration that he emphasizes the obscurity in which all intellectual endeavors subsist and counsels for modesty and moderation. Insofar as this spirit infuses the *Federalists* and infused the Convention itself, perhaps the framing of the United States Constitution was a time when some of the most influential American statesmen justified political moderation in terms akin to Hume's mitigated skepticism.

"Of the Standard of Taste": Judgment and Its Relationship to Nature

Descriptions of how we judge begin by observing judgment in action. Our considered descriptions and evaluations are based on "sentiments more public and social" than they usually are. Improved judgment requires a reflection on ourselves brought about by a change in our circumstance. It requires an enlarged view or an extended sphere (in James Madison's formulation from *Federalist 10*).[18] Enlarging our view to encompass a variety of parties, interests and passions allows for the refinement of sensibilities and the tempering of precipitate judgments. Hume's account of improving judgment parallels Alexander Hamilton's defense of legislative debate. "In a legislature," Hamilton writes, "promptitude of decision is oftener an evil than a benefit. The differences of opinion, the jarring in that department of government, though they may sometimes obstruct salutary plans, yet often promote deliberation and circumspection, and serve to check excesses in the majority."[19] Hamilton hopes that the closest approximation of the public interest or the common good can result from a deliberative legislative process (and the other checks in the Constitution). Hume has similar hopes that correct judgment comes from the jarring of opinions. "The intercourse of sentiments... in society and conversation, makes us form some general unalterable standard, by which we may approve or disapprove of characters and manners" (EPM 229). The exchange of ideas improves judgment by sharpening the description of the actions of men, by calling forth an individual from selfish or prejudicial considerations, by engaging the emotions and sentiments of others, and by, in the end, approximating some "general unalterable standard" against which actions can be evaluated. Without the clash of ideas, men would either be too self-interested, too disinterested, or lack sufficient grounding in common opinion to make correct judgments. The standard of judgment emerges from an internal clash of different faculties—faculties that correct, restrain, modify, qualify, and supplant each other—rather than from an attempt to conform to an external standard.

The study of history reproduces the virtues of conversation. Each forces human beings from their circumstances and encourages them to consider the actions of others in the correct manner. "When a man of business enters into life, he is more apt to consider the characters of men, as they have relation to his interest, than as they stand in themselves; and has his judgment warped on every occasion by the violence of passion" (E 567–8). This "man of business" Hume contrasts to the philosopher, who "contemplates characters and manners in his closet."[20] Philosophers are unable to judge soundly because they are insufficiently engaged in common life and fail to recognize their dependence on sentiment: "The general and abstract view of the objects leaves the mind so cold and unmoved, that the sentiments of nature have no room to play." History "keeps in a just medium betwixt these extremes" of the overly engaged man of business or partisan and the disengaged philosopher, "and places the objects in their true point of view." Writers and readers alike can be interested enough in the characters to feel sentiments of praise and blame, and can be relatively immune from prejudice to have their sentimental judgments corrupted (E 568). Besides encouraging the disposition essential for the acquisition of a refined judgment, history expands the understanding and provides materials for judgment.

> Indeed, if we consider the shortness of human life, and our limited knowledge, even of what passes in our own time, we must be sensible that we should be for ever children in understanding, were it not for this invention, which extends our experience to all past ages, and to the most distant nations; making them contribute to our improvement in wisdom, as if they had actually lain under our observation. A man acquainted with history may, in some respect, be said to have lived from the beginning of the world, and to have been making continual additions to his stock of knowledge in every century. (E 566–7)

In providing a storehouse for knowledge, history exceeds conversation in degree if not in kind. History can teach limits and possibilities, force one to judge after transporting oneself to a different time and place, reveal the range of human types, provide portraits of human excellence and depravity, and show the prejudices of particular epochs. Hume's liberal science is for people who shun intellectual echo chambers and the din of the crowd in a concerted effort to achieve better judgment.

Exchanging views and increasing the materials for correct judgment does not guarantee the cultivation of correct judgment. The difficulty lies in ascending from the conversation and the study of history to achieve a "general unalterable standard" as a basis for sound judgments. "Morals and criticism," Hume writes at the end of the first *Enquiry*, "are not so properly objects of the understanding as of taste and sentiment" (EHU 165).

What is needed is a standard of taste. The "Standard of Taste" frames Book I of Hume's *Essays*: the first essay of Book I is "Of the Delicacy of Taste and Passion" and the last is "Of the Standard of Taste."[21] History reveals an amazing diversity of taste about the beautiful and good. The "most careless enquirer" notices this diversity—the difference between the modes of ancient Sparta and modern England, for example. Upon closer inspection, the variety of taste is "still greater in reality than in appearance." All countries use the language of virtue and recommend certain actions or styles, but when "critics come to particulars, this seeming unanimity vanishes." Everyone blames coldness and affectation in writing (in Hume's example), but many disagree about whether a piece is cold or affected. "We are apt to call *barbarous* whatever departs widely from our own taste and apprehension: But soon find the epithet of reproach retorted on us. And the highest arrogance and self-conceit is at last startled, on observing an equal assurance on all sides, and scruples, amidst such a contest of sentiment, to pronounce positively in its own favour" (E 227). History reveals diversity, confusion and heated disagreement on the most important matters.

The diversity of opinion on matters of taste is an occasion for wonder and an impetus to search for a standard. In this confusion "it is natural for us to seek a *Standard of Taste*; a rule, by which the various sentiments of men may be reconciled; at least, a decision, afforded, confirming one sentiment, and condemning another" (E 229). Those seeking a "*Standard of Taste*" are not merely interested in having a standard confirm their predilections. Some persons seek order in the larger, cross-cultural diversity of opinion. They desire a basis from which to confirm and condemn sentiments and judgments. The desire to secure a "*Standard of Taste*" is no guarantee that it can be found, yet that desire is the *beginning* of wisdom.

The search for wisdom is not necessarily consistent with success in securing a "*Standard of Taste*." There is a "species of philosophy, which cuts off all hopes of success in such an attempt, and represents the impossibility of ever attaining any standard of taste" (E 229). This "species of philosophy" divorces judgment from sentiment, and sides with sentiment because it "has a reference to nothing beyond itself, and is always right, wherever a man is conscious of it." On this account, the "determinations of the understanding," in contrast, "are not right; because they have a reference to something beyond themselves, to wit, real matter of fact" (E 230). This appears to be an almost postmodern ethic of authenticity or emotivism or the basis of positivistic science, though Hume characteristically does not provide examples of those who entertain this "species of philosophy."[22] The separation of sentiment from judgment and the preference for pure sentiment in matters of taste "seems to have attained the sanction of common sense" (ibid.). This "species of philosophy" appears as a feature of common life—people believe beauty is in the eye of the beholder. This "species of philosophy" endorses a rather democratic, perhaps postmodern, "natural equality of tastes" (E 231) with no way to correct sentiment. A philosopher of common life cannot discount this conclusion, and Hume attempts to come to grips with the truth in it. There is at least a feint similarity between this "species of philosophy" and Hume's own view: Both found moral distinctions on sentiment.

This is true only with qualification. Hume counters the common sense view that beauty and moral distinctions are in the eye of the beholder with the common sense distinction between good and bad judgment. There is a "species of common sense" which opposes or "at least serves to modify and restrain" the position of cultural relativism implicit in the purely sentimental "species of philosophy." Specifically referring to literary taste, Hume writes,

> Whoever would assert an equality of genius and elegance between OGILBY and MILTON, or BUNYAN and ADDISON, would be thought to defend no less an extravagance, than if he had maintained a mole-hill to be as high as TENERIFFE, or a pond as extensive as the ocean. Though there may be found persons, who give the preference to the former authors; no one pays attention to such a taste: and we pronounce without scruple the sentiment of these critics to be absurd and ridiculous. (E 230–1)

Once we distinguish good from bad judgment, we must face the question of what constitutes good judgment. Ranked order can be accomplished by referring to a kind of superiority noticed by creditable judges. This perspective implies refinement or ranking, and is cautious about postmodern democratic equality and democracy as such. Hume reconciles the democratic view that beauty or a standard is in the eye of the beholder with the aristocratic view that some beholders have better judgment than others. Better judgers are more moderate in conversation, are more learned from the study of history or from a storehouse of relevant experience, are understanding the trade-offs or choices authors or statesmen or artists face, and can articulate these complexities to learned and unlearned alike. They manifest a distance from what they are watching or studying. Not all manifest these hallmarks of good judgment, and the passionate or ignorant may not recognize its authority, but that speaks to their poor, unformed judgment. In fact, few (and fewer, perhaps) may recognize this standard of taste, though it is the touchstone for those who aim to achieve wisdom.

Hume equates good judgment with a "delicacy of taste" (E 235), which calls attention to the first essay, "Of the Delicacy of Taste and Passion." A delicacy of taste "enlarges the sphere both of our happiness and misery, and makes us sensible to pains as well as pleasures, which escape the rest of mankind" and "enables us to judge the characters of men, of compositions of genius, and of the productions of the nobler arts" (E 5, 6). "Standard of Taste" puts forward the method of correct judgment through the illustration of literary beauty: "Delicacy of Taste" applies that method to moral sentiments and extends it to politics. A liberal education above all promotes the delicate taste.

> In order to judge aright of a composition of genius, there are so many views to be taken in, so many circumstances to be compared, and such a knowledge of human nature requisite, that no man, who is not possessed of the soundest judgment, will ever make a tolerable critic in such performances. And this is a new reason for cultivating a relish in the liberal arts. Our judgment will strengthen by this exercise: We shall form juster notions of life: Many things, which please or afflict others, will appear to us too frivolous to engage our attention. (E 6)

Essential to the cultivation of a delicate taste is "*practice* in a particular art," which involves repeated study and "*comparisons* between the several species and degrees of excellence" (E 237, 238). Frequent observations train the eye to see all that is relevant to a particular performance, character, or object, so that nothing passes "unnoticed or disregarded" (E 241).[23] A critic should obviously have a "mind free from all *prejudice*" (E 239). Lastly, a delicate taste requires what Hume calls "*good sense*" to check the influence of prejudice and to ascertain the design of the object under consideration (E 240). Perhaps people can work themselves toward a general delicate taste through learning a particular thing well (e.g., novels, history) and then expand through that exercise to other areas and all areas.

In the rare person who has these traits of delicate taste "is the true standard of taste and beauty" (E 241). This is a second point of agreement between Hume and those who advocate the "species of philosophy" which divorces sentiment from judgment. Hume follows the "species of philosophy," which holds that "beauty is no quality in things themselves" (E 230).[24] Both argue that notions of beauty and morality arise from within the spectator or judge. People of good judgment help others feel the right sentiments and find the right words to describe things. They have the best judgment about what *merits* our contempt, praise, or attention. What we mean by this, however, is different than the common sense of the matter suggests. Common folks may think that the person of good judgment has special insights into the reality of things, into the "nature of Beauty," the "Idea of Beauty" or "the Form of Beauty." Such a person has special insights, but does not apprehend objective value reflecting a natural order. The person of good judgment is a person of much experience, a cultivated taste, proper detachment, and proper engagement, whose special insights are not based on a penetrating apprehension of nature. Nature or any other general idea is assembled by the mind after a refining and sifting process culminating in the achievement of a standard that exists *in* the investigator. No special grid conveys this standard from one to another—only long, difficult refining work can initiate one to it; and we cannot expect those with good judgment to agree in the same manner as they agree about the number of corners in a triangle.

On this account, Hume seems to be well within the modern school of thought, which emphasizes how human beings *make* nature or *make* standards. The imagination is the faculty involved in "mixing, compounding, separating, and dividing" ideas so that we can distinguish fact from fiction, good from bad (EHU 47). Hume emphasizes the care and viewer-centered "objectivity" necessary to carry out this assembling of nature. Nature emerges only from a rigorous encounter with particulars. Hume's working hypothesis is that nature can be impartially made by human imagination, judgment, and feeling out of the materials of common life. The building is done with natural equipment, which becomes finer the more it is used. Hume's delicate taste as the standard of judgment prefigures Adam Smith's notion of the "impartial spectator." Fine judges are reliable in several ways. Their guidance is trustworthy: people can repose confidence in fine judges and test their judgments against the matters under consideration. This is not inter-subjectivity, though inter-subjective agreement among learned judges provides evidence for that standard. It is testing people's ability to assemble and judge by an appropriate standard of taste. The reliability of any scientific theory emerges from the particulars and can be judged as trustworthy by particulars.

Hume suspends judgment about the character of history. On one hand, Hume's emphasis on historical imagination and subjective construction elevates the role of the historian in the telling of history. Never satisfied with authoritative histories, the critical historian comes to embody the standard of judgment for telling the general direction of history and for constructing the "given" facts out of which history will be retold. The historian's imagination is the touchstone for decisions about historical facts, patterns, and processes. On the other hand, the imagination must represent the things that happened; it must be proportioned to the evidence or to the reality outside the historian if history is to be different (in degree, perhaps) than fiction. Historians are creative, subjective, and constructivist, but not arbitrary or *purely* creative, subjective, and constructivist and not novelists or dreamers. It is a mixed science involving the creative, subjective making of data and the creative, objective discovery of data.

After responding to an objection raised by the persistence of "a bad critic, who might always insist upon his particular sentiment" (E 241),[25] Hume makes an important and potentially troubling concession about our ability to build a natural standard of judgment. "Notwithstanding all our endeavours to fix a standard of taste," Hume writes, "there still remain two sources of variation, which are not sufficient indeed to confound all the boundaries of beauty and deformity, but will often serve to produce a difference in the degrees of our approbation." The "different humours of particular men" and "the particular manners and opinions of our age and country" (E 243) shape even the most delicate taste, to an extent. The strength and reasonableness of these variations suggest that a "certain degree of diversity in judgment is unavoidable" and that "we seek in vain for a standard, by which we can reconcile the contrary sentiments." The young prefer different authors than the old; some people prefer comedy, others tragedy, others yet satire. "Such preferences are innocent and unavoidable, and can never reasonably be the object of dispute, because there is no standard, by which they can be decided" (E 244). This would seem to suggest that we can form judgments about which is the best comedy and which is the best tragedy, but that choosing between the genres of comedy and tragedy cannot reasonably be the object of dispute; they are matters of taste divorced from judgment. If the young and old have different tastes in authors, whose opinions are to be more regarded in general? Is the young's view superior to the old's or vice versa? If we apply this thought to the influence of "the particular manners and opinions of our age and country" on our taste, our capacity for moral evaluation would seem to be historically conditioned. Has Hume rehabilitated the cultural relativism that he has sought, at least, to "restrain and modify"?

We must not rush to such extremes. The objects of our evaluation are particular and particulars must be judged by a suitable standard. Arriving at a standard of taste in any particular genre requires a person to study, compare, and practice first within a genre. "There is no standard, by which [disputes across genres] can be decided" only when we "feel a predilection for that which suits our particular turn and disposition" (E 244). If literary genres are evaluated in the same manner as moral character and culture, the delicate taste is *to an extent* culture bound. A delicate taste takes its bearings from the conventions and norms of a given culture and never completely escapes them. One moves toward a philosophic perspective by expanding one's horizons beyond delicate taste in one field and by eliminating predilections for particular objects or characters; delicate taste steps toward philosophy, but is not philosophy. Comparing across genres or cultures demands that one has arrived at a reasonable understanding of the genres or cultures under consideration. Hume's account of the delicate taste points beyond itself to a philosophic engagement across horizons.

This problem of gaining proper perspective illustrates the tension between theory and practice. As a philosopher, Hume shows great respect for what we might see as the self-sufficiency of particular genres or of common life or of the historical practice of a particular era because he worries that philosophy can distort common life as it tries to "methodize and correct" common life; philosophy can lose its proper bearings in common life. His presentation is designed to discourage such philosophic distortion. Those with a taste for philosophy must preserve the appearances, while evaluating them. Hume's concession preserves the rather lofty perspective of delicate taste. His argument points beyond itself toward philosophic judgment or a philosophically informed delicate taste. Philosophy enters common life to investigate, but hopes not to disturb it overmuch unless it can improve common life (as when it opposes superstition or system). Theory must have a proper orientation if it is to enter into common life, and Hume shows what that orientation is. Seeking a standard by which to judge tastes requires that one take the correct perspective in relation to the particular thing under examination. Evaluation of the particular requires that we have some recourse to a general rule or to a general storehouse of thoughtful observation. An excessive "particularity" precludes the critical distance necessary for evaluation; an excessive "generality" fails to do justice to the phenomena under examination. Delicate taste requires a horizon or historical context in order to point beyond an immediate horizon or historical context; there are successive layers of context that can be ascended by those with a taste for philosophy. A proper science accommodates itself to the in-between, contradictory character of our faculties. Philosophy finds in

"Our Mixed Kind of Life": Science as a Window to the Human Condition

I have canvassed Hume's account of human faculties and shown how those faculties shape our engagement with nature. Human faculties are our only window to the world. The window is foggy and we have difficulty explaining how appearances are mediated through the window. Hume's account of human understanding yields "mixed" results. His naturalistic side emphasizes the place of non-rational elements in the formation of correct judgment. Belief in necessary connection and personal identity comes from imagination and natural sentiments as conveyed to the imagination. Our ability to distinguish truth from falsehood is a matter decided by a "more vivid, lively, forcible, firm, steady" sentiment. Sentiments and feelings are indispensable features of a sound understanding, but, left to themselves, they are apt to lead to prejudice. The problems with sentiment do not send Hume careening to the opposite extreme. He does not suggest that reason alone can explain human understanding or moral evaluation. Just as our belief in our rational faculties must be mitigated by a skeptical awareness of "the strange infirmities of human understanding," so also must our "naturalism" be mitigated by an awareness of the problems inherent in pure naturalism. Prejudice and flights of imagination are the "strange infirmities" of our natural faculties. Our ability to know the world is shaped by a skepticism that is mitigated by natural suppositions and by natural suppositions that are discovered and sometimes corrected by critical reasoning. Each standing alone renders a correct understanding impossible. Critical reasoning mixes with common life and common faculties. Hume's understanding of "correct Judgement" mixes these natural and skeptical features in a proper proportion. This proper mixture is difficult to achieve and is perhaps unsteady once it is achieved.

In addition to mixing natural and skeptical traits, a "correct Judgement" exists between the general and particular or the whole and the parts. Our capacity for science must be grounded in common life and try to ascend from common life without distorting common life. In the last lines of his *Natural History of Religion*, Hume writes, "The whole is a riddle, an aenigma, an inexplicable mystery. Doubt, uncertainty, suspence of judgment appear the only result of our most accurate scrutiny" (NHR 76). Although "the whole" is an "inexplicable mystery," the thrust of Hume's philosophy of common life suggests that we can secure some knowledge of parts. Mere knowledge of particular appearances does not satisfy those with a taste for philosophy. If human understanding is confined to knowledge of parts or individual appearances, "men could never think or talk steadily on any subject; while their fluctuating situations produce a continual variation on objects, and throw them into such different and contrary lights and positions." Philosophy grounds itself in particulars, must transcend mere particulars or appearances toward general maxims and standards, but cannot expect to understand "the whole." Human beings are the only animals capable of looking upward, but it is not clear how much looking upward assists the cause of knowledge. We inquire with feet on the ground and eyes in common life. Lifting eyes from common life can cause flights of fancy characteristic of an actively sovereign mind.

The "in-between" character of Hume's scientific mix serves as a metaphor for the human condition. Irresolvable tensions between reason and ignorance, universals and particulars, subjective making and somewhat objective discovery, and our natural equipment and critical faculties characterize our condition. Hume's most direct discussion of the human condition appears in the context of a comparison between an insufficiently critical "easy and obvious philosophy" preferred by "the generality of mankind" and an isolated, closet-bound "abstruse philosophy" (EHU 6, 7). The "most perfect character is supposed to lie" between the abstract philosopher and the ignorant (EHU 8). After describing this "most perfect character," Hume writes,

> Man is a reasonable being; and as such receives from science his proper food and nourishment: But so narrow are the bounds of human understanding, that little satisfaction can be hoped for in this particular, either from the extent or security of his acquisitions. Man is a sociable, no less than a reasonable being: But neither can he always enjoy company agreeable and amusing, or preserve the proper relish for them. Man is also an active being; and from that disposition, as well as from the various necessities of human life, must submit to business and occupation: But the mind requires some relaxation, and cannot always support its bent to care and industry. It seems, then, that nature has pointed out a *mixed kind of life* as most suitable to human race, and secretly admonished them to allow none of these biasses to draw too much. (EHU 8–9, emphasis supplied)[26]

This characterization of the human condition, neglected by Hume scholars, provides, perhaps, the key insight to Hume's thought and his account of human nature in particular. Hume seeks to reconcile philosophers to this "mixed kind of life." The "negative" side of this project involves exposing pretentious attempts to illuminate what cannot be illuminated; it constitutes, in effect, a warning to philosophers that their attempts to make sense of certain key concepts partake of a bias that draws too much toward the reasonable or scientific or general side of the human mix. Shunning sentiment and imagination, modern philosophy has drawn too much toward reason and, unbeknownst to itself, asserted a sovereignty of reason that collapsed reason into fancy.

Hume's "positive" project holds that the perspective of common life abides more closely to a correct understanding of our "mixed kind of life." The characterization of human life as a mix between knowledge and ignorance, and the implication that man can hope for little "either from the extent of security of his acquisitions" is intended, like "mitigated scepticism," to promote moderation, modesty and humility in inquirers. It is notable that Hume's discussion of our "mixed kind of life" appears in the introduction to the first *Enquiry*. The book testifies to the philosophy of common life as a mix of heterogeneous elements. The blend is so complete that it is difficult to recognize the original elements, and it is not clear that Hume wants us to identify each element after we understand that human understanding is a mixture.

Ours is a "mixed" condition in another way. Everything human and mortal is a "mixed" blessing. It is the task of philosophy to articulate the mixed blessings as a means of promoting moderation and describing our condition:

> It belongs, therefore, to a philosopher alone, who is of neither party, to put all the circumstances in the scale, and assign to each of them its proper poise and influence. Such a one will readily, at first, acknowledge that all political questions are infinitely complicated, and that there scarcely ever occurs, in any deliberation, a choice, which is either purely good, or purely evil. Consequences, mixed and varied, may be foreseen to flow from every measure: And many consequences, unforeseen, do always, in fact, result from every one. Hesitation, and reserve, and suspence, are, therefore, the only sentiments he brings to this essay or trial. Or if he indulges any passion, it is that of derision against the ignorant multitude, who are always clamorous and dogmatical, even in the nicest questions, of which, from want of temper, perhaps still more than of understanding, they are altogether unfit judges. (E 507; also 130–1)

Hume echoes the same sentiment near the end of the *Natural History of Religion*.

> Good and ill are universally intermingled and confounded; happiness and misery, wisdom and folly, virtue and vice. Nothing is pure and entirely of

> a piece. All advantages are attended with disadvantages... The draughts of life, according to the poet's fiction, are always mixed from the vessels on each hand of JUPITER: Or if any cup be presented altogether pure, it is drawn only, as the same poet tells us, from the left-handed vessel. (NHR 74)

Examples of mixed blessings abound. The human imagination is essential to a coherent engagement with the world, but also tends to lead human beings astray and to undermine reason.[27] The sentiments are the foundation of our ability to distinguish virtue and vice, but are also liable to lead us astray with prejudice. It is one of Hume's great insights that reason itself is a mixed blessing, that reason is has its advantages and disadvantages. Reason is not only, as Locke would have it, "our only Star and compass"[28] because reason unmoored undermines itself and becomes unreasonable. Reason is a necessary corrective of the sentiments and allows us to speak steadily on a topic amidst the fluctuating appearances. Reason is also a source of systematizing distortions and dangers when not added to the "gross earthy mixture" of common life. That reason is a mixed blessing is seen in Hume's critique of Locke's political principles. Locke's actively sovereign imagination designed a theory that was supposed to establish a politics of peace, tolerance, and humanity. Theory without moorings in common life cannot guide people to a moderate political practice.

CHAPTER 5

THE LIBERAL IMAGINATION AND THE PROBLEM OF ABSTRACT SPECULATIVE PRINCIPLES IN POLITICS

> Above the real society, whose constitution was still traditional, confused, and irregular, where laws remained varied and contradictory, ranks were separated, status was fixed, and burdens were unequal, there was slowly built an imaginary society in which everything seemed simple and coordinated, uniform, equitable, and in accord with reason. Gradually the imagination of the crowd deserted the former to concentrate on the latter. One lost interest in what was, in order to think about what could be, and finally one lived mentally in that ideal city the writers had built.
>
> —Tocqueville, *The Ancient Regime*, Book 3, Chap. 1.

Hume initiated a critique of modern ideology that came to prominence after the French Revolution in the writings of Edmund Burke, Hegel, and Tocqueville. Hume's critique grows out of his concern about modern rationalism's actively sovereign imagination. Social contract theory and its attendant doctrines are political equivalents of philosophic doctrines such as primary and secondary qualities or personal identity. Just as Hume had criticized those philosophic doctrines in part to prepare the way for a philosophy of common life, Hume's criticisms of social contract and other political principles lead him to defend the commercial republic as the arrangements most suited to our "mixed kind of life." There is a crucial difference between Hume's intervention into philosophy and his treatment of political theories. Philosophical conundrums such as those viewed in the previous chapters are revealing, though they do not engage deep human emotions. Merely philosophic errors are "ridiculous" (T 272); arguments over abstruse topics are more likely to induce sleep than riots. Theoretical intrusions into politics implicate strong passions, established institutions, and the basis for political community. Political systemizers seek to remold institutions and customs inconsistent with their principles. If they are opposed by another system, passion can run especially high and civil conflict can ensue. Abstract systems unopposed can lead to a violent utopian politics. Philosophic debates about the nature of perception or the source of our belief in continued existence are one thing; the French Revolution (to which this chapter's epigram refers) is another.

The problem that theory and philosophy pose for politics is as old as philosophy itself. Plato's *Republic* concerns the construction of an ideal polity, a city in speech, which some—rightly or wrongly—believe to represent Plato's theoretical blueprint for reforming Greek society. Aristotle too mentions a meddling theoretician in *The Politics*, Hippodamus, who proposes a geometric solution to the problems of politics (*Politics* 1267b22ff.). The question of how theory relates to practice takes on a greater urgency in modern thought, which re-conceives the traditional understanding of philosophy and politics. Aristotle and, arguably, Plato show the obstacles to a theoretical remaking of politics by defending the proposition that political communities are caves, based on opinions and sub-rational passions that are unsettled by abstract political plans. Modern advocates of Enlightenment before Hume are not as interested in pointing out the obstacles to theory remaking practice as they are in removing obstacles to a more rational political practice. They seek to enlighten the cave and to guide political practice directly through their principles. This modern re-conception of theory and political practice finds its most popular expression, as Hume understands it, in Locke's Whig political teaching.

Prioritizing theory begets several practical problems, especially if the theory is not properly embedded to the political climate. Systematizing politicians view politics as a canvas on which their ideals can be impressed. Public-spiritedness often masks an inhumane pleasure of contemplating a political system in one's own mind or as an extension of one's own will. In Hume's context, theoretical parties—especially Whigs—threatened to cultivate a dangerous factionalism that would undermine what Hume regarded as Britain's uniquely excellent constitution. Those taken with pure, theoretical insights are, more than most, inclined to political action and actuated with great confidence in their vision. Hume sees a kinship between religious and political fanaticism and hopes he can help cure politics of these diseases.

Humean Politics: An Overview

Given the complexity of Hume's thought—the often misunderstood relation between Hume's destruction of modern constructs and his purpose in describing our "mixed kind of life"—it is not surprising that there is great controversy about his politics. Some, seizing on Hume's destruction of Whig principles, see Hume as a conservative political philosopher. Frederick Whelan, for instance, contends that "Hume's resort to history for guidance in moral and political questions and his appreciation of the paramount role of habit or custom in sustaining artificial moral rules...are conducive to a conservative approach to practice."[1] Generally, on this view, Hume's account of human understanding translates into limits on the reform he thought to be desirable and could lead to his questioning the possibility of progress. His rejection of social contract theory and his decision not to found a political teaching on individual rights even call into question Hume's credentials as a liberal. As a result, Thomas Jefferson had profound worries about Hume. Concerned principally with the *History of England*, Jefferson often writes of Hume's Tory sentiments and the danger Hume's thought posed to the cause of human liberty. John Adams agreed. "That history," Adams complained to Jefferson, "has only increased the Tories and diminished the Whigs."[2]

Yet Hume advocates for progress. His condemnation of priestly power and religious enthusiasm and his advocacy of progress in the arts, separation of powers and checks and balances in government, the representative principle, and modern commercial arrangements lead one commentator to conclude that Hume is a liberal who introduces "experimental reasoning into moral subjects...to bring about reform, change for the better."[3] Reason contributes to achieving a society of toleration, commercial prosperity, and limited, free government. Counteracting modern theory with theory is part of this intention, but so is providing human beings with an alternative way of understanding the moderation and humanity implicit in modern practice. Hume suggests there might be ways that the benefits of modern life might be extended as well.

Two views could hardly seem more dissimilar. One emphasizes the *limits* of reason in bringing about reform; the other emphasizes the *power* of reason to contribute to reform. The first may emphasize the frivolity of politics when viewed from a sufficiently philosophic perspective; the second aligns itself with the great, unique achievements of modern commercial society. The first suggests that intervention in exploding religious myths may be a matter of indifference; the second might seek to undermine (at least) certain kinds of religious conviction. As Wolin writes, "to have fathered squabbling children is always something of an embarrassment, but particularly so when one is, like Hume, temperamentally averse to taking sides."[4] Could Hume not have "taken sides" on such an important matter?

Scholars offer two approaches to this David Hume Problem. First, some locate Hume in a conservative universe of discourse typical of the mid-1700s, wherein the gains of the Glorious Revolution and the emergent modern economy were consolidated without threatening the quasi-feudal sociopolitical order in Great Britain.[5] The temptation to reconcile these seemingly contradictory strands in Hume's political teaching with reference to contingent features in Hume's political environment is understandable since occasional issues gave rise to many of Hume's political essays. Hume's concern about the intrusion of Whig political theory was perhaps the most significant political issue about which Hume wrote, and Hume was worried about the unsettling effects of the emancipated imagination unloosed by Whig theory. Notwithstanding its merits this approach has in directing attention to Hume's contemporary concerns, its adherents leave open the question of Hume's broader philosophic intention. Hume claims to offer a durable teaching about society as such through an examination of the political situation in the Britain of his time. If Hume sees matters of permanent importance in particular British events or in other historical investigations, Hume's participation in occasional debates would point beyond immediate context to permanent issues. In the modern iteration of the actively sovereign imagination Hume saw persistent problems posed by the theoretical perspective. It is safer to assume that Hume's political teaching is consistent with his theory of judgment and to see that his political teaching speaks to a broader context in addition to his immediate context.

Others resolve the problem by reading Hume's moderate but modern political teaching in the light of his worry about the adverse political implications of modern rationalism in politics. Pierre Manent thinks Hume's political conservatism grows from his modern skepticism. All ideas, including Locke's idea of rights, are products of human imagination without support in nature; we cannot know the difference between right and wrong in terms of rights. This skepticism about universal human rights leads Hume's science to investigate common experience as expressed in moral sentiments, which reveals that people distinguish right and wrong in common life. Political investigations aim at revealing the principles of human nature as they manifest themselves in different societies. Hume embraces the charm and importance of local variety against Locke's embrace of universal human rights. "That is why," Manent concludes, "Hume's more radical and in some way ultimate skepticism leads...to a much more conservative practical viewpoint than Locke's does."[6] Hume's conservatism may follow from his judgment that tradition is a source of order in a world shorn of intelligibility.[7] Not unlike Aristophanes as he his commonly understood, Hume seems to defend the city in the quarrel between the city and philosophy.

Seeking to preserve the statesmanlike perspective against the destructive tendencies of modern rationalism, this reading risks missing how Hume seeks to upset portions of the English tradition and it risks missing the purpose in Hume's skepticism. Hume welcomes pretty radical changes to England's religious character, as we see in chapters 8 and 9. Hume criticizes modern Enlightenment to place Enlightenment on different grounds. Hume avoids a theory of rights, the state of nature, and a contract theory of political obligation because they are founded on an over-estimation of human capacities and a misreading of the human condition.[8] The "reason" to which such efforts appeal is the actively sovereign imagination attempting to flee the inescapable contradictions and mixtures of our condition. Hume's selectivity toward tradition prompts readers to search for a philosophy, taking it bearings from "our mixed kind of life," that can serve as a standard for judgment for evaluating tradition.

Hume almost comes across as a dissident political thinker in his criticisms of Whig theory and the problems endemic to the modern theoretical stance. Hume relates in his autobiographical essay that, during his day, members of "the Whig party were in possession of bestowing all places, both in the state and in literature" (E xxxviii.). Hume worried that Whiggism would be politically unsettling unless it was arrested or moderated. Pursuant to the end of arresting its spread, Hume concentrated on exposing its deficiencies. Of the 39 essays appearing in the final edition of Hume's *Essays*, 28 pertain to political issues;[9] almost all of these political essays directly or indirectly challenge Whig ideology in theory and in practice. Hume also saw the rise of an actively sovereign imagination in politics to be a predictable historical development grounded in human nature that features of the social environment had long restrained. That which had restrained the sovereign imagination eroded in modern times, which means that either modern politics will be unusually factious or there must be a new philosophic cure for the malady. Without a solution, imputations of human sovereignty over politics and a belief in the rectitude of one's actions might foster a partisan zeal inimical to sound political order. This chapter's subject matter is political; it aims to illuminate Hume's philosophical perspective against the perspective of modern theory.

"Philosophers who have embraced party"

"Parties from *principle*," Hume writes, "especially abstract speculative principle, are known only to modern times, and are, perhaps, the most extraordinary and unaccountable *phenomenon*, that has yet appeared in human affairs" (E 60).[10] What are parties founded on "abstract speculative principle"? Why have they arisen only in modern times? What dangers do they pose to sound humane politics?

Formerly, factions may have divided over policy or economic interests traceable to disagreements over the nature of justice or the good; modern parties include all of these conflicts, but they sustain them with a broader superstructure (I am tempted to say) in which preferred politics or interests can be conceived. "No party," Hume begins, "in the present age, can well support itself, without a philosophical or speculative system of principles, annexed to its political or practical one; we accordingly find, that each of the factions, into which this nation is divided, has reared up a fabric of the former kind, in order to protect and cover that scheme of actions, which it pursues" (E 465). The prevalence of parties based on abstract speculative principles means that disagreements between parties are more difficult to mediate and partisans aim to bring political reality into line with their systems. Speculative parties come to have an ideological (as opposed to a material) interest in reform, leading them to demand reforms to well-functioning institutions and practices. Hume's Britain was divided between the Tories and the Whigs.

> The one party, by tracing up government to the DEITY, endeavour to render it so sacred and inviolate, that it must be little less than sacrilege, however tyrannical it may become, to touch or invade it, in the smallest article. The other party, by founding government altogether on the consent of the PEOPLE, suppose that there is a kind of original contract, by which the subjects have tacitly reserved the power of resisting their sovereign, whenever they find themselves aggrieved by that authority, with which they have, for certain purposes, voluntarily entrusted him. These are the speculative principles of the two parties; and these too are the practical consequences deduced from them. (E 466)

Reform or revolution is the consequence of the Whig system; deference and passive obedience of Toryism. Reformers point toward a man-made, consensual and representative government; Tories to the established order or to turning back the clock a bit. Whigs hope to clear up the representative principle; Tories to leaving what is alone. How could citizens believing in such different principles live together in peace? "Dangerous parties are such as entertain opposite views with regard to the essentials of government, the succession of the crown, or the more considerable privileges belonging to the several members of the constitution; where there is no room for any compromise or accommodation, and there the controversy may appear so momentous as to justify even an opposition by arms to the pretensions of antagonists" (E 493).

Abstract speculative parties would be problematic if there were only one seeking to remake politics in light of an abstract image. Hume envisions the problem of one (abstract) party rule: the Whigs appear to be vanquishing the Tories. In fact, one hegemonic party based in abstract speculative principles is more problematical political phenomenon. Like Locke,[11] Hume thinks human beings thirst to have their opinions confined by their followers. "Such is the nature of the human mind, that it always lays hold on every mind that approaches it; and as it is wonderfully fortified by an unanimity of sentiments, so is it shocked by any contrariety. Hence the eagerness, which most people discover in a dispute; and hence their impatience of opposition, even in the most speculative and indifferent opinions" (E 60–1). Hume goes further than Locke, noting that unanimity tends to have an abstract, speculative character in modernity. Abstract partisanship inspires a group with a sense of omniscience and may derive from an unfulfilled desire for transcendence. Perhaps with humane intentions, the followers of political orthodoxy become impatient with attempts to "educate" the heterodox and come to see their continuing opposition as intransigence that must be overcome by force or, perhaps, as a sign of their lack of participation in common humanity. To borrow a phrase,[12] such "intolerance traceable to the aspiration to orthodoxy" justifies attempts to realize utopian systems of politics by eradicating opposition to the enactment of utopian schemes. Abstract principles often lead to destructive schemes of reform. Burke developed Hume's critique of abstract principles in reaction to the French Revolution[13] as did Tocqueville in his depiction of the French Revolution as part of the advance of modern democracy.[14]

Modern Politics and the Development of Parties based on Abstract Speculative Principle

If the sources of faction based on abstract speculative principles are sown in human nature, why have such parties been "known only to modern times?" Addressing this rarely observed riddle helps to clarify Hume's view on how abstract parties become violent and how they might be contained. As the desire for orthodoxy "is universal in human nature," Hume writes, "its effects would not have been confined to one age, and to one sect of religion, did it not there concur with other more accidental causes, which raise it to such a height, as to produce the greatest misery and devastation" (E 61).[15] The pantheistic, non-universalist, almost unbelievable religious doctrines of pre-Christian times tamed the actively sovereign imagination and the thirst for orthodoxy in politics. In medieval times, superstitious Catholicism checked the sovereign imagination by encouraging submission to papal and political authority. Catholicism adapts "itself to the senses, and enjoin[s] observances, which enter into the common train of life" (H IV.14). Contact with and assimilation to common life tames its abstract speculative principles and serves to make polytheists and Catholics more at home in the world than Protestant enthusiasts. In fact, as Hume understands it, Catholicism is a fundamentally ancient (even polytheist) religion in its mode of worship (e.g., the cult of Mary and the emphasis on saints)[16] and in its hostility to human pride. "Most religions of the ancient world arose in the unknown ages of government, when men were as yet barbarous and uninstructed, and the prince, as well as peasant, was disposed to receive, with implicit faith, every pious tale or fiction, which was offered him" (E 61). An examination of the *Natural History of Religion* reveals why "idolatrous," polytheistic religions prevented speculative religious parties from arising. In fact, *Natural History of Religion's* treatment of the movement from polytheism to theism can be seen as a metaphor for how the actively sovereign imagination arises in modernity. Abstract speculative parties are founded on transcendent longings similar to those commonly associated with religious faith— beliefs of special insight into the human condition that apply to all regardless of time and place. The desire to re-make the world is related to the somewhat noble desire to escape the particular and here and now. As long as polytheistic religion reigned and ecclesiastical and civil authority were fused the tendency of human beings to embrace parties founded on abstract speculative principle did not manifest.

The key factor in taming the actively sovereign imagination and in preventing the rise of abstract speculative parties is a broad submission to ordinary or common life. Barbarous polytheists keep their heads down without being tempted to entertain flights of imagination or an abstract orthodoxy. Without leisure to wonder about how the world began or to marvel at the orderliness of nature, polytheists are actuated by passions of fear and happiness in the face of necessity. "No passions, therefore, can be supposed to work upon such barbarians, but the ordinary affections of human life; the anxious concern for happiness, the dread of future misery, the terror of death, the thirst for revenge, the appetite for food and other necessities" (28). Many gods come from the many concerns that human beings have; in this way polytheistic gods stay close to normal human concerns and natural diversity. Polytheists "deify every part of the universe, and conceive all the conspicuous productions of nature, to be themselves so many real divinities" (38). Gods rule distinct provinces of nature and human affairs—a goddess of love, a god of war, a god of the sea, and so forth. Polytheists do not have a grand, sovereign idea of God, one who rules or saves or creates or destroys all. Theirs are confined gods with smaller spheres of influence that arise directly from the natural operation of the human mind and passions. "In all nations, which have embraced polytheism, the first ideas of religion arose not from a contemplation of the works of nature, but from a concern with regard to the events of life, and from the incessant hopes and fears, which actuate the human mind" (NHR 27). Hence another paradox: polytheistic societies, while hardly home to sound philosophy and progressive science, are free from the furious partisanship that can accompany progressive philosophy.

With a qualification that I discuss near the end of this chapter, Hume contends that polytheistic religions are more conducive to tolerance and mutual forbearance. "By limiting the powers and functions of its deities," Hume writes, a polytheistic religion "naturally admits the gods of other sects and nations to a share of divinity, and renders all the various deities, as well as rites, ceremonies, or traditions, compatible with each other" (NHR 48–9).[17] Citizens that believe themselves ruled by polytheist gods do not demand orthodoxy of neighboring cities or perceive the gods of the neighboring cities as threats. The polytheistic cast of mind prepares people to accept many gods.[18] The non-scriptural, doubtful nature of polytheist faith makes people less attached to their gods. The influence of polytheist religion was universal, Hume contends, "though it was not so great. As many people gave their assent to it; though that assent was not seemingly so strong, precise, and affirmative" (NHR 60; also E 62). Agreeing to disagree about the nature of the gods in the polytheist world is easier because no one deeply believes in such gods anyway. The tolerating spirit of idolaters (NHR 50, 49) and the tentative assent given to ancient religions (65) prevent the rise of a furious, speculative sectarianism. Hume credits the melding of religious and civil power typical of polytheistic cities for also preventing the rise of abstract speculative parties. In ancient polities, "the magistrate embraced the religion of the people, and entering cordially into the care of sacred matters, naturally acquired an authority in them, and united the ecclesiastical with the civil power" (E 61). Magistrates adopting the religious consensus of a particular nation do not experience intrusions by pious non-politicians into political affairs, as would Christian polities. Systematic theology was not needed to conjure up opposition to earthly powers because religious and secular powers were fused. Polytheist dogma does not, in short, appeal to the actively sovereign imagination.

Though partly salutary politically in confining potentially abstract mind to common life, polytheist religions are inherently unstable. In fact, according to Hume, societies subsist within a "flux and reflux" between polytheism and theism (NHR 46–8). Psychological and social factors explain the changes from one religious system to another. Men are led from primitive polytheism to theism by eulogizing and exaggerating the powers of formerly limited deities until those powers reach "infinity itself" (43). Anxiety and fear give rise to polytheism, but, as people believe divine assistance is needed, they elevate "their deities to the utmost bounds of perfection, [and] at last beget the attributes of unity and infinity, simplicity and spirituality" characteristic of theism (47). In the cycle of religious beliefs, theism deteriorates into polytheism because adherents cannot grasp "infinity" or pure "spirituality" without inventing more concrete "demi-gods or middle beings" which, in turn, become the chief objects of devotion (46–8). Polytheism leads to theism, and theism to polytheism.

Theism, especially enthusiastic theism, begets abstract speculative *religious* parties, which cross national borders, inspire conversions and crusades, and are more likely to persecute those who will not convert. Emancipated from common life and grasping for infinity, theism demands orthodoxy and flatters the sovereign imagination (H IV.14). Theist religions also lead to a melding of religious and political authority, as religion becomes the intellectual foundation for politics (i.e., God's sovereignty mirrors a prince's). Christianity began as an insurgent religion that gained power by arguing for the separation of ecclesiastical and civil authority, but it became the "established religion" later (E 61–2). A deeper, accidental cause of the final emergence of the natural tendency to embrace speculative parties in theistic times lies in the convergence of Christianity and scholastic philosophy. Philosophy is an agent on the border of common life that could mollify the melding of theology and philosophy.

> As philosophy was widely spread over the world, at the time when Christianity arose, the teachers of the new sect were obliged to form a system of speculative opinions; to divide, with some accuracy, their articles of faith; and to explain, comment, confute, and defend with all the subtlety of argument and science. Hence naturally arose keenness in dispute, when the Christian religion came to be split into divisions and heresies: And this keenness assisted the priests in their policy, of begetting a mutual hatred and antipathy among their deluded followers. Sects of philosophy, in the ancient world, were more zealous than parties of religion; but in modern times, parties of religion are more furious and enraged than the most cruel factions that ever arose from interest and ambition. (E 62–3)

Philosophy was disabled from being that corrective because it was "at every turn perverted to serve the purposes of superstition" and eventually gains "a kind of appetite for absurdity and contradiction" (NHR 54; also 53). Theism tends to fill people with a sense of righteousness that supplements the natural human aspiration for orthodoxy and fosters the partisanship known only to modern times (NHR 49). The marriage of philosophy and Christianity has spread "the greatest misery and devastation" and has been a "poison of human society, and the source of the most inveterate factions in every government" (E 60–1).

Catholicism is associated, in Hume's view, with profound ignorance, barbarism, stupidity, self-abnegation and individual submissiveness to all authority.[19] Bigoted and intolerant, superstitious people lack the pride and philosophic pretensions to form parties founded on abstract speculative principles. Catholics are also grounded in common life, paying homage to saints of smaller causes and concerned to serve those around their parishes with humility. As Hume charts the ascendancy of parties founded on abstract speculative principles, he charts the waning of superstitious public opinion in England and the rise of enthusiastic religious sects. (See chapter 7 for a detailed account of this transition.) As the character of religious devotion in England and in Europe changed, the philosophic speculation restrained by superstitious religious dogmas was emancipated.[20] The rise of enthusiasm is a great accomplishment, in a sense, because such parties do not arise in a pre-civilized age. In showing how these parties arise Hume is not pining for a return to the superstitious beliefs that prevented their ascension. What he does is subtler, and more consistent with his philosophic project of identifying mixtures that define the human condition. Curiosity, innovation, and the revival of arts and letters dissolve superstitious ignorance (to our great benefit) but they unleash new problems associated with modern ideology (to our dismay). Even such goods as curiosity and arts and letters are mixed blessings, for they are often associated with intellectual arrogance among the self-styled learned and with false philosophy.

Modern philosophy took on the form of Christian theology in its attempt to hasten the decline of Protestant enthusiasm and offer itself as an alternative. The demand for purity, disputatiousness, contempt for common experience, the spirit of innovation, and personal investment in ideas that define Puritanism prefigured the same characteristics in its secular Whig cousins. Modern philosophic teachings may also borrow its desire for complete sovereignty over the universe from Christianity.[21] However this is, Locke's political teaching was designed to be free of the difficulties incident to the abstract speculative parties in religion. Not only did Locke recognize the dangerous partisanship that can flow from designing elites, he sought to mitigate partisanship by announcing a non-teleological, secular, almost de-ontological political creed. For Hume, Locke's theoretical principles contradict his political goals: they were liberal in principle but not in practice. Modern theory imputes to mankind the ability to know political principles divorced from ordinary experience and to institute reforms based on these principles. This abstract reasoning, however perfect in itself, wraps one's particular will, desires and reason into universalist language. Locke's principles are products of emancipated imagination that would result in party rage and the destruction of conditions for good government. Some think Hume's argument has wider, contemporary application.[22]

Parties Founded on Abstract Speculative Principles in Hume's Time

With the shadows of religious wars receding in England and on the continent, parties from abstract speculative religious principle were less threatening. Political partisanship could, as we learn from the French Revolution, be just as problematic. In England, the possibility of furious, violent partisanship seemed far away and life itself did not appear to be on the line. Whigs supposed that enacting procedural reforms in the British Constitution would liberalize it. Applying their speculative systems to the complexities of political life, aspiring partisans wanted important elements of the nation's political machinery jettisoned in the name of theory. Hume aimed to dampen the cry for reform and to promote political moderation by exposing shortcomings in systems of reform. His *History of England* acts against the partisan claims of both Whigs and Tories. Many of Hume's *Essays* "show that neither side" is "so fully supported by reason as they endeavour to flatter themselves." This is designed to encourage "moderate opinions" and persuade "each [party] that its antagonists may possibly be sometimes in the right" (E 494). I first examine the dangers he saw in the Whig's theoretical demands and then outline Hume's efforts to tame the emancipated imagination of these reformers.

There are, Hume writes, "parties of PRINCIPLE involved in the very nature of our constitution, which may properly enough be denominated those of COURT and COUNTRY" (E 65). The country party worried above all about parliamentary corruption, by which the king maintained a working majority in the House of Commons by dispensing parliamentary offices to friends of monarchy. The practice served as an informal check on the Commons, which otherwise might have had unchecked control of the government. The country party worried that royal control of parliamentary affairs undermined the independence of parliament and the viability of popular rule. Underneath this worry was Locke's political system. Locke had posited a close connection between the separation of the legislative from the executive powers and representative government on the one hand and the maintenance of the rule of law on the other. Locke writes, "The *first and fundamental positive Law* of all Commonwealths, *is the establishing of the Legislative* Power." No edict can have the force of law which "has not its *Sanction from* that *Legislative,* which the publick has chosen and appointed" (*Second Treatise,* Para. 134). Based on this, Locke concludes that absolute monarchy is "*inconsistent with Civil Society,* and so can be no form of Civil Government at all" (Para. 90).[23]

Hume first questions Whig theory as such and then investigates the likely practical consequences of Whig reforms (E 494). On the level of theory, Locke's Whig account "leads to paradoxes, repugnant to the common sentiments of mankind, and to the practice and opinion of all nations and all ages."

> The doctrine, which founds all lawful government on an original contract, or the consent of the people, is plainly of this kind; nor has the most noted of its partizans, in the prosecution of it, scrupled to affirm, *that absolute monarchy is inconsistent with civil society, and so can be no form of civil government at all*; and *that the supreme power in a state cannot take from any man, by taxes and impositions, any part of his property, without his own consent or that of his representatives.* What authority any moral reasoning can have, which leads into opinions so wide of the general practice of mankind, in every place but this single kingdom, it is easy to determine. (E 486–7)

Legitimate and enforceable laws flow from cultural, non-legislative sources. Absolute monarchies are often consistent with civil society in the modern world. Hume discusses the relationship between absolute government and the rule of law in "Of the Rise and Progress of the Arts and Sciences."[24] There is no necessary link between representative government and the establishment of the rule of law as he describes the great improvements experienced under modern monarchy. Whig theory's failure to understand the true sources of constitutional moderation and the true sources of the rule of law is bound to have practical implications.

On a practical level, Hume shows that the Whig desire to end parliamentary corruption and to propagate belief in the right to revolution would upset Britain's well-functioning British Constitution. I examine these issues in turn.

Parliamentary Corruption. The question of how the British Constitution could be improved "is not concerning a fine imaginary republic, of which a man may form a plan in his closet." It is a practical question that requires an analysis of the peculiar characteristics of the British system. The British Constitution was vulnerable, in Hume's judgment, to majority faction exercised through the House of Commons. Locke's political teaching encouraged assertions of popular sovereignty. "The share of power, allotted by our constitution to the House of Commons, is so great, that it absolutely commands all the other parts of the government." Kings possessed only a veto in the framing of laws, which Hume thought was of "little moment," and the exercise of an "altogether subordinate" power to execute laws made by another body (E 44). An unchecked commons would lead to majority faction and perhaps to the dissolution of the British Constitution.

> If the House of Commons, in such a case, ever dissolve itself, which is not to be expected, we may look for a civil war every election. If it continue itself, we shall suffer all the tyranny of faction, subdivided into new factions. And, as such a violent government cannot long subsist, we shall, at last, after many convulsions, and civil wars, find repose in absolute monarchy, which it would have been happier for us to have established peaceably from the beginning. (E 52–3)

Whig theory is too complacent in its reliance on theoretical clarity. Only by investigating how the British Constitution moderates and improves the new forces of democracy does Hume think we can gain a proper scientific account of the British Constitution. What Whig advocates call corruption or dependence is in reality the most effective restraint on the ambition of the House of Commons and preserves the balance of power in the government. "The interest of the body is here restrained by that of the individuals, and... the House of Commons stretches not its power, because such an usurpation would be contrary to the interest of the majority of its members" (E 45), just as it would be contrary to the preservation of the constitution itself. Members of parliament owing their offices to the crown have no interest in advocating for the elimination of dependent seats or an extension of parliamentary power. What is in the interest of many members of parliament (and repugnant to Whigs) serves good government by checking the otherwise unchecked parliament. Hume chides Whigs for ignoring evidence about corruption. "Instead then of asserting absolutely, that the dependence of parliament, in every degree, is an infringement of BRITISH liberty, the country-party should have made some concessions to their adversaries, and have only examined what was the proper degree of this dependency, beyond which it became dangerous to liberty." This leads to a conclusion consistent with Hume's science of our "mixed kind of life": high questions of principle are really matters of degree, where statesmen must weigh competing goods in a zone of twilight and uncertainty. The theoretical view of politics elevates one of these goods beyond its true, limited importance. In this case Whig theory elaborates a conception of consensual government above other goods. A mixed science sees how excessively consensual government can upset stability and how stability too promotes liberty and the ability to live a good, happy life.

The Right to Revolution. Hume examines other *"practical* consequences" for politics drawn by Whig theory (E 488). Locke argues that the right to revolution is connected to the proposition that legitimate governments are founded on the consent of the governed. The American Declaration of Independence follows the logic of this connection. Consent ensures that government respects the rights of its citizens. Those rights are insecure in the state of nature and a just government is instituted to secure those rights. If the government becomes destructive to those rights or if these rights become insecure again, individuals retain the right to remove the cause of the insecurity. Consent and the right to revolution serve the same end, securing individual rights.[25] Frequent reference to the right to revolution is designed to promote an ethic of popular jealousy and to encourage a heightened regard for the first principles of government. One can see a simulacrum of these rights in Jefferson's proposal to have each generation fix its own constitution. His aim was to keep the first principles of government in the citizens' minds by institutionalizing the rights to consent and revolution.

Hume sees danger in the Locke-Whig-Jefferson position. Common experience does weigh in favor of revolution sometimes. "Common sense teaches us, that, as government binds us to obedience only on account of its tendency to public utility, that duty must always, in extraordinary cases, when public ruin would evidently attend obedience, yield to the primary and original obligation" (E 489). Despite this agreement, Hume argues that the principled defense of revolution by Whig theorists misshapes public opinion. It encourages the citizenry to feel an untrammeled sense of right and power, an active *popular* sovereignty. A population embracing the right to revolution will be more likely to practice forms of civil disobedience, which will undermine the duty to obedience and may lead to the fraying of the social bond based on the rule of law. Politics is always conflict- and faction-ridden, as groups have different interests, passions and opinions. In such a situation, political harmony depends on obeying laws even as groups may jockey to change them, as laws are the established, agreed-upon framework for living together. Groups may not love each other, but they can obey laws. The right to revolution and its attendant doctrines tend to upset that harmony and may lead to a loosening of the social bond, civil war or tyranny. "Besides the mischiefs of a civil war, which commonly attends insurrection; it is certain, that, where a disposition to rebellion appears among any people, it is one chief cause of tyranny in the rulers, and forces them into many violent measures which they never would have embraced, had every one been inclined to submission and obedience."[26]

These dangers flow from Whig abstract speculative principles and from the attempt to ascend from the limits of common life. This is a case when what philosophers teach and how they teach it can affect practice in common life. Philosophers would be "better employed in inculcating the general doctrine" of obedience than "in displaying the particular exceptions, which we are, perhaps, but too much inclined, of ourselves, to embrace and to extend." They should also not announce principles based on the extreme case, but rather concern themselves "with regard to the degree of necessity, which can justify resistance, and render it lawful or commendable." Even so, while philosophers may be excused for arguing that rules of obedience should be "dispensed with in cases of urgent necessity," passionate politicians cannot be excused for entertaining this general principle. Hume asks, "What should we think of a preacher or casuist, who should make it his chief study to find out such cases, and enforce them with all the vehemence of argument and eloquence? Would he not be better employed in inculcating the general doctrine, than in displaying the particular exceptions, which we are, perhaps, but too much inclined, of ourselves, to embrace and extend?" (E 490–1).

Popular philosophical speech made by "philosophers who embrace party" shapes how political actors speak. American experience testifies to the shaping influence of Locke's Whig rights-based political theory. This mode of thought tended, in Hume's judgment, to exacerbate problems of securing obedience. James Madison saw a similar problem in Jefferson's attempt to draw the people directly into the government. Madison writes, "The danger of disturbing the public tranquility by interesting too strongly the public passions is a still more serious objection against frequent reference of constitutional questions to the decision of the whole society."[27] Madison, like Hume, is concerned to shape public opinion toward a reasonable obedience to a reasonable government. Frequent appeals to the people about fundamental principles would give rise to a dangerously passionate partisanship tending to undermine veneration for the constitution and to dissolve national fellow feeling. *The Federalist Papers's* silence on the right to revolution is in keeping with Hume's thought on this matter, though Publius does not go as far as Hume in criticizing the mode of thinking that gives rise to the right to revolution.

Hume's analyses of parliamentary dependence and the right to resistance reveal the problems with parties based on abstract speculative principles. The utopian cast of mind and underlying assumptions about human nature embraced by abstract reformers suggest a dangerous notion of human sovereignty over our affairs. By flattering and even liberating the human capacity for choice from the contingencies of common life, Whig theory risks inaugurating a period where individual willfulness will decide the direction of political changes. The Enlightenment would become an age of obscuring poetry aiding the cause of perpetual political making, unmaking and remaking, not an age of moderation, happiness, and industry. The expressive nature of human choice directed by restless imagination and elevated by Locke's political psychology undermines rational political order.[28] This intrusion of empty and arbitrary ideology gave Hume pause about rationalism in politics. When ideologies clash, the problem turns violent. When one ideology predominates, the time-tested traditions and subtly influential institutions of society would come under attack as inconsistent with the principles of the reforming party.

In his later years Hume believed that he saw British constitutional government coming to an end in the events surrounding the Wilkes and Liberty riots.[29] I rely on Hume's private correspondences about the events of 1769–72 to discern his fears about the future of British government and to illuminate his criticisms of modern rationalism in politics. Hume's reaction to this crisis reflects his worries about modern rationalism as expressed in his published work, so I do not fear using private letters as a source.[30] John Wilkes returned from fugitive exile in France, where he fled to escape parliamentary expulsion and criminal prosecution for seditious libel. Despite this, in 1769, electors in Middlesex elected Wilkes to the Commons three times. He was expelled from the House after each election. Riots ensued, where constituents of Middlesex and people committed to democratic reforms of the British Constitution demanded that Wilkes be allowed to take his seat.[31] These events showed Hume that politically "factious prejudices are more prevalent in England than religious ones" (Letters II.233).

The "factious prejudices" to which Hume refers are the kind of "unaccountable *phoenomenon*" of abstract political parties Hume treated in "Of Parties in General." In a letter to the Rev. Hugh Blair, Hume states that the abstract political parties are *more* difficult to understand than abstract religious parties. "This exceeds the Absurdity of Titus Oates and the popish Plot; and is so much more disgraceful to the Nation, as the former Folly, being deriv'd from Religion, flow'd from a Source, which has, from uniform Prescription, acquir'd a Right to impose Nonsense on all Nations & all Ages: But the present Extravagance is peculiar to Ourselves, and quite risible" (Letters II.197). The Wilkes rebellion was peculiar for two reasons, which Hume relates in letters to the French statesman Turgot in June 1768. The British people riot, Hume writes, "without any Grievance, I do not only say, real, but even imaginary; and without any of them being able to tell one Circumstance of Government which they wish to have corrected." Instead reformers "roar Liberty, tho' they have apparently more Liberty than any People in the World; a great deal more than they deserve; and perhaps more than any men ought to have" (Letters II.180). Hume saw cries of "Wilkes and Liberty" as signs of a general "Progress of Madness and Folly and Wickedness in England" and of having a "stupid" and "barbarous and absurd" basis for action.[32] The grievances surrounding the Wilkes affair were purely speculative, made by the imaginations of men alienated from common life.

The folly of suggesting constitutional changes where no changes were needed is evident. The reformers were "barbarous" in that they did not understand how their calls for reform would destroy the foundation of a well-functioning government. As Livingston argues, in their state of sophisticated ignorance the reformers attempt to remake a world they did not understand.[33] "The Madness and Wickedness of the English... appear astonishing, even after all the Experience we have had. It must end fatally either to the King or Constitution or to both" (Letters II.226). The death of the constitution and the destruction of the monarchical element of the constitution would spell years of faction for Britain, culminating most probably in "absolute monarchy... the easiest death, the true *Euthanasia* of the BRITISH constitution" (E 53).[34]

Concerns about the Wilkes Riots overturning the British government and renting the union with Scotland asunder may appear in retrospect to be the ravings of a crank. Britain survived and even thrived in the era after the Wilkes incidents. If Tocqueville is correct, Britain found a way to mitigate the effects of abstract thinking in politics with free institutions.[35] However this may be, what Adam Smith calls a "love of system" in politics became an important feature of modern politics generally. Hume's warnings about the problems of revolutionary ideology were not without foundation. The French Revolution, which began just over a decade after Hume's death, provides a glimpse of the dangers associated with visionary ideology and actively sovereign imaginations.

"Political Polytheism" and the Subordination of the Sovereign Imagination

One development associated with abstract principles that Hume embraced was the establishment of religious tolerance as official policy in England and Holland. Though these countries "embraced the principles of toleration, this singularity has proceeded from the steady resolution of the civil magistrate, in opposition to the continued efforts of priests and bigots" (NHR 50). "Civil magistrates" pursued policies of tolerance at the goading of popular opinion shaped by thinkers such as Locke and because the increasing diversity of sects made religious establishments less tenable. State policies of toleration reflected the citizens' willingness to live with the religious doctrines of others. In fact, it seems that one of the main motivations behind the move toward toleration is the practically polytheistic, though explicitly latitudinarian, premise that our ignorance about theological matters is so profound that we must rest satisfied with a variety of theological opinions (H III.186). Tolerance is enthusiasm with a tincture of skepticism, a reality functionally equivalent to the tolerating spirit of polytheist idolators that Hume praised in the *Natural History of Religion*. The advent of a tolerant religious practice was one place where philosophic intervention into politics seemed welcome, in Hume's judgment.

As religious partisanship waned, partisanship based on abstract speculative principle became the problem. With the expected convergence of modern philosophy, a waning Christian theism, and parties based on abstract speculative principle, the full weight and fury of the natural human aspiration for orthodoxy would settle in politics. The British experience with parties suggested to Hume that abstract systems or "ideologies" would be part of modern politics. The dangers involved in such a politics include the prospect of armed factional conflict, political instability, the destruction of conditions necessary to maintain moderate government, the corruption of established social practices, and perhaps the advent of tyrannical government.

Hume criticizes modern political philosophers from a point of agreement with them. He does not question whether philosophy should play a role in shaping politics—his diagnosis of political problems caused by the intrusion of modern rationalism is proof of the role he believes he has in shoring up the cause of modern commercial society by correctly shaping public opinion. He worries about the form that the philosophic advice takes or the understanding of philosophy reflected in the advice. Hume's concern about the effects of abstract principles in politics indicates the direction his political science would tend. Instead of promoting the tendency of viewing politics in black and white terms, Hume attempts to lower the temperature of politics and to inculcate moderation by showing that politics always involves questions that are shades of gray. Parliamentary dependence and the question of rightful resistance are questions of degree to be examined by acute political observers and statesmen. Politics specifically and human life as such involve a complex mix of important human goods. Statesmen seek to vindicate these goods and balance them. Political problems occur when one of the goods is either insufficiently realized or blown out of proportion. Philosophers must understand balance and help statesmen to understand it and to convey it to their citizens or subjects. This political science is part of a project aimed at reconstructing public opinion so that the natural human aspiration to orthodoxy is counteracted by other tendencies of the human mind. Hume attempts to reform how people think about modernity so that people can enjoy its fruits.

Hume's concerns about rationalism in politics can be summarized in a different way. By imputing to mankind a flattering account of human reason that does not acknowledge the prevalence of natural beliefs and sentiments, Locke emancipated imagination from its moorings in common life. There is a deep irony in Locke's self-understanding. Where Locke purports to follow reason divorced from the imagination, Hume sees the imagination distorting Locke's account of reason. This elevated liberal partisanship imputes to human beings sovereignty over their politics and, by extension, their own nature, an ability to reform society according to the dictates of abstract reason. Against this view, Hume demands that the political imagination be subordinated to the dictates of practice or face the consequences of the goose that laid the golden egg. It is not so much Whig institutions that foster liberty, though they are not unimportant; institutions are not secure without the liberal culture or way of life. Attributes of this liberal culture include a moderate popular jealousy of political power, a concern for public affairs, the spread of property ownership, the growth of a middling class, the acceptance of the commercial spirit, and a decline in superstitious reverence for priestly authority and doctrine. The importance of manners in shaping the tone of government blunts the liberal faith in manipulating institutional mechanisms. The priority of the cultural over the institutional and of habits of the heart over constructions of the imagination points to the fundamental insight of Hume's political teaching, and the most difficult challenge to modern *theory*. If theory as it is commonly asserted can damage the healthy political practice, what is a political theorist to do? This challenge points to a fundamental challenge to Hume's own perspective too. Has Hume placed reason into an inescapable box of culture? Does the priority of culture over imagination and reason lead to the displacement of reason and imagination? Does Hume's turn to history require a turn to History?

CHAPTER 6

HUMANITY AND COMMERCE

> *We have finally reached the age of commerce, an age which must necessarily replace that of war, as the age of war was bound to precede it. War and commerce are only two different means to achieve the same end, that of possessing what is desired... War then comes before commerce. The former is all savage impulse, the later civilized calculation.*
>
> —Benjamin Constant, *The Spirit of Conquest and Usurpation*, Pt. I, Chap. 2.

Hume's dissatisfaction with modern political philosophy led him to the study of history as a mirror to "the constant and universal principles of human nature" (EHU 83). This study of history, while it led him to insist that there was an enduring human nature across time, also led him to appreciate the unique accomplishments (and problems) in political practice of modern Europe of his time[1] and to see the political arrangements of ancient regimes as almost unbelievable distortions of human nature. For Hume, ancient political institutions are peculiar, violent, immoderate, and generally undesirable, while modern practice is gentle and moderate and fosters happiness and human flourishing. How can Hume reach this conclusion about the superiority of modern to ancient times? How are we to understand his turn to history as a mirror of nature when it comes to studying human nature?

Previous turns to history—those characteristic of Whig politicians, for instance—were laden with dubious metaphysical and theoretical assumptions, which Hume's *History* explodes (see chapter 7). Hume seeks to investigate history, shorn of these assumptions, as a fount of empirical evidence from which to draw general rules or conclusions about the mixed character of human affairs (as I argued in chapter 4). There seem to be two broad objections to such a view of history. From a classical perspective, Hume's view of history appears overly optimistic in its hopes of revealing the permanent, enduring nature of human nature by looking at particular past actions. "The unbiased historian had to confess," argues

Leo Strauss, "his inability to derive any norms from history... 'the historical process' revealed itself as the meaningless web spun by what men did, produced, and thought, no more than being unmitigated chance—a tale told by an idiot."² This criticism is based on an understanding of history as found in Aristotle's *Poetics*, where Aristotle argues that history is less philosophic and less worthy of attention than poetry because it is concerned with particulars rather than universals. History appears to be mere event unable to provide universalistic illumination about things and as something only concerned about "things which have happened" instead of what "might have happened."³ History appears as a science of single events; that is, not a science at all. Poetry and philosophy, in contrast, investigate universal concerns. From this perspective, Hume's attempt to ground a political teaching in history expects too much from history (in revealing universal principles of human nature) and too little from philosophy (by subordinating it to what it has seen in history divorced from human ends).

The second objection builds on Hume's own reservations about this ancient understanding of history and philosophy, but develops those reservations in a radically skeptical direction. Hume's rejection of ancient metaphysics and teleology turns him to investigate empirically derived human constants instead of human ends. History itself, Hume seems to contend, provides standards by which to judge history. The hope that history itself can provide a standard of judgment cannot survive the observation, not foreign to Hume, that history is governed mostly by "accident and chance" (H II.525). If history cannot provide standards of judgment, the only standards available, absent a resurrection of ancient teleology or revealed knowledge, are subjective or procedural in character. This is the conclusion drawn by the Historical cum Nihilist school of thought characteristic of nineteenth century German philosophy and culminating in Nietzsche. Pinning such high hopes on history—hopes that it can provide guidance for moral judgment—leads to the debilitating nihilistic conclusion that all thought is conditioned by fate or one's own political horizon. On this view, Hume steps toward acknowledging our desperate situation, but he naively and unjustifiably clung to Enlightenment pretensions to universality; Hume lacked the courage of his convictions.

These objections provide the philosophic impetus for a discussion of Hume's defense of modern commercial arrangements. Hume seeks a different way to conceive of the relationship between history, philosophy and nature. The ancients conceived of history too narrowly. Aristotle, for instance, based his *Politics* on observations of continuity and change in many constitutions. His *Athenian Constitution* and other lost studies form the basis of his *Politics* just as Hume's *History of England* forms part of the basis for Hume's *Essays*. The study of many cases (Aristotle) and history (Hume) yield knowledge about the possibilities, tensions, and remedies, in political life. Aristotle too had recognized development in political life; that is, how Greek political life differed from savage and barbarous life and how times had changed even within Greek life to make monarchy and aristocracy less thinkable than they were "in ancient times" (1319a8, 10). Aristotle's science, while dismissing historical investigations in word, assimilated them in fact. For Aristotle, such studies provide the fund of experiments revealing our complex accounts of justice, the incommensurable goods toward which we strive in political life, the various legitimate claims to rule, and the possibilities of politics. Philosophy meanwhile uses the stuff of history to account for the mixed nature before it continues to chase after given human ends. Nor does Hume embrace a providential or dialectical "historical process." New phenomena may arise in history: Hume nowhere holds that these are products of a process and such a thought is not commanded by the idea that there are new developments. Hume's explanation for the rise of parties based on abstract speculative principle as a new, modern phenomenon does not include an account of how they emerge from a mysterious historical process. Such parties arise from a human tendency combined with the removal of that which had prevented that tendency from manifesting itself in practice (see chapter 5).

This chapter tests Hume his endorsement of modern commercial arrangements. Hume's endorsement is controversial because it is "hazardous," as Butterfield writes, "for the historian to venture on certain historical investigations—for example to pretend that he can show that one generation was really more happy than another."[4] How can Hume claim that the modern commercial republic is the best arrangement for human beings? How can his understanding of one human nature survive given the decisive differences he sees between the prodigy Sparta and the historically unique, most perfect system of liberty in England? How can he make judgments in our mixed condition? This chapter proceeds in two parts—the first showing why Hume rejects ancient practice and second why he endorses modern arrangements. The larger issue of Hume's conception of history unites this chapter and the next.

Ancient Violence and Distortion

Political virtue [in republican government among ancients] is the renunciation of oneself, which is always a very painful thing.

Montesquieu, *The Spirit of the Laws*, IV.5.

The distinction between the ancient and modern worlds is as significant for Hume as the distinction between democracy and aristocracy is for Tocqueville. This should come as no surprise because Hume, like Tocqueville, was a great student and admirer of Montesquieu, who, as much as Hume, is responsible for articulating a non-dogmatic defense of commerce and the English Constitution.[5] Like Montesquieu, Hume sees deep similarities between the ancient's classical republican virtue and austere Christian religious orders, both of which are defined by violent repression of humane, universalistic passions.[6] The Christian and ancient traditions had often seen themselves as competitors because they aspired toward different ends: Christians aim toward salvation or heaven; and ancient politics toward the service of the public good. Montesquieu and Hume criticize these traditions first by denying the reality or authority of their respective ends, and then by collapsing these distinct traditions into one defined by subordination, obedience, violence, and irrational self-denial. Both the ancient political tradition and Christianity, as they see them, distorted nature by insisting that passions be ordered by the rule of reason.[7] Each tradition conceived of human beings as lost, or certainly imperfect, without the instruction toward the end. Hume places his hopes in the conception of man underneath or prior to the distorting instruction engendered in each tradition, a conception defined as our "humanity."

Let us follow Hume's argument. Ancient republics were "violent, and contrary to the more natural and usual course of things." Sparta in particular is justly esteemed a "prodigy" by all who have "considered human nature as it has displayed itself in other nations, and other ages."[8] Even "though the ROMAN and other ancient republics were supported on principles somewhat more natural," only "an extraordinary concurrence of circumstances" relating to the need to be prepared for almost continual warfare made people submit to "such grievous burthens" (E 259). Ancient cities were "fortified camp[s]" where "a passion for public good" was infused "into each breast" (262). Citizens were animated by a rigorous public spirit or love of fatherland (259 and 404). Individual sacrifice for the public was the defining virtue of these free and martial republics. The extreme case, Sparta, illustrates this approach. Lycurgus thought men too naturally egoistic to trust them to subordinate their private desires to their public duties. Spartan citizens were deprived of opportunities to accumulate private wealth because arts, money, and commerce were banished. In the place of private endeavors and attachments, citizens were educated to devote their lives to public duties in war, in the assembly and in office; slaves performed non-public chores such as gathering food. Such public spirit, moral order and self-renunciation can only be attained through intrusive legislation, violence, and rigorous statesmanship. Citizens must embrace their chains, are devoted to their chains with enthusiasm, and see their chains as their own freedom; they live for the glory of their chains.⁹ Hume's characterization of ancient republicanism differs little from Rousseau's; both see ancient cities as animated by something akin to a "general will" promoting a simple, undivided education for citizenship.

Hume sees deep similarities between the intrusive legislation seen in ancient republics, such as Sparta, and Christianity.¹⁰ Like Montesquieu who compares Sparta's singular institutions to the religious fanaticism witnessed in monasteries,¹¹ Hume complains of a "dismal dress" that has been sown by "many divines, and some philosophers." This dismal morality demands "useless austerities and rigors, suffering and self-denial" (EPM 279). Christianity's "monkish virtues" of "celibacy, fasting, penance, mortification, self-denial, humility, silence, solitude" especially seem to cultivate rigorous self-denial for no discernible individual gain and no lasting public benefit. These "virtues," as Hume sees them, "serve no manner of purpose; neither advance a man's future in the world, nor render him a more valuable member of society; neither qualify him for the entertainment of company, nor increase his power of self-enjoyment" (EPM 270).¹² Monks (and Christians) embrace rules that mortify the flesh, and Hume does not think that self-mortification serves the higher end of salvation.

In each case, the end proposed violates a proper understanding of our "mixed kind of life." Ancient public spiritedness draws human beings too far to the social side of the human mix, holding that human beings could simply identify themselves with their city. Contradicting human nature, they also caused severe problems for the political community (as we shall see). Christian faith lent certainty into the area of the unknown and was traceable to the imagination ungrounded in common life. Virtues must in the first place be traceable to benefits in common life, which provide a standard for distinguishing moral goodness from its opposite, but Christian virtues did no such thing, as Hume sees it. One indication that the principles animating ancient republicanism and austere Christianity violate our "mixed kind of life" is the violence needed to sustain them. "The less natural any set of principles are," Hume argues, "the more difficulty will a legislator meet with in raising and cultivating them." Ancient republics were founded on principles "too disinterested and too difficult to support" and maintained by a "violent method" that proved for the most part "impracticable" (E 260, 263, 262) for improving the individual or enriching the public. Sparta was relatively successful in establishing and securing the perpetuation of its political and educational institutions, yet we are led to wonder if a life dedicated to Sparta would be satisfying. Spartans defined virtue as the negation of one's own interests, passions, and attachments. Their self-abnegation becomes almost an end in itself because the end it serves is not in reality satisfying to mixed human creatures. If this is the case, is self-denial for Sparta (normally) tenable over the long term? The cultivation of the blinding devotion necessary to sustain ancient republicanism requires disfiguring violence and intrusive public censoriousness that breed fanaticism and factionalism and foster an extreme desire for glory through war.[13] Ancient politics were hence inconsistent with political moderation (E 407 and 414).[14]

There is a parallel between the city and the soul. Political subordination, like the psychological subordination in the relationship between master and slave, is sustained by violence and repression while licensing violence and repression. According to the ancient practice of slavery, "all checks were on the inferior, to restrain him to the duty of submission; none on the superior, to engage him to the duty of submission" (E 384). The unchecked relationship of noble and serf was a defining element of the feudal order as well. Inequality pervaded feudal institutions to such a degree that nobles were hardly regarded as of the same species as lesser subjects. This is evident from the actions of King Edward III with respect to the praising of his fellow nobleman Ribaumont, who was freed for showing such spirit on the battlefield, and the citizens of Calais, who, though showing similar courage, Edward condemned to die (H II.238–41). Murders of or by nobleman were different in law than murders of or by commoners under the feudal constitution (H V.47). Ancient and feudal polities, where "a severe, jealous Aristocracy" ruled "over discontented subjects," were defined by a political inequality sustained by violence (E 416). No matter how much ancient cities depended on some level of material and political equality among citizens, the gap between citizens and non-citizens (i.e., slaves) was so profound as to constitute a defining commitment of the regime.

Christianity was also a breeding ground for violent factions (E 61, 76–8; T 272). A political and humane Christianity for Hume is maintained through a violence similar to what is seen in ancient republics. Salvation is even less to be seen than the public good of ancient republicanism, and it forms an even more fanciful, dangerous basis for political disagreements. Faith is maintained, on Hume's account, through a suppression of, or violence against, the intellect and its natural curiosity enforced by priests or public opinion generally.

How profoundly the modern constitutions that Hume describes differ from ancient ones and from Christian faith! Liberty, a more robust commitment to equality, the presence of commerce, and the softening of mores define modern constitutions. Ancients lived in continual war, ignorance and poverty, while the commerce characteristic of modern times promises peace, knowledge and prosperity. Ancient laws were rigorous and violent, but modern constitutions are gentle and moderate, though Hume does not abandon some elements of the ancient belief that constitutions (somehow) educate the people.[15] Christians claim to be concerned about the next life; modern commercial people about this one.

If history gives few such examples of modern commercial societies, and if indeed the weight of historical evidence tells against the prevalence of modern commercial republics, how can Hume justify those arrangements as natural and regular without recourse to what he regards as dubious metaphysical categories such as the rights of man? On what basis does Hume shun Sparta and embrace England's Constitution? What is the humanity to which Hume refers and why does he think it is a live, *natural* possibility?

Liberty and the Humane Alternative

These questions demand that we confront the importance of modern commerce. Commerce is one of the most important developments in history (E 416–20), in that it has contributed to a moral revolution. Hume's most complete discussion of human happiness appears in his essays about the nature of commerce, implying that commerce is connected with the greatest of human concerns. The most thorough discussion of happiness appears in "Of Refinement in the Arts." This essay, which originally appeared under the title "Of Luxury," is one of Hume's three great defenses of humane, modern arrangements (the others are "Of the Populousness of Ancient Nations" and "Of Commerce"). "Refinement" follows "Of Commerce," and it deals with a chief objection to modern commercial society "Of Commerce" leaves unanswered. In "Of Commerce," Hume argues that the cultivation of manufacturing, trade, and commercial agriculture characteristic of modernity contributes to the greatness of a state more effectively than the ancient practice of direct, almost universal citizen participation in the military. In ancient republics, where commercial activities were discouraged, there "seems to be a kind of opposition between the greatness of the state and the happiness of the subject" (E 257). Citizen armies and navies in ancient times were involved in almost constant warfare. Commerce was antithetical to the rigorous cultivation of citizen-soldiers. This ancient policy did not make for strong states, though it could produce men of outstanding individual virtue. "Though the want of trade and manufacturing, among a free and very martial people may sometimes have no other effect than to render the public more powerful, it is certain, that, in the common course of human affairs, it will have a quite contrary tendency" (E 260). As Hume presents it, ancient polities are based on a miscalculation about how to augment public power rather than on a delusion (as he suggests Christianity is). Ancients thought that constant vigilance and direct service to the city made for powerful political constitutions, but they ignored that power came from inventions, improvements, audacity, thinking for oneself and technical innovation; a happy, hopeful people also reproduce, making for more potential inventors and improvers. Ancient cities did not understand that public power rests on private power, so they were usually weak and unable to sustain great efforts. Modern states must sometimes embrace the direct, comprehensive sacrifice characteristic of ancient policy when they wage war. The ancients had mistaken the extreme case for the normal case (a mistake mitigated the fact that the normal case in the ancient world *was* waging war). Throughout "Of Commerce" and "Refinement" Hume argues that the promotion of manufacturing and commerce increases the power of the sovereign more than direct service in the military.

Further details of Hume's argument about the augmentation of public power need not detain us. Let it suffice to say that Hume's defense of modern commerce is incomplete at the end of "Of Commerce." The superiority of modern over ancient policy depends not only on the aggrandizement of the public, but also on the happiness and morality of individuals in commercial times. Hume asserts in "Of Commerce" that modern arrangements are more consistent with "the most natural course of things" (E 260) and more conducive to individual happiness and virtue. In "Refinement" Hume defends this proposition against powerful and persistent objections similar to those implied by the ancients and articulated by Rousseau. "Men of severe morals," writes Hume, "blame even the most innocent luxury, and represent it as the source of all the corruptions, disorders, and factions, incident to civil government" (E 269). Philosophic and religious proponents of "monkish virtues" think luxury is inimical to a properly ordered disposition.[16] The condemnation of luxury is especially prevalent among those whom Hume sees as taken with "frenzies of enthusiasm" (E 268).

This is another instance where Hume puts theory in the service of combatting false or partial theories. Theories condemning commerce and refinement and technology threaten the sound practices of commerce and a politics of humanity. Hume's defense of commerce is tied to his defense of humanity, which, as we have seen, is the virtue best reflecting our "mixed kind of life." Modern political communities are likely to follow what Hume considers the "best policy," which is "to comply with the common bent of mankind, and give it all the improvements of which it is susceptible" (E 260). Instead of creating artificial, repressive obligations as ancient and feudal polities had, modern communities liberate the soft mores and humane virtues. "Our modern education and customs instill more humanity and moderation than the ancient" (E 94; also 404, 414). The rise of soft, humane mores coincides with the rise of modern liberty; in fact, it seems that Hume posits a cause-effect relationship. "To one who considers on the subject" of comparing the ancient and modern worlds, Hume writes, "it will appear, that human nature, in general, really enjoys more liberty at present, in the most arbitrary government of EUROPE, than it ever did during the most flourishing period of ancient times" (E 383). Liberation from repressive laws and unnatural superstition allows humane nature itself to arise. Ancient and Christian practice had acted as governors on human nature and removing the governors finally allows nature to emerge. Humanity arises almost spontaneously in an atmosphere of freedom; humanity is the central moral commitment of a nation that abjures the rigors of ancient governments and the moral teaching of the Church.

Again, like parties based on abstract speculative principles, this humane way of life is, paradoxically, natural *and* something new in human affairs when viewed in light of the experience of pre-modern times. History, as Hume understands it, does more than reveal the permanent principles of human nature and show how these principles are shaped by different regimes. History does not *introduce* contradictions and divisions of society as Rousseau had thought; it reveals them. History is not something to be stripped away to reveal human nature as the state of nature theorists held; it is a fund for discernment about what is permanent and accidental that will guide properly modest enquirers. History does not reveal the end goal of human striving, but it melds with a new philosophy to articulate and defend our "mixed kind of life." History is not moved by a providential spirit or reflective of a process; it is something old and something new, always with costs, always with contradictions that cannot be radically resolved. History shows our mixed condition—between knowing and now knowing; between society and self; between sovereignty and dependence; between reason and imagination.

Superstitious austerities and the imposed virtue of ancient cities weaken and disorder "the internal frame" from which humane actions spring (NHR 68). The historical record, where human passions have been bent and broken by peculiar and repressive institutions, does not establish the centrality of humanity. There is a sense in which Hume repeats the pattern seen in state of nature theories. He thinks that there is a moment when the potential of human nature—what he repeatedly refers to as the original human nature[17]—is liberated and blossoms. Human nature contains uncorrupted passions or pre-rational convictions that are reliable and enduring enough so that, though they have been for the most part suppressed by the dark history of superstitious religious practice and ancient-feudal institutions, they account for what Hume sees a natural, humane, civil psychology that ascends in modernity. A series of agreeable original passions, such as those giving rise "to self-love, affection between the sexes, love of progeny, gratitude" (NHR 21), some of which fall under the general rubric "humanity," express themselves in the absence of repressive regimes of virtue. Again like parties based on abstract speculative principles, humanity has been there but repressed by superstition and excessive parochialism.

No matter how close Hume may appear to the liberal state of nature theories in this respect, the humane substance of what Hume finds underneath repressive regimes separates his defense of modernity from theirs. Instead of stripping away artificial conventions and finding selfish people bent on their own preservation and power,[18] Hume finds a genuinely more complicated, sociable syndrome of passions in our native frame. Language provides a clue to our complex nature. We are both "selfish" (i.e., particular, self-regarding beings) and "humane" (i.e., beings belonging to a common species known as human beings) (EPM 270–2). The word "humane" or "humanity" refers to something transnational and trans-religious, in that it implies that there is some durable "human" nature underneath or beside the accretions of national character. Differences seen in national characters—traceable to moral differences to be sure (E 203ff.)—mask an important reality, for Hume: That which makes us different from one another need not be as great that which unites us in our common humanity.[19] Only the "sentiment of humanity" is so "common to all mankind" and "so universal and comprehensive" as to "be the foundation of morals"; the "humanity of one man is the humanity of every one, and the same object touches this passion in all human creatures" (EPM 272–3; also 231). Strange, unnatural conventions stopped this common element from being noticed or acted upon; they perverted the feelings that give rise to humane moral judgments. The modern world sees the eclipse of particularistic virtue and the ascension a more general, "humane" virtue (E 94).

> Among the ancients, the heroes in philosophy, as well as those in war and patriotism, have a grandeur and force of sentiment, which astonishes our narrow souls, and is rashly rejected as extravagant and supernatural. They, in their turn, I allow, would have had equal reason to consider as romantic and incredible, the degree of humanity, clemency, order, tranquility, and

other social virtues, to which, in the administration of government, we have attained in modern times. (EPM 256–7)[20]

Hume uses humanity in at least two senses. First, it is a moral faculty similar to sympathy—that which allows us to enter into the lives of others and make judgments about the propriety of actions. Virtuous conduct "communicates a pleasure to the spectator" (EPM 277), indicating that the good corresponds with the pleasant or produces pleasure on some level.[21] The approbation accorded to virtuous conduct proceeds from a pleasure, though the pleasure to which it corresponds is not one's own pleasure. The pleasure that culminates in the bestowal of praise is prompted not by a consideration of one's own interests or one's personal pleasure, but rather by a pleasure shared by the humanity of all human beings. Judging others demands that we unite with the feelings and situation of others. Second, humanity is a particular virtue resembling general benevolence and gentleness. There is a clear relationship between these two senses of the word humanity. As the strange, unnatural conventions of earlier times wear away, the mechanism of humanity will judge by the standard provided by the virtue of humanity. The more the virtue of humanity arises, the more one can expect the moral mechanism of humanity to be sharpened.

To reverse Rousseau's formulation, modern people, insofar as they become more humane, are emerging from the woods, shedding their distinctive ethnic and religious clothing, and converging on the same spot: their own essentially complex humanity.[22] Hume looks forward to the day when virtue's "dismal dress falls off" and mankind can slip into something more comfortable and conformable to humane nature (EPM 279). The contrast with Rousseau, Hume's one-time friend and companion, is important and telling. Both are repulsed by the "selfish system of morals" found in the early liberal state of nature theorists who seem to ignore that human beings have within themselves a general humanity (Hume's formulation) or "natural pity" (Rousseau's) for their fellow man.[23] This general sentiment prompts us to "feel only a general sympathy with him or a compassion for his pains" (EPM 298). It is not a passion that admits in action on behalf of the person, but a general benevolence or fellow-feeling ultimately serving as the source of morality and our sociable nature. While Rousseau and Hume make the relationship between history and nature a centerpiece of their thought, the contrast between them reveals different conceptions of that relationship. For Rousseau, a human being, when seen stripped of history's accretions, is simple and necessitous, defined by a unified soul centered on the mere desire to exist and a general sentiment that others should exist as well. Hume emphasizes that human nature is a complex set of steady, contradictory and easily distorted passions as revealed by a study of history, the mirror to nature. Rousseau sees these contradictions as products of our entry into civil society, as an eradicable part of man's plastic human "nature." The contradictions between self and society and between reason and imagination are, for Hume, in contrast, ineradicable features of the human condition. Rousseau, who shares many of Hume's reservations about liberalism's moral theory, is furthest from Hume's assessment among all of the state of nature theorists because Rousseau more radically denies the existence of human nature (even and especially if those features are contradictions within human nature). Hobbes and Locke used the state of nature historically, as an inference from passions attendant to human nature as seen in history; they meant, in a sense, to describe civilized man as they described natural man because human nature was necessary for both. They prefigured, in short, Hume's position, that history was a mirror to human nature, though their view of what history taught about human beings was too simplistic for Hume. Rousseau insisted more radically on the state of nature's actual historical existence and more radically on the simplicity of natural man. Hume's argument against Rousseau was therefore deeper than his against Locke and Hobbes. Not only did Rousseau invent a fanciful, supposed historical epoch of man's history as the others had, he also neglected to see the channels and structure of an enduring complex human nature when he invented the simple, unified, unself-conscious soul of "natural man."

Humanity is the virtue that best reflects the contradictions and tensions that define human life. The great modern virtue of humanity appears to be philosophic modesty refracted into social life. Gentle mores reflect the proper social reaction to our "mixed kind of life," in that they are self-effacing, corrosive of excessive pride, reasonable, productive of action, and friendly (EPM 263–5). Just like scientific modesty, humane virtue is easy, not violent. Humane virtues provide a context for deciding conflict by sympathetic, civilized debate, instead of calls to arms and for peaceful assertions of personal ambition (i.e., commerce) instead of violence and fraud. Human beings are interesting and diverse enough when viewed in light of their complex and contradictory humanity. Adding layer upon layer of artificial barriers between human beings only serves the interests of superstition and ancient virtue Such artifices make it difficult to notice the human beings because they focus attention of the distinctions between believer and non-believer (or orthodox and heretic/infidel) or citizen and stranger. These artificial categories are akin to the philosophic constructs that hide the natural contradictions in the human mind by inventing new obscurities. If this reading is correct, humanity as a characteristic of human psychology is natural in reflecting the most reasonable reaction to original contradictions in the human constitution. Humanity, if not natural in the sense of being historically first or original, is natural in its effects. It is not a permanent feature of the human condition (and it was ignored as a social virtue throughout much of history), but it is the virtue best reflecting a proper understanding of our condition. Great revolutions of history bring forth humanity as a mass social virtue; Hume's philosophy shows how this revolution reveals or reflects the naturally mixed human condition.

The virtue of humanity—the tendency to treat one another as human beings instead of as Spartans or Catholics—finds its home in commercial ages. The psychology of humanity is related to the psychology of commerce; they are part of an "indissoluble chain" (E 271). Earlier modern accounts of why men might engage in commerce emphasized the link between necessity and labor. Ancient thinkers and, if we abstract from the differences, Christian thinkers emphasized that many must work so that a few (the nobles or priests) are freed from necessitous labor and enjoy a leisured good life. Modern thinkers debunked aristocratic and Christian pretensions to be free from the dictates of necessity. They held that all people must work for their own preservation and aggrandizement. Hume took a different tack in explaining the naturalness of the desire to engage in commerce. It is not something low such as avarice or a re-channeling of religious dread into productive unease that Hume sees in this turn to commerce.[24] Nor does Hume contend, as Adam Smith appears to, that man's commercial inclinations for "truck and barter" explain the ascension of commerce.[25] Hume's defense of commerce takes a high road, in a sense, because he refuses to provide a theory of human motivation that reduces itself to a single passion or to a complex of narrowly selfish passions. Motivations for engaging in commerce are, according to Hume, a mixture of selfish concerns, ambition, curiosity, and a desire for employment. Human beings often "resolve" these contradictions by religious inspiration, but such resolutions lead only to pretentious theology, the suppression of commerce, and inhumane religious persecution. As Hume relates it, people work or occupy themselves for the sake of work or of occupying themselves; human beings love action because they love action, or because they find inaction or leisure insufferable. People want to lose themselves in action to distract themselves from those insurmountable contradictions endemic to the human condition. Those contradictions are so many affronts to human pride and imagination, affronts that proud, dignified creatures would rather not think about. Deep melancholy and delirium can be relieved with games, lively conversation, or commercial activity. Commerce allows human beings to forget problems they cannot solve and to live in peace with one another.

If people express this desire for employment in a "lucrative" way, human beings come to have gain in their eyes, and they "acquire[], by degrees, a passion for it, and know[] no such pleasure as that of seeing the daily encrease of [their] fortune[s]." These passions are transferred from person to person because they appeal to natural tendencies in human psychology. Commerce acts in the same manner as evangelizing universalistic religions, which aspire to convey their messages to all people: commerce "conveys [industry] readily from one member of the state to another" (E 301);[26] but unlike such religions, commerce treats people according to their natural passions (instead of creating passions) and holds out the hope that all people will see and sympathize in their essential unity. Commerce enlightens the regions of the human mind subjected to the Kingdoms of Darkness and Virtue. Industriousness born of commerce, trade and manufacturing "satisfies" the mind's "natural appetites, and prevents the growth of unnatural ones, which commonly spring up, when nourished by ease and idleness." Too much ease (as that enjoyed by priests and aristocrats) and too much agitation (as that experienced by war-like peoples) lead people to superstition, while engaging in commerce provides the proper mix between ease and agitation (E 269).

For Hume, commerce succeeds in taking "a man from himself" (E 270), while encouraging the conquest of chance by peaceful, scientific means. In commercial arrangements minds awake, curiosity is whetted, and "improvements into every art and science" are discovered (271). Commerce attracts people to commercial centers, where those that were under the influence of superstitions or local customs are freed to pursue their desires in the presence of one another. The "wise" and "foolish" congregate in clubs of learning; the sexes meet in "an easy and sociable manner." Artificial barriers are destroyed by a growing equality of rank wherein every person enjoys "the fruits of his labour, in full possession of all the necessaries, and many of the conveniences of life" (265). As relationships among people multiply and people become familiar to one another, the impetus for persecution and prejudice corrodes. Easy, natural expressions of human passions allow people to experience common humanity and cultivate a recognition that the desires of humane people are to be respected. "The very habit of conversing together, and contributing to each other's pleasure and entertainment" leads people to "feel an encrease of humanity" (271).[27] These advantages take place within and among nations trading, manufacturing, and producing for one another.[28]

National character and local peculiarities wane, as can be inferred from the fact that the English, among whom commerce has made its greatest strides, have "of any people in the universe...the least of a national character" (207).[29] When arts increase in one state, skills and industry are roused in others, who "desire to have every commodity in the utmost perfection" and everyone is a winner by the trade (329). Commerce among nations brings "a very close communication together, either by policy, commerce, or travelling" and nations "acquire a similitude of manners, proportioned to the communication" (206).

The humane world is not a world where suffering is common or communal ties are so strong as to distort human passions much. It is not a place defined by the charms of local attachment in small agricultural communities as Livingston and those favoring the paleo-conservative reading of Hume favor. It is a world united in pleasure, enjoyment, and amusement, where chance is not out of control, prosperity has spread, and further material and scientific progress is the common aim. The foregoing leads Hume to conclude that there is an "indissoluble chain" among "*industry, knowledge*, and *humanity*" (E 271).

There appears to be no greater advocate of the political and personal benefits of knowledge, technology, and Enlightenment than Hume. Ignorance of causes and the attendant unwillingness to relieve persistent poverty lead people to strange kinds of devotion, to superstitious beliefs, and to warfare (NHR 30, 75). Consider the following: "Can we expect, that a government will be well modeled by a people, who know not how to make a spinning-wheel, or to employ a loom to advantage? Not to mention, that all ignorant ages are infested with superstition, which throws the government off its bias, and disturbs men in the pursuit of their interest and happiness." Technological knowledge and improvements in the "arts of government" beget "mildness and moderation, by instructing men in the advantages of humane maxims above rigor and severity, which drive subjects into rebellion, and make the return to submission impracticable, by cutting off all hopes of pardon" (E 273–4).

Hume again raises the important objection to his own defense of commerce in this context; it is an objection that leads to a deeper understanding of what Hume means by humanity and to a qualification of Hume's endorsement of commerce. Citing an interpretation of Rome's decline prominent in his time, Hume recalls the "severe moralists" who have declaimed the spread of luxury and commerce as corrosive of martial ferocity and the virtues of citizenship and courage. Hume's response to this objection is a portrait of politic argument, taking place on a number of levels. I trace these levels as they manifest themselves in "Refinement" in the rest of this section and in the next. Hume concedes that the nature of war, and hence citizenship, is changed by the spread of humanity, and he thinks the changes are progress. Foreign wars "abate of their cruelty; and after the field of battle, where honour and interest steel men against compassion as well as fear, the combatants divest themselves of the brute, and resume the man." Anger loses "somewhat of its asperity" when tempered by considerations of honor, "politeness and refinement." Discipline is added to courage, as a military is professionalized and civilized. Losing their ancient ferocity does not cause people to "lose their martial spirit, or become less undaunted and vigorous in defence of their country or their liberty." A recognition of our common humanity, presumably, causes people to lose the desire to begin waging war and tempers the effects of war once it ends (E 274).[30] If foreign wars, as Hume believes, are less cruel and barbarous, we can expect that distinctions between armies and civilians to be better recognized and respected as people recognize a common humanity. Modern soldiers have martial spirit and dauntless, vigorous courage, and those passions are more humane, orderly, and reasonable in modernity. Hume promises a more effective way of waging war, while more quietly suggesting that commitments to humanity will indeed change and pacify one's passions.

This does not get at the nub of the objection made by the "severe moralists." The ferocity characteristic of ancient citizenship is a political manifestation of the rigor and severity necessary to lead people to virtue. While it is tempting to see Hume presenting objections only from ancient thinkers and modern admirers of ancient practice such as Rousseau, one must include Montesquieu—that humane advocate of commerce!—among these severe moralists. "Commerce," Montesquieu writes, "corrupts pure mores, and this was the subject of Plato's complaints; it polishes and softens barbarous mores, as we see every day."[31] Pure morals appear to belong, for Montesquieu, to barbaric countries, while civilization undermines virtue proper and the purity of sentiments. This objection raises questions about soft morals and true virtue or, perhaps, commerce and human thriving. This ultimately reflects a worry about the possibility that nobility and pure virtue will die in modern commercial nations.

Hume's response to this criticism at first appears to be the most emphatic in the history of political philosophy (and to violate his theory of mixed blessings). The cultivation of commerce and the arts has, he writes, "no such effect in enervating either the mind or the body" because the industrious mind, if roused, adds "new force to both" (E 274). The advantages of modern commercial society are not "attended with disadvantages, that bear any proportion to them" (E 271). Hume wants to show that there are no political disadvantages attendant to embracing commerce—armies are better disciplined, the total wealth of the country makes it less burdensome to wage war, and so on. It is more important for Hume to show that commerce conduces to individual happiness and fulfillment. For Hume, the passing of ancient citizenship is not the passing of "pure mores," as many thinkers—both advocates and opponents of modern commercial arrangements—seem to think. Hume's emphatic answer to this challenge reflects his unwillingness to romanticize the past or to see the virtues connected with barbaric times divorced from the terrible violence and oppression with which they were necessarily associated. (His *History of England* bears testimony to this attempt to strip away romantic longings of an ideal ancient constitution.[32])

This judgment has practical and theoretical roots. To those seeking a return to "the maxims of ancient policy," Hume answers that such a return is "almost impossible" (E 259). Hume's contemptuous rhetorical treatment of ancient politics emphasizes the undesirability of ancient and feudal arrangements and he denies the authority of ancient thinkers and ancient politics more thoroughly than Montesquieu. This serves his purpose in reconciling human beings to the narrower possibilities that characterize the modern condition. There is simply no use in being taken with the austere ancient virtues, and only a truly repressive, discordant modern ideology would attempt to re-introduce such measures into the more easy-going modern world. How could anyone, especially one arguing from within the modern world itself, be a humane advocate of the ancient world as Hume describes it? This rhetoric is not mere rhetoric, nor does he counsel a self-forgetting about the possibilities within human nature. Hume's deprecation of ancient possibilities reflects his judgment about the nature of the moral imagination. Judging commercial virtues requires a proper horizon or perspective from which to judge those virtues. The perspective from which the standard of judgment necessarily originates, for Hume, as we have seen, is within the horizon of commercial society itself.

While such an argument reflects Hume's statesmanlike perspective about the limits of politics at any particular time, it is a position that depends on an argument showing that the virtues of humanity are new, enduring, and good. How do we know that easy, humane politics are best and most natural? The commercial solution is more natural for Hume, as I have argued, for its *natural effects*, its tendency to promote the virtues of humanity, and its congruence with our "mixed kind of life." There is no spring within human nature that embraces commerce or explains its naturalness. Humanity and commerce reflect the totality of human nature, and the virtue of humanity reflects the proper moral reaction to contradictions and diversity in human nature. While Hume does not use this formulation, the naturalness of humanity is seen in its spontaneous ascension in an atmosphere of freedom. Humane virtues and commerce may be associated with "narrow souls" (EPM 256). The emphatic endorsement of commerce is part of Hume's effort to be consistently non-teleological and to see efforts to defend a teleological view of human nature and implement it in politics as manifestations of oppressive violence. Human happiness is not defined in the light of a *telos*, but as the liberation of natural passions and humane feelings from the constraints of ancient polities and superstitious authorities and as the reflection of the humane mix when so liberated. Commercial liberty is associated with the soft virtues characteristic of commercial nations. Never recommending elevation in politics, one sees a flattening of the moral world to humane virtue—a virtue connected to the overcoming of superstitious ignorance and warlike dispositions. Hume sees the political equivalent of what he considers this salutary flattening in modern middle class politics.

Humanity and the Middling Element

I continue to be occupied with the singularly complex topic of humanity's naturalness. On the one hand, ancient rigors are associated with elevated, almost unbelievable individual virtues in philosophy and politics. Violent laws seem to serve a purpose for Hume in elevating some human beings to some degree. Perhaps rigorous conventions come to the aid of nature in producing some human greatness, which, apparently, does not rise as much of its own accord by following the easy modern method. On the other hand, stripping away artifices may lead to "narrow souls," but these narrow souls are, in Hume's judgment, more natural. Nature and humanity seem to be associated with narrowness and, perhaps, superficiality, while unnatural rigors and violence are associated with depth of soul and greatness. If this is the case, then does not Hume's contention that the advantages of commercial societies are not "attended with disadvantages, that bear any proportion to them" ring hollow? Does this not show that Hume, in contrast to Smith, Tocqueville, Rousseau, Montesquieu, and Nietzsche, underestimates the costs and dangers inherent to modern commercial society?

Only by continuing with "Refinement" can I fully address this question. I mentioned that "Refinement" is a complex, multi-layered argument. This is nowhere more evident in ascertaining the relationship between the essay's two sections. The first section—that which has concerned us heretofore—defends "ages of refinement" as both the "happiest and most virtuous" (E 269; see 269–78). In this section we find Hume's emphatic defenses of the benefits of adopting modern commercial practices. This first section culminates with Hume's praise of the modern middle class, which I turn to presently. The second section argues that there is a point where refinement or "luxury ceases to be innocent" and is "pernicious, though perhaps not the most pernicious, to political society" (E 269; see 278–80). This second section qualifies the observations made in the first.

We can grasp the relationship between humanity and modern political and social arrangements by comparing Hume's thoughts on the middle class with Aristotle's in *The Politics*. For Hume, modern "*political* customs and institutions" are responsible for the full flourishing of human life in the modern world (E 400). The specific factors Hume cites in claiming the superiority of modernity are the relative absence of war, the elimination of slavery, the relative lack of violence among class-based factions, the cultivation of arts and sciences, and the presence of a strong, regular police power (E 404–21). Modern arrangements destroy feudal and aristocratic social arrangements; they are egalitarian in that they open up the desire for "exercise and enjoyment" to most everyone. "Without commerce, the state must consist chiefly of landed gentry, whose prodigality and expence make a continual demand of borrowing; and of peasants, who have no sums" (E 301–2).[33] The most important result of commerce is the rise of a middling rank suited for republican liberty. Hume writes:

> Where luxury nourishes commerce and industry, the peasants, by a proper cultivation of the land, become rich and independent; while the tradesmen and merchants acquire a share of the property, and draw authority and consideration to that *middling rank of men*, who are the best and firmest basis of public liberty. These submit not to slavery, like the peasants, from poverty and meanness of spirit; and having no hopes of tyrannizing over others, like the barons, they are not tempted, for the sake of that gratification, to submit to the tyranny of their sovereign. They covet equal laws, which may secure their property, and preserve them from monarchical, as well as aristocratical tyranny. (E 277–8, emphasis supplied)

This middling rank resembles the middling element from Aristotle's most possible good regime. Those with a middling fortune are, Aristotle writes in the fourth book of *The Politics*, "readiest to obey reason, while for one who is overly handsome, overly strong, overly well-born, or overly wealthy—or the reverse of these things, overly indignant, overly weak, or very lacking in honor—it is difficult to follow reason. The former sort tend to become arrogant and base on a grand scale, the latter malicious and base in petty ways; and acts of injustice are committed either through arrogance or through malice." Aristotle's middling element, like the middling rank for Hume, is praised more for lacking the aristocratic vice of haughtiness and the democratic vice of slavishness than for possessing positive political virtues. Because the middling element avoided the most dangerous extremes of political life, Aristotle found "the political partnership that depends on the middling sort [to be] best" (1095b5–10, 35).

The essay "Of the Middle Station of Life" illustrates how Hume's praise of the middling rank of men goes beyond Aristotle. This essay appeared only in the second edition of the *Essays* and was withdrawn, perhaps because it was thought by Hume to be "frivolous" or trite given the clarity of his praise of the middling rank in "Refinement."[34] Hume begins the essay by reiterating that the middle class is most likely to heed the voice of reason or least likely to entertain dangerous passions. Avoiding the pretentious aristocratic imagination without lapsing into the slavish self-concern of the poor and tending to steer a course between luxurious aristocratic slothfulness and the servile drudgery of the poor, the middling rank implicitly accepts the "mixed kind of life" that defines the human condition. "The Middle Station, as it is most happy in many Respects, so particularly in this, that a Man, plac'd in it, can, with the greatest Leisure, consider his own Happiness, and reap a new Enjoyment, from comparing his Situation with that of Persons above or below him" (E 546).

> The middle station is here justly recommended, as affording the fullest *Security* for Virtue; and I may also add, that it gives Opportunity for the most ample *Exercise* of it, and furnishes Employment for every good Quality, which we can possibly be possest of. Those, who are plac'd among the lower Rank of Men, have little Opportunity of exerting any other Virtue, besides those of Patience, Resignation, Industry and Integrity. Those, who are advanc'd into higher Stations, have full Employment for their Generosity, Humanity, Affability and Charity. When a Man lyes betwixt these two Extremes, he can exert the former Virtues towards his *Superiors*, and the latter toward his *Inferiors*. Every moral Quality, which the human Soul is susecptible of, may have its Turn, and be called up to Action. (E 546–7)

The quiet peaceful reflection on one's character presupposes the good character of the "Middle Station" and "the greater Leisure" to "consider [one's] own happiness." People of middling rank are uniquely capable of self-reflection or "repose" amidst active lives. Their easy sociability disposes them to enjoy the company of their fellows even as they live active lives. They are also well situated to pursue scientific or even philosophic investigations (on Hume's model). A middle class man "has a better Chance for attaining a Knowledge both of Men and Things, than those of a more elevated Station" (E 547). The intellectual ambitions of the middling rank mix critical reason with an appreciation for our natural equipment. Ambitious to attain knowledge, the middling rank grounds science directly in common life, directly in men and things. At the same time, people in the middling rank are not satisfied with prejudice and they seek to correct reflections of common life. Besides the natural, easy familiarity with which these men enter into life and life's trials, a middle class man has "the Motive of Ambition to push him on in his Attainments; being certain, that he can never rise to any Distinction or Eminence in the World, without his own Industry" (E 548).

For Hume, a middling rank beyond Aristotle's middling element arises through non-Aristotelian or even anti-Aristotelian practices of technological science and commerce. We can see this by comparing Aristotle's critique of luxury with Hume's defense of it, which follows behind Hume's defense of the middling rank in the second section of "Refinement." Aristotle saw "expertise in exchange" as "justly blamed since it is not according to nature but involves taking from others" (*Politics* 1258b1). Trading activity or the desire for wealth as a means of securing household goods often corrupts into the desire for wealth itself. When it does, this obscures the difference between the good life and mere life and tends to destroy that which is highest in human beings.

Hume, in contrast, sees the establishment of commercial republics as an effective, legitimate, and even virtue-promoting way of creating a middling rank of men, though following Hume's logic allows us to comprehend the disadvantages that come with the modern commercial order. Hume begins with a distinction that could be accepted on Aristotelian grounds: "Innocent luxury" differs from "vicious luxury." Innocent luxury can serve the public or household, while vicious luxury "engrosses all a man's expence, and leaves no ability for such acts of duty and generosity as are required by his situation and fortune" (E 278–9). Excessive indulgence in sensual delights is "vicious luxury." Advancement of refinement, if it fosters "vicious luxury," may be consistent with a waning of duty and a reduction of services to economic calculations. There may be less heart-felt desire to help one's fellow man, less true generosity or charity, but more people will be better housed and fed. After acknowledging these results of "vicious luxury," Hume does not recommend that rooting it out be made an object of public policy; he does not advocate a modern variety of sumptuary taxes, for instance. He asks a more prudential question: What human activities would likely replace those activities that are involved in vicious luxury? If those engaged in economic activities and sensual delights were to turn their attention toward concerns such as the proper education of children or relief of the poor, banishing vicious luxury might prove beneficial to society. If banishing vicious luxury would lead people to lives of sloth, the benefits of ridding society of the vice of excessive indulgence in sensual delights would be outweighed by the greater vice of a loss of spirit. "By banishing *vicious* luxury, without curing sloth and an indifference to others, you only diminish industry in the state, and add nothing to men's charity or their generosity" (E 280). This kind of reformation in the concerns of mankind—the cultivation of whole-heartedly charitable, generous, self-effacing, and industrious citizens—is not to be expected. "All plans of government, which suppose great reformation in the manners of mankind, are plainly imaginary" (E 514). He recommends that magistrates permit the indulgence of even vicious luxury as the lesser of two evils. "Luxury, when excessive, is the source of many ills; but is in general preferable to sloth and idleness, which would commonly succeed in its place, and are more hurtful both to private persons and to the public" (E 280). Where Aristotle suggests that magistrates might fight the indulgence of vicious luxury as something detrimental to the pursuit of the good life, Hume would permit such indulgences as the lesser of two vices from which magistrates must choose.[35]

This comparison with Aristotle allows us to see the last level of Hume's defense of commerce and humanity. Whereas the first section of "Refinement" leads Hume to overstate the virtues of commerce against the critics of commerce, the second shows that eras of commerce are attendant with disadvantages and vices, perhaps even those Montesquieu adverted to. Vicious luxury is not the worst vice because stamping out vicious luxury requires perhaps curtailing human industry and relegating human beings to a life of sloth. This is not the end of the story.

We glimpse Hume's concerns about the dangers modern commercial life may pose to human happiness by visiting his praise of the just life with which he ends the second *Enquiry*. The so-called happiness of the "sensible knave" bespeaks a character that is willing to sacrifice "inward peace of mind" and "consciousness of integrity" for the acquisition of "worthless toys and gewgaws." Specifically with a view to pleasure, the knave sees the "feverish, empty amusements of luxury and expense" to be greater than the "peaceful reflection on one's own conduct." The self-interested commercial activity of modern life may encourage the ascension of such a "sensible knave." Pursuing wealth is often made an end in itself, as Aristotle had expected. The prevalence of market activities may encourage people to confuse "feverish, empty amusements" with the repose of mind at the heart of "natural pleasure." This confusion might be one of the "many ills" brought on by the pursuit of excessive luxury. It may draw people too far toward the active or agitated side of the continuum that characterizes our mixed kind of life. Among others, Adam Smith notices just such a possibility in recounting the sad story of the empty old man who wasted his life on the accumulation of empty goods, but who forgot the meaning of happiness.[36] It may be that Hume and Smith saw the difficulty of pursuing the correct understanding of happiness—the problem of King Midas—to be a fundamental human problem more than a modern problem. Modern commercial arrangements democratize the problem of King Midas, at the very least.

Other disadvantages attend modern arrangements. For all of his criticisms of the unnatural austerities in ancient republics, Hume admires their grandeur and depth of soul. Hume illustrates his discussion of greatness of soul with only ancient examples. What is impressive about these ancient virtues is the "elevation of sentiment, disdain for slavery, and... the noble pride and spirit, which arises from conscious virtue" (EPM 252). Courage too has a "noble elevation inseparable from it," and it is found "among all uncultivated nations" (EPM 254, 255). The repressive ancient laws that disfigured human nature occasionally promoted an almost superhuman virtue, and superhuman ferocity and cruelty. Ancient grandeur is immoderate and fragile; it reflects a politics with "little humanity and moderation" (E 414). Modern souls are narrower, and moderns "rashly" believe that this ancient elevation is no longer possible. In our humanity we often fail to grasp that these virtues are beautiful. We tend to concentrate only on the dangers these virtues pose to humane, peaceable political communities.

Modern morality is more humane, and humanity is more democratic than the grand, elevated ancient morality. The moral revolution accompanying the advent of commerce is associated with a democratic political revolution. This democratizing revolution in morals has a democratizing effect on politics. Political problems in the modern world are associated with democratic government for the most part. Practice under democratic and republican governments has always been especially vulnerable to the problem of majority faction. In ancient Rome the "unbounded" power to legislate was "possessed in a collective, not in a representative body," but soon was transferred to demagogues (E 16). "Democracies are turbulent" and quite susceptible to "the force of popular tides and currents" (E 528). Jealous and agitated people are more likely to rent a polity with faction. People emerging from absolute monarchies tend to have exaggerated opinions of popular power and exaggerated views of the dangers posed by the remnants of monarchy. Britain bore out these expectations. The "watchful jealousy" of the British press tends toward "licentiousness" in Hume's mind (E 12). This licentious press is "one of the evils, attending to those mixt forms of government" (E 13). Hume's diagnosis of the problem of democracy would therefore be helpful to the American Founders, who were concerned to cure "the diseases most incident to republican government."[37]

Whig theory exacerbates this problem. This seems to be where the problem of abstract speculative principles collides with a politics of humanity. Modern ideological parties become prevalent precisely because human beings come to see themselves as so similar to one another as they embrace a vision of humanity. Students of Hume tend to blame modern philosophers for the rise of the unaccountable phenomenon of parties from "abstract speculative principle" that are "known only to modern times" (E 60). Abstract political systems not unlike those of Locke and the Whigs had been propagated before in the history of the world. Only in the modern world had these abstract systems become the basis for political parties. "No party, *in the present age*, can well support itself, without a philosophical or speculative system of principles" (E 465, emphasis supplied). The people are "very rude builders, especially in this speculative way... it is natural to imagine, that their workmanship must be a little unshapely, and discover evident marks of that violence and hurry in which it is raised" (E 466). The popular appeal of those abstract political theories is a matter of great concern because it locates the success of those appeals in the populace instead of in the announcement of them by philosophers. When people are very different from one another, when masters rule slaves and French do not understand the ways of the English, trying to reduce practice to one principle is, on its face, ridiculous and contrary to common experience. When people are defined by the same feelings and the same virtues and when they live in the same manner as their fellows, there is a fertile ground for parties based on abstract speculative principle.[38] In this crucial respect the politics of humanity and commerce can come to resemble the universalizing tendencies in Christianity.

There are deep intractable problems associated with abstract speculative parties in an era of humanity: a politics of humanity may beget inhumane, abstract politics. The way of life most consistent with our "mixed kind of life" can produce a politics ridden with abstract speculative factions. The concerns of chapter 5 derive from the virtue around which chapter 6 is arranged, and they seem connected to one another: the more successful the industry and knowledge leading to a politics of humanity, the more free from necessity people are, the less they will be satisfied with a politics of common life. The advantages of industry and humanity are mixed with disadvantages after all.

CHAPTER 7

RELIGIOUS REVOLUTION AND ENGLAND'S HUMANE POLITICAL CONSTITUTION

> *A great democratic revolution is taking place among us.*
>
> —Tocqueville, *Democracy in America*, Intrc.

The humane virtues are the proper reaction to the "mixed kind of life" to which nature has consigned human beings. In its tranquility, order, moderation, and gentleness, the commercial polity reflects the fortified temper, softened passions, self-conscious reflections and relatively steady equilibrium central to a happy disposition (cf. E 177n with EPM 256–7). Hume's *History of England* shows how the unique achievement of England's humane constitution arose in history and how the constitution relies on a complex set of mores to arise and sustain itself. No one in the depths of the Middle Ages would have predicted that England, of all places, would lead the world into an era of humanity and liberty. Only when the superstitious edifice of feudalism crumbled did an ethos of humanity, learning, and industry arise. The edifice crumbled in unexpected ways (through enthusiastic religion) as initiated by unexpected people (the Tudors). This chapter outlines the destruction of the feudal order so we can understand the political, economic, and social underpinnings for a humane polity.

This chapter also shows how Hume's philosophy of common life manifests itself in the *History* and raises questions about the adequacy of Hume's approach. These questions center on the relationship between history and nature and the extent to which Hume's turn to history entails an endorsement of historicism. Philosophers became preoccupied with historicism and historical consciousness within 50 years of Hume's death. According to historicism, all human thought (human action is the instantiation of thought) is made, assembled, and created, and that making assembling, and creating are done in reference to one's historical situation. When this view is supplemented with a belief in progress or scientific history (as with Kant, Hegel, and Marx), creations of previous eras appear as contributions to the making of a higher point in history or an absolute moment in history; history appears to be a deterministic process whereby later philosophers place earlier achievements in making and thought in a logical, progressive context; previous thought is comprehensible as part of that logical development.

Much in Hume smacks of this school of thought. His elevation of the imagination as the assembler and judge of "all our thoughts and actions" (T 225) marks an important step toward the assumptions of the historical school of thought. Hume also is willing, as I have shown in chapter 4, to begin his judgment of historical actions by grounding it in the particular historical situation from which those actions arose. Further, for Hume there appears to be little permanence in human nature. Consider, for instance, the following: "The manners of a people change very considerably from one age to another; either by great alterations in their government, by the mixtures of new people, or by that inconstancy, to which all human affairs are subject" (E 205–6; see also 255–6). Despite his kinship to historicism, there is something—a belief in human nature[1] and a standard of judgment—that restrains Hume from swallowing historicism whole. This chapter examines whether these restraints survive Hume's telling of history.

It also forms a test case for the claims propounded in previous chapters. The *History* traces England's magnificent "system of liberty" to accident and chance and not to the announcement or discovery of abstract speculative principles. The *History* instructs curious inquirers, as Hume writes in the final words he penned of the *History*, "in the great mixture of accident, which commonly concurs with a small ingredient of wisdom and foresight, in erecting the complicated fabric of the most perfect government" (II.525). There is also much in Hume that tells against the idea that England's system of liberty was brought about mostly through accident or that the only viable historical causes in this case are accident and wisdom/foresight. Most important is Hume's claim that the minds of people, all over Europe, were awakened at the same time and in the same political direction. That seems too coincidental to be traceable only to accident and chance and too broad to be traceable to human wisdom. Other elements of Hume's *History*, we shall see, force us to question precisely what history is and whether his account is an inescapable feature of common life. Included among these is the idea that the most recent developments in politics—the well-structured system of liberty in England and the political improvements on the continent—have been a boon for human nature and human flourishing. It almost seems as if history (or History) is headed toward a particular goal—a system of liberty and humanity. The treatment of history combined with the importance of humanity as best reflecting our "mixed kind of life" *could* reveal that Hume sees the coming of the best of all possible worlds or the End of History. Such outcomes are obviously contrary to the theme and spirit of Hume's thought, which emphasize that ours is a mixed situation with mixed blessings and which opposes such "high and distant" inquiries as outside the sphere of common life.

We must grasp how and why Hume's account of our nature survives his telling of history. Common life philosophy assumes the common sense of the matter in the concept of history. Yet common sense points in contradictory directions in his telling of history—toward both the idea of a permanent, timeless human nature and to the idea that the manners of people change "considerably from one age to another" (E 205, also E 255–6). Hume's *History* is where these competing suppositions about history clash and where Hume's philosophy of common life is stressed to the breaking point.

Nature and Humanity in Hume's *History of England*

Nature is hidden, distorted, corrupted, and, finally revealed in history. History does not add value to nature, though it does bring about phenomena (i.e., parties based on abstract speculative principles and a politics of humanity, at least) never before seen in human history. These new phenomenon are traceable, Hume insists, to timeless principles of human nature (EHU 83) that long-standing, countervailing influences in history have suppressed or distorted. Hume sifts through historical accretions or strips away the artifices to get at the natural. Yet the historical also reveals the natural, in that it shows the contradictions and mixtures that constitute human nature. Hume's teaching, as we have seen, holds that history covers or reveals nature and sometimes the covering consists in the revealing. How can this be?

Hume denies that we have unmediated knowledge of eternal verities or timeless structures (the human self or "nature"). All judgments about morality and politics begin as judgments grounded in time and place. *The History of England* contains Hume's narrative of how liberty and humanity emerged within the English Constitution. That Hume presents the virtue of humanity through a historical narrative suggests that his moral teaching introduces contingency, convention, time and culture into his account of human nature. Let an example suffice to illuminate the conflict between the natural and contingent. Commenting on the severities in Charles I's administration, Hume concludes: "It seems unreasonable to judge of the measures, embraced during one period, by the maxims, which prevail in another" (V.240). These comments counsel people against judging Charles too harshly and are in keeping with Hume's comparative and statesmanlike approach to moral and political judgment. Individuals, institutions and ethical codes must *first* be understood and evaluated in the climate from which they arise. Judgments divorced from context fail to see that actions, actors, and mores must, initially, be seen in light of viable alternatives. A thorough, sympathetic understanding of context is the beginning of wisdom. This embedded, comparative approach grounds moral imagination against flights of fancy, excessive abstraction, and utopian ambitions.

This emphasis on the importance of context does not and need not lead Hume to consign his thinking to particulars in a historical situation. Comparative judgments would be impossible were there no stability in human nature. Those who make comparative judgments about an era must be able to transcend their own time and place to a degree. Critical, sympathetic moral reflection implies that some, at least, are not bound by custom. Judgment requires us to enter into the situation of others *and* to stand at a critical distance from others and ourselves. Thus a non-dogmatic, yet guiding "standard of judgment," informed through much investigation and experimentation, cannot be divorced from and is not reducible to history.

Hume's concept of nature and his treatment of how history relates to nature contain all the inexactitudes in a "standard of judgment" with greater problems of discernment. The existence of a permanent human nature appears to be the reasonable assumption—the "natural supposition," to revert to the language of chapter 3—informing Hume's political philosophy. One can reasonably wonder if that assumption can survive Hume's telling of history. England's humane, orderly, tranquil constitution came about on the crest of "a general, but insensible revolution" in "the minds of men" (H V.18). If the "minds of men" can undergo such a revolutionary change, Hume's claim that there is a constant human nature may seem to be an endorsement of either formalism or human passivity. As the climate changed, human minds changed. Human nature appears to go with the flow of history, in the same way that the flow of water changes with the topography.[2] It acts like other bodies in nature act by obeying predictable, almost mechanical laws. Note that Hume often describes human nature as a passive agent in this general revolution. As the Reformation burst on the scene in Europe, "the minds of men, somewhat awakened from a profound sleep in so many centuries, were prepared for every novelty" (H III.140). As the Reformation spread to France, "it was during this period, when men began to be somewhat enlightened" (H IV.57; see also V.18). What student of history could question this (seeming) deliverance of common sense? Something *did* happen to make people change their ways and modes of thinking.

Yet as the climate changed, human minds changed in predictable ways—not randomly or by chance but steadily and in the same direction. The underlying logic of the mixed creature characterized by mixed blessings pulled this way and that way is a fact about human nature. Hume often refers to substantive, natural principles of humanity that cannot be reduced to custom and that presumably are less radically subject to such revolutionary changes or more difficult to suppress through violence. Again, this alternative view is sanctioned by common sense: we refer to people as human beings, at the least. This tension shows that human nature is caught between nature and history and between passivity and action. Neither characteristic is absent and neither can be vanquished. There is a definite division within the deliverances of common sense on the matter of history and nature and it is not clear if and how both deliverances can be supposed as the foundation of inquiry.

This chapter, primarily concerned with outlining the spiritual change, pushes the limits of the philosophy of common life as well. Consider the similarities and differences between Tocqueville and Hume. Both wrote monumental philosophic histories about the fall of the feudal order— Tocqueville's *The Old Regime and the Revolution* chronicles the decline of the feudal order in France and Hume's *History* does the same for England. Hume's *History* is, to be sure, more of a narrative than Tocqueville's *Old Regime*, which is analytical and topical. These works are united in purpose and spirit and, broadly, in their arguments. Hume paved the way for Tocqueville in recognizing the first stirrings of modern politics when Europe was in the depths of its feudal constitution. Both date the stirrings of this revolution from roughly the same time. Hume fixes the ascension of the humane revolution of politics from the point between the Norman Conquest in 1066 and the discovery of Justinian's Pandects in 1130 (II.519–20). In *Democracy in America*, Tocqueville (written circa 1830) recounts how he took himself "back to what France was seven hundred years ago" (circa 1130) and found that one finds "no great events in seven hundred years that have not turned to the profit of equality." Like Tocqueville, Hume shows how non-Enlightened religious fanatics and absolute monarchs such as the Tudors benefit the cause of humanity and the establishment of England's humane constitution, though this was far from their intention. People throughout Christendom have aided the advancement of this leveling spirit, according to Tocqueville, who emphasizes the role played by the Bourbon kings and the Church in preparing the way for the Revolution: "Those who had in view cooperating for its success and those who did not dream of serving it; those who fought for it and even those who declared themselves its enemies; all have been driven pell-mell on the same track, and all have worked in common, some despite themselves, others without knowing it."[3] Hume, like Tocqueville who shows that this revolution "is not peculiar to France," sees the moral revolution taking place throughout Europe. On a most general and profound level, Tocqueville's contrast between aristocracy and democracy resembles Hume's between feudalism and the constitution of liberty.

For all their similarities, Hume, unlike Tocqueville, is averse to making generalizations about history or seeing grand Ideas at work in history. He never discusses the revolution in politics, as Tocqueville does, in terms of an abstract idea or even a condition such as equality of conditions. Hume's reticence in this regard is, no doubt, traceable to his philosophy of common life and his aversion of "high and distant" inquiries that take him from the stuff of common life. For our purposes, we must ask if Hume's reticence is complete and consistent with insight and philosophy and whether it can be justified on his principles.

The Early Stages of English Political Development

Volume I of Hume's *History* depicts the creation of the powerful "ideology" of feudalism after the Norman Conquest; later volumes depict its dissolution. Danford shows that civilization rises from the ashes of feudalism due to three analytically distinct causes: the peculiarities of England's situation; historical accidents outside England that affect the English Constitution; and the natural mechanism of human nature where the establishment of the rule of law leads to the advancement in science and the establishment of a humane commercial republic. The last of these features, Danford argues, "is universal in its operation, but...it was not of sufficient force to overturn feudalism in the absence of other factors."[4] Danford's account of the fall of feudalism concentrates on the rule of law as it establishes personal property ownership, a distinguishing feature of the civilized era.[5] Describing the transition from barbarity and feudalism to civilization in terms of a transition from martial valor to civilized industriousness, as Danford does, while compelling, omits a more fundamental transition from superstition to enthusiasm to something resembling Enlightenment.[6] Hume's *History* shows that the waning of superstitious religious belief antedates the rise of a commercial ethic. Civilization advances on several tracks—economic, political, and religious—simultaneously. Hume does not provide a thematic or systematic analysis untangling these factors, and it is difficult, on his analysis, to assign the priority of the economic over the political or the religious over the economic. The "gradual progress of improvement" (II.522) and the breaking of superstition could not have proceeded if factors indigenous to England had not conspired with broader, continental factor to cause the waning of superstition. Breaking of superstition is not a part of the natural course of things, and Hume is careful to trace how accidental causes contribute to its waning in England.

Hume describes England's feudal constitution as "rough and licentious" and "ignorant and barbarous" (I.185, 53). The virtues given pride of place among the Saxons were "valour, and love of liberty" (I.15). For the first millennia (until the Norman conquest in 1066), they lived in a "rude state of nature," where a poor, nasty, brutish, martial, undisciplined people placed themselves in the service of local lords (I.167).

> Violence universally prevailed, instead of general and equitable maxims. The pretended liberty of the times, was only an incapacity of submitting to government. And men, not protected by law in their lives and properties, sought shelter, by their personal servility and attachments, under some powerful chieftain, or by voluntary combinations. (II.521-2)

Protection provided by quasi-feudal lords was inconsistent with personal liberty and secure property. England under the Anglo-Saxons possessed "much less true liberty, than where the execution of the laws is the most severe, and where subjects are reduced to the strictest subordination and dependence on the civil magistrate" (I.168-9).[7] Government lacked the power to control its people and a regular plan of liberty provided by the rule of law. Anglo-Saxon government was "extremely aristocratical" (I.165) and subjects owed allegiance to capricious local chieftains more than they did to the king. Its society was broken into armed and hostile bands. Even the most determined king lacked the institutional power to enforce peace among the local rivals. The power of the most impressive Saxon king, Alfred (871-901), came entirely from his great abilities. Personality alone would not serve the purpose of instituting steady rules for society.

The "continual intestine war" was "pernicious to industry, as well as to the execution of justice" (I.350), but just as pernicious was the prominence of the Catholic Church and Christian superstition. "Superstition and jealousy of military honour" were the two "ruling passions of the age" (I.366). England's embrace of Catholicism brought unintended benefits, but many more political and moral problems. The Church benefited the English by connecting the barbarous Anglo-Saxons to the "more polished states of Europe"; this connection eventually contributed to "banishing their ignorance, or softening their barbarous manners" (I.51; see also I.32; II.14). On the negative side, the Church fostered a civilization "destructive to the understanding and to morals." Adoration for God, a cult of religious reverence, the belief in miracles, and the spread of monastic observances led people to neglect research into "natural causes" (I.51). Catholicism's doctrines of atonement, forgiveness, and penances allowed people to wrap violent actions in the garb of service to the Church. The emphasis placed on pilgrimages and meritorious works of devotion distorted natural moral calculus and fostered terrible political problems.[8]

Most damaging was the reverence for and deference to the clergy (I.51), the superstitious attachment to Rome, and the continual controversies in theology. Clergy checked tyrannical, baronial rule with priestly tyranny: they made monetary demands on the barons, kings, and laity; they incited people to make sacrifices in Crusades; and they undermined national institutions with foreign papal authority. The prominence of foreign authority on English soil inhibited kings from checking baronial rule because it added a "foreign" resistance point to the domestic one. Kings who believed in papal authority submitted to the erosion of their own authority when pontiffs so demanded. Popes were emboldened "by this blindness and submissive disposition" and advanced continually on the independence of English churches and English political authority (I.51–2). Saxon, Briton, Scottish and English religionists continually disputed until the Roman hegemony was established over England after the Norman Conquest (I.53–4). This beginning of national unity came at the price entrenching superstition throughout the island.

Let us pause to consider how the Anglo order stifled the natural mechanism of progress. Several human goods follow one another in the natural mechanism of progress: "From law arises security: From security curiosity: And from curiosity knowledge." The beginnings of this process are "altogether necessary," but the latter steps are "more accidental" (E 118). This natural mechanism culminates in an ethic of "*industry, knowledge, and humanity*," discussed in chapter 6, which "are linked together by an indissoluble chain" (E 271). The primacy of war and martial virtues, the division of political authority between national and foreign powers, and superstitious ignorance left property insecure, personal freedom insecure, the people poor and ignorant, and laws nonexistent. The Anglo-Saxon regime promoted neither law, security, curiosity, nor knowledge; there was little industrious cultivation of arts and sciences; and the virtues of humanity, while present, perhaps, beneath the surface, were not observable. That which stifled humanity had also stifled parties from abstract speculative principles. The Anglo-Saxon constitution seems to be the pure case of how a superstitious, martial constitution acts as a governor on the virtues of humanity.

The Norman Conquest formalized Anglo political arrangements into the feudal system. William the Conqueror divided England among his most powerful subjects. These "great barons, who held immediately to the crown, shared out a great part of their lands to other foreigners, who were denominated knights and vassals, and who paid their lord the same duty and submission in peace and war, which he himself owed to his sovereign" (I.203–4). Commoners and serfs owed their property rights and liberty immediately to the barons, and by extension to the king, because the barons enjoyed their property and liberty at the pleasure of the king. This order formally increased royal power, as the king controlled the military, courts of law, inheritance among the nobility, and public revenue (I.471–8). The first 130 years of Norman rule witnessed an expansion of the crown's prerogatives. Invested with only a few prerogatives, the king's "large demesnes and numerous retainers rendered him, in one sense, the greatest baron in his kingdom; and where he was possessed of personal vigor and abilities (for his situation required these advantages) he was commonly able to preserve his authority, and maintain his station as head of the community, and the chief fountain of law and justice" (1.464, also 1.437). William the Conqueror (I.225), Henry I (I.276), and Henry II (I.370) expanded royal power with their impressive abilities. No regular, legal guidelines hemmed in kingly prerogatives.

It is important not to exaggerate the powers of Norman kings or the stability of the feudal system. No matter how extensive their prerogatives, the public remained weak and the constitution remained aristocratic. Each great baron "considered himself as a kind of sovereign within his territory" (I.485).[9] In England, "a kind of Polish Aristocracy prevailed; and though the kings were limited, the people were as yet far from being free" (II.525). Great kings could rein in nobles with exertions of personal power to a degree.[10] Less able kings—the lazy, cowardly John among them—were beaten back by the barons.[11] This pattern intensified after John signed the Great Charter. It was "a government of will, not of laws" (II.174; see also II.284). Under this barbaric aristocracy, "all was confusion and disorder; [there was] no regular idea of a constitution; force and violence decided everything" (I.362).

The syndrome of domestic and foreign events that preceded the spread of a more Enlightened and independent spiritual attitude—England's geographic isolation rendered the need for perpetual war preparation less necessary (II.522); raids from the Danes ceased; free cities or corporations expanded—need not detain us here. The unstable rivalry between the king and barons left the people weak, ignorant, and ignored (II.284, 525).[12] Let us pause to consider the problems baronial rule caused in feudal times because this has a direct bearing on how the feudal system would collapse. Local barons and priests oversaw the details of daily life to a greater degree than a distant arbitrary monarch could. Barons and priests could ferret out and try to correct every misdeed, while monarchs faced difficulties entering into details of administration in their larger realms. Barons and priests were fierce enemies of freedom because every extension of freedom was a derogation of their power. The people, paying fealty to local nobility, held the king in higher esteem because kings caused fewer grievances.[13] One is tempted to go further. In fact, the barons were natural enemies to the people, and a king had a chance to become a natural ally of the people against their oppressors.[14]

As baronial tyranny deepened, so also did superstitious attachment to, and the power of, Rome. "After an insensible progress during several ages of darkness," the pope "began... to lift his head openly above all the princes of Europe" (I.151; see also I.265). The Normans depended on English submissiveness to settle their claim to rule conquered England. "Devoted attachment to Rome continually encreased in England; and being favoured by the sentiments of the conquerors, as well as the monastic establishments... it soon reached the same height, at which it had, during some time, stood in France and Italy" (I.207). Monkish historians praised Church policies that led to the greatness of the Church in temporal affairs. From humble beginnings and without relying on arms, the Church established a "universal and almost absolute monarchy in Europe." The instrument that the Church availed itself of, however, in Hume's judgment, was not brilliant policy as much as it was "the ignorance and superstition of the people," which is "so gross an engine, of such universal prevalence, and so little liable to accident and disorder, that it may be successful even in the most unskilful hands" (I.264; also I.237). When kings such as William Rufus or Henry I asserted power over the investiture of prelates or control over revenues, the Church emerged victorious from the conflict (I.422). The people were more attached to the Church than their relatively powerless kings; allegiance to a foreign power made it difficult to establish the rule of law domestically. The Crusades combined the two "ruling passions" (I.237) of the age—piety and martial valor—in the service of a transnational cause that prevented the ascension of national power.

Amid these realities, the natural mechanism of progress was released by the first stirrings of civilization. As Danford catalogues,[15] the feudal system, where serfs occupied land in exchange for promised military service, gave way to an arrangement where serfs held land on annual contracts, then for life, and finally as part of an inheritance. "The idea of something like property" stole on minds (I.458). The recovery of the Pandects of Justinian (AD1130) abetted the move from dependence on feudal barons to independent land ownership. Ideas of property and law percolated for two to three hundred of years before Hume notes the rise of commerce, arts, and sciences. A hundred years after the Pandects gained attention, "regular administration was [still] not any where known," commerce was "in a wretched condition," and "bad police" rendered "all communication dangerous, and all property precarious" (II.20, 69).[16] Even during the reign of Edward I (1272–1307) when the "foundations of great and important changes in the government" were laid, the "feeble execution of the laws had given licence to all orders of men" (II.99, 95).[17] Throughout Volume II, Hume shows that trade and manufacturing was "at a very low ebb" (II.178 and 279) and that the kingdom "abounded...little in commodities" (II.275). Ruffians, thieves, robbers, and murderers lurked behind every bush as late as the reign of Henry V (1413–22), and, despite Edward I's achievements, "no law could be executed against those criminals" (II.279). Where laws existed, they did not provide security to property, personal freedom, progress in arts and sciences, or commerce. Only forceful kings such as Edward I and Edward III overcame obstacles to the steady execution of the laws in the feudal constitution. Corrupt barons, lawless popular habits, irregular institutions, and the primacy of tribal loyalties left the enforcement of the law dependent on royal whim.[18]

Between 1140, when the Pandects of Justinian were first discussed in English circles (II.520) and these later stirrings of a commercial ethos, there was a momentous change in English religious convictions. Superstitious popular opinion had arrested the natural mechanism of progress by inhibiting the rise of curiosity and the development of national law. Superstition was the glue of the feudal constitution: it encouraged submission to civil and ecclesiastical authorities; and it encouraged belief in and fear of "invisible and unknown" powers that must be appeased by "equally unaccountable...ceremonies, observances, mortifications, sacrifices, presents, or in any practice, however absurd or frivolous, which either folly or knavery recommends to a blind and terrified credulity" (E 74). While superstitious attachment to Rome persisted, political authority remained tenuous, the administration of law unsteady, property insecure, and progress in arts and science unrealized.

The waning of superstition is the theme of Volume II just as the stifling of law and commerce are. Superstition waned due to indigenous English and the imported European causes. Unchecked papal supremacy tempted religious authorities into all kinds of abuses: the pope obtained 1/10 of all revenues; ecclesiastical pardons and offices were openly sold;

favors and forgiveness could not be obtained without bribery; the church demanded that sovereigns contribute soldiers and treasure for crusade after crusade; church officials lived extravagantly; threats of excommunication and interdiction peeved princes; and the pope insisted on filling most offices with foreigners (as he hoped to extend his influence). The "rapacity" of Rome, from which the English suffered, "became so evident as to be palpable to the blindness of superstition itself" and was "the ground of general complaint" (II.23–4). During Henry III's reign (1216–72),

> papal power was at its summit, and was even beginning insensibly to decline, by reason of the immeasurable avarice and extortions of the court of Rome, which disgusted the clergy as well as laity, in every kingdom of Europe. England itself, though sunk in the deepest abyss of ignorance and superstition, had seriously entertained thoughts of shaking off the papal yoke; the Roman pontiff was obliged to think of new expedients for riveting it faster upon the Christian world. (II.70)

Edward I seized Church property and announced that Catholic priests would not be afforded protection of the laws; he encouraged people to "throw off that respect for the sacred order, by which they had so long been overawed and governed" (II.116).[19] Exertions of papal power diminished it (II.124) because papal rapacity offended sensibilities favorable to individual property ownership, justice, and national feeling; the Chruch's grip on the popular imagination, which is weak, as Hume thinks, in the nature of things, loosened insensibly, though it had a great height from which to fall.

This "insensible" decay became, over a century later, "a sensible decay of ecclesiastical authority"; the country was "very much weaned...from superstition" due to the "numerous usurpations both of the court of Rome, and of their own clergy" (II.325). Two incidents reveal this change: John Ball's insurrection (1381) in the name of equality and liberty (II.289–92) and John Wickliffe's (d. 1385) more popular and enduring attempt to reform the Church. Wickliffe especially endorsed the principles that would be "propagated by the reformers in the sixteenth century"; the Church's power had waned so much that Wickliffe was not punished for his enthusiastic heresies. Wickliffe died, but his movement, which some writers think represented half the kingdom, gained proselytes in England and abroad (II.326–29). Soon (1414) the Lollards embraced Wickliffe's doctrines (II.355–7). In retrospect, Hume concludes that the age "seemed strongly disposed to receive" Wickliffe's doctrines, but "affairs were not yet fully ripe for this great revolution; and the finishing blow to ecclesiastical power was reserved to a period of more curiosity, literature, and inclination for novelties" (II.329). Likewise the Lollards.

> Common sense and obvious reflection had discovered to the people the advantages of a reformation in discipline; but the age was not yet so far advanced as to be seized with the spirit of controversy, or to enter into those abstruse doctrines, which the Lollards endeavoured to propagate throughout the kingdom. The very notion of heresy alarmed the generality of the people: Innovation in fundamental principles was suspicious: Curiosity was not, as yet, a sufficient counterpoize to authority. (II.357)

Such movements were unthinkable only 50 years before; they were not yet thinkable enough to be successful as the Tudors ascended to the throne.

Let us assess the changes afoot in the late feudal constitution where even the beginning points in the natural mechanism of progress had not been fully realized yet. Political authority became more regular due to Edward I's reforms, but not regular enough to prevent barons and the Church from corrupting the rule of law. Superstition was waning, but not yet enough to kick off the Roman yoke. Commerce was "at a very low ebb," but slightly better than it had been during Anglo-Saxon times. As Hume presents it in the *History*, the waning of superstition and popular disgust with Rome antedate all other factors that would destroy the feudal constitution. Every element of the natural mechanism—law, security, property, curiosity, and knowledge—rose marginally in the pre-Tudor years. Hume traces the release of this natural mechanism to chance events—the discovery of the Pandects, the rapacity of the Roman clergy, the incorporation of cities, and so on. Hume also admires the actions of legislators such as Alfred and Edward I, who shaped the constitution through action (consider I.72–7 and II.141). At least a degree of foresight contributed to advances in the constitution.

Hume's tendency to deprecate prudence and foresight and to elevate accident is connected to his wish, as Eugene Miller argues, "to protect the English Constitution by discouraging a destructive rationalism."[20] Against shallow rationalists, Hume emphasizes (perhaps over-emphasizes) the fragility of the humane English Constitution: what chance has given, it can also rip away.[21] Hume's emphasis on chance seems to be in keeping with the philosophy of common life, the feeling that things could have been otherwise if just this event or that event had not happened. The *History of England* assigns paramount meaning to that which is apprehended in "daily life and experience." To relate Hume's view by metaphor, he sees several boats—commercial, religious, political—rising at the same time. His philosophy of common life precludes him, in contrast to Tocqueville, from positing the existence of some ineffable, insensible, uniquely historical or spiritual tide on which the boats rest. Hume can date the discovery of documents and record incidents that express popular disgust with Rome, but not so with an ineffable historical spirit. Locating a "high and distant" historical spirit seems to require that one occupy a point outside of history from which to view history; it requires that one possess theoretical insights into what moves history or to make tenuous inferences absent what is real. His emphasis on chance events is part of what keeps Hume from offering a deterministic, providential, unidirectional, or even cyclical[22] view of history. He seems to believe that the history of England could have gone in any number of directions had chance events not happened. The natural mechanism of progress, universal in operation, could have been distorted or suppressed for another thousand years if, for instance, English cities had not been incorporated or Justinian's Pandects not been found. A history grounded in common life shows the importance of accident, the permanent springs of human nature, and the presence of a great revolution in human affairs.

Such a complex and even contradictory "in-between" view—in keeping with Hume's general description of our "mixed kind of life"—can be criticized from several sides. Allow me to expand on this problem through a critical analysis of Hume assigning great historical importance to the discovery of the Justinian's Pandects. It was, as Hume relates in his summary comments about the rise of the English Constitution, a catalyst for the spread of jurisprudence and gave birth to professions in the law (II.520). Hume's analysis of the Pandects begs a fundamental question. What is more interesting—the discovery of the Pandects (which would assign importance to chance) or the fact that many were interested in the discovery of the Pandects (which would assign import to the general revolution in public opinion)? Would the barbarous Anglo or Saxon kings have been as anxious to mine the Pandects for guidance in establishing the rule of law? I doubt it. Would the discovery of the Pandects have aided the Tudors' absolute, arbitrary governance? I doubt it. The age was ripe for receiving the Pandects: their discovery was a case of a chance meeting the fruitful spirit.

Interest in the Pandects is more an effect of civilizing tendencies than their cause; history or culture seems to be the true, but ineffable, "high and distant," and almost undetectable cause of things. This line of criticism is especially compelling if *most or all* chance events point in the same direction as the humane revolution. Suppositions in Hume's philosophy of common life preclude such an analysis—those suppositions concentrate on the boats and not the tides. The presentation of history in the

History forces us to ask if Hume's self-imposed limits on the philosophy of common life—limits that tell against shallow rationalism and relativism alike—might distort Hume's view of history or whether Hume's claims about the primacy of chance might smuggle controversial assumptions about history into this telling. When most or all chance events turn to the profit of the humane revolution, when the humane revolution profits from the actions of its enemies, perhaps we should not refrain from positing the existence of a "high and distant" reality. If this revolution took place throughout Europe at the same time in roughly the same manner, it may be safer to infer, with Tocqueville, the existence of something spiritual, providential, or Historical at work?[23] I consider this problem in greater depth in the conclusion of this chapter.

The Tudors and the Humane Revolution

The Tudors ruled England from the ascension of Henry VII (1485) until the death of Queen Elizabeth (1603). The Tudor volumes (Volumes III and IV) chart the rise of virtually unlimited monarchical power, the eclipse of superstitious religious belief, and the rise of an ethic propitious to the arts and sciences. Barons were ascendant since the signing of the great charter. The Tudor monarchs reversed this trend and gained the power lost by the barons partly as a result of their victory in the War of the Roses. More essential was the tacit alliance between the Tudor monarchs and the commons, which began in some measure earlier.[24] Henry VII used an "almost absolute authority... to pull down these disorderly and licentious tyrants, who where equally averse from peace and from freedom" in order to establish a "regular execution of the laws" (II.525; also III.49). The English people loved the Tudors because they vigorously wielded absolute power against oppressors, sacred and profane. "Instead of checking and controuling the authority of the king, [the commons] were naturally induced to adhere to him, as the great fountain of law and justice, and to support him against the power of the aristocracy, which at once was the source of oppression to themselves, and disturbed him in the execution of the laws" (III.109). The Tudors occupied the "interval between the fall of the nobles and the rise of [the commons]"; they "took advantage" of the situation to aggrandize themselves as they contributed to England's development (IV.384).

Hume likens Tudor monarchy to Eastern despotism (III.322–3; IV.346, 358, 360), but this overstates the arbitrary nature of their rule. "This situation of England [under the Tudors], though seemingly it approached nearer, was in reality more remote from a despotic and eastern monarchy, than" the England of Hume's day, where, in Hume's judgment, the commons threatened a democratic despotism. The power of the Tudors, "though really unlimited, was exercised after the European manner, and entered not into every part of the administration." Property was more secure under the Tudors than it was under arbitrary and corrupt baronial rule or under the priestly thumb.[25] The "tacit check" of custom "maintained the government in that medium, to which the people had been accustomed" (IV.370).[26] The Tudors obliged the commons, despite themselves sometimes,[27] by granting the commons protection and "*personal* freedom" (II.524).

Henry VIII rose to power as the commitment to martial valor was waning and a new order concerned with property, luxury, the arts and sciences, and the rule of law was rising.[28] The discontinuity between the pre-Tudor and post-Tudor constitutions could not be more dramatic. Henry VIII's ascension coincides with "a general revolution...in human affairs throughout this part of the world," wherein people "gradually attained that situation, with regard to commerce, arts, science, government, police, and cultivation, in which they have ever since persevered" (III.81). The study of history from that point forward, Hume writes in a remarkable passage, is "useful" and "agreeable," while "researches into preceding periods" beget little "knowledge of public affairs, or the arts of government" (III.82). This "general revolution" occurs throughout Christendom, suggesting that it is not caused predominantly by national events. Speaking of the most fundamental "event" in this general revolution, Luther's Reformation, Hume writes as follows: "All Saxony, all Germany, *all Europe*... roused from that lethargy, in which they had so long slept, began to call into question the most ancient and most received opinions" (III.139; emphasis supplied). Unlike the statement in the first *Enquiry* (EHU 83), Hume in this context suggests that the "experiments" before the Tudor era (including presumably investigations into the ancient world) are not useful for the acquisition of political knowledge. Hume must mean here that statesmanlike models and political questions after the Tudors are relevant guidance for statesmen of his day. Acts of political judgment in the modern world resemble the "experiments" conducted after the Tudor's reign. Earlier researches are still relevant for acquiring philosophical knowledge of our mixed condition and for informing more philosophical standards of judgment.

Henry VIII's reign, the era when England kicked superstitious habits, is the key to how this revolution unfolded in England.[29] Hume is preoccupied with religious matters more than anything else in the Tudor volumes; Henry's reign is redolent with the theological and political ramifications of the reformation. Henry's reasons for reforming the church were ostensibly marital, though Hume shows how Henry's humor comports with changes afoot in Europe and England. Ground for the Reformation was prepared in England by Lollards. Henry (1521) won papal praise for penning books that opposed these innovations. But his desire for a divorce and re-marriage soon brought him in line with profound popular discontent with the Church. If it had not been divorce that separated Henry from the Church, something else probably would have initiated it. The issue, for Henry as for the English people, was papal authority's effect on royal power and the rule of law.[30] The Church inhibited the "execution of justice" by exempting clergy from criminal and civil penalties and by offering sanctuary and forgiveness to criminals (III.324).

> The higher dignities of the church served, indeed, to the support of gentry and nobility; but by the establishment of monasteries, many of the lowest vulgar were taken from the useful arts, and maintained in those receptacles of sloth and ignorance... And as the hierarchy was necessarily solicitous to preserve an unity of faith, rites, and ceremonies, all liberty of thought ran a manifest risque of being extinguished; and violent persecutions, or what was worse, a stupid and abject credulity took place every where. (III.136)

Afraid to presume too far on the passive obedience of his subjects (III.160), Henry established the regular administration of justice by restraining several impositions of the clergy (III.186–7), closing monasteries,[31] and seizing Church property. The suppression of the monasteries was especially important. The presence of monasteries was "the radical inconvenience of the catholic religion" just as the nobles had been the inconvenience of feudalism: "Papal usurpations, the tyranny of the inquisition, the multiplicity of holidays; all these fetters on liberty and industry were ultimately derived from the authority and insinuation of monks" (III.227). The people were thereby prepared for a complete break with Rome as each parliament "retrenched somewhat from the power and profits of the pontiff." Henry taught "the nation, that a general council was much superior to a pope" (III.203).

Henry's consolidation of authority into the Church of England ended an important political intrusion into the functioning of English Constitution.

> A way was also prepared for checking the exorbitancies of superstition, and breaking those shackles, by which all human reason, policy, and industry had so long been encumbered. The prince, it may be supposed, being the head of the religion, as well as of the temporal jurisdiction of the kingdom, though he might sometimes employ the former as an engine of government, had no interest, like the Roman pontiff, in nourishing its excessive growth; and, except when blinded by his own ignorance or bigotry, would be sure to retain it within tolerable limits, and prevent its

abuses. And on the whole, there followed from this revolution many beneficial consequences; though perhaps neither foreseen nor intended by the persons who had a chief hand in conducting it. (III.206–7)

Henry apprehended the danger such "great innovations" could wreck on his rule (III.190), but the population was devoted to him as the author of their deliverance from the Church. The rejection of Rome would have opened a religious and political Pandora's box were it not for Henry's "decisive authority" (III.227).[32] Henry's absolute authority and his uncommon popularity were necessary prerequisites for a break with Rome and the relatively peaceful religious settlement that followed. In Hume's development theory, absolute political rule appears to be an essential moment in establishing the rule of law and destroying political and religious forces inimical to progress. Henry was England's Ataturk; and the pope his Caliphate.

Henry's rule was complicated not merely by the existence of superstition but also by the existence of religious faction between Catholics and Protestants. Forging this reformation required a theological revolution. Maintaining some doctrines from the old religion and establishing some from the new, Henry was able to appease all to an extent and please no one completely. Reformers glorified "private judgment" over Church authority, but Henry opposed this move out of interest and inclination because "in proportion as the practice of submitting religion to private judgment was acceptable to the people, it appeared, in some respects, dangerous to the rights of sovereigns, and seemed to destroy that implicit obedience, on which the authority of the civil magistrate is chiefly founded" (III.212). Henry's "political machine" initiated this "furious movement, and yet regulate[d] and even stop[ped] its career: He could say to it, Thus far shalt thou go and no farther" (III.244).

Henry's ambiguous conduct redounded to the benefit of Protestants (III.214, 251). For example, he commissioned a translation of the Bible in deference to those exalting private judgment. Upon its completion, Henry insisted that only a few be disseminated and that those few be chained inside churches, in deference to the desire to maintain submission to religious authority. Later he would sanction a general dissemination of it, thus reviving the "spirit of research and curiosity" (III.231, 251, 273). Henry hoped publishing the Bible would promote unity of opinion in religious matters; he published tracts outlining pure religious doctrine too.

> Henry laboured incessantly, by arguments, creeds, and penal statutes, to bring his subjects to an uniformity in their religious sentiments: But as

he entered, himself, with the greatest earnestness, into all those scholastic disputes, he encouraged the people, by his example, to apply themselves to the study of theology; and it was in vain afterwards to expect, however present fear might restrain their tongues or pens, that they would cordially agree in any set of tenets or opinions prescribed to them. (III.290)[33]

Henry and his daughter and true heir Elizabeth could maintain this delicate balancing act; however, Henry unleashed forces—Hume's natural mechanism of progress, in fact—that royal authority could not contain in the long term. The English deferred to the Tudors out of religious conviction, out of fear of religious faction, and out of hatred for Catholicism (IV.367).[34] Even as they protected personal freedom and reformed the church, the Tudors presumed to dictate religious opinion and opposed civic freedom. Their efforts would prove untenable.

Let us pause to place developments in a broader context. Superstition had insinuated itself into common life and distorted or suppressed the natural mechanism (IV.14). The Catholicism under which the English suffered had come to resemble law-based revealed religions such as Islam or orthodox Judaism that reveal economic, political, scientific, and culture practices to which followers must submit; Catholicism had become a comprehensive religion—one that taught what to believe, how politics should be structured and how all aspects of life should be organized. Progress was impossible under this comprehensive superstitious religious establishment. The Tudors ruled during the destruction of the Catholic consensus. That which suppressed and distorted the natural course of improvement corroded throughout Europe, and absolute monarchies were everywhere agents of this corrosion. Beating back lawless barons and unproductive superstitions, absolute monarchs set themselves up as founts of law, security, orthodoxy, and commerce. "The minds of men, somewhat awakened from a profound sleep of so many centuries, were prepared for every novelty, and scrupled less to tread in any unusual path, which was opened them" (III.140). No longer would the Church impede the administration of justice. No longer would it inhibit the spread of an ethic of humanity and industry. No longer would it prevent novelties and innovations from being introduced into all spheres of human existence. No longer would science be superstition's handmaiden. The Tudors were agents of development and modernization, despite their dedication to absolutism and their somewhat conservative religiosity; they oversaw creeping democratic changes to English culture, while they tried to keep a governor on the democratization of political power. Only when the desire for property took possession of the English mind would the English insist on a functioning rule of law, and this desire for property came after the erosion of superstitious belief. Though England was largely cured of superstitious habits before and during the Tudor years, commerce and a "spirit of industry" began to flourish only after Henry's death (III.386–7).

The Tudors cleared away all obstacles but one to the flourishing of commerce and the execution of regular justice. Only the Tudors' absolute, arbitrary rule—and their laws retarding the spread of commerce—stood in the way of a regular rule of law and a humane constitution. Less than 50 years after the Virgin Queen died, England's political settlement crumbled on the scaffolding at Whitehall.

Enthusiasm and the Humane Constitution

Tocqueville thinks modern England's effectively established a *true* aristocracy, the rule of the best instead of the rule of the well-born. England was the "only country where the caste system had not been merely changed but really destroyed." The rich or well-born in England could achieve great public stature by entering into politics and serving the public. The public benefited from this service without resenting the aristocracy.

> It is interesting to see how the English nobility, pushed by its own ambition, has known how to mingle on familiar terms with its inferiors when necessary, and pretend to consider them its equals... The English aristocracy was more haughty than the French aristocracy, and less inclined to be familiar with those who lived beneath it; but the necessities of its situation required it to do so. It was ready to do anything to lead.[35]

England succeeded by this means in reconciling nearly all elements of society to a modern republican political settlement. Hume's analysis of England's uniqueness does not differ in principle from Tocqueville's, though Hume emphasizes the religious basis for England's achievement. England emerged from the Reformation having destroyed the feudal *and* Catholic hierarchies. In England commerce was considered "*honourable*" (E 93; III.327). The move from superstitious reverence to modern republicanism and religious tolerance (NHR 50) was instigated (ironically) by Protestant enthusiasm; enthusiastic forms of Protestantism—remnants of Lollards and their predecessors—emerged triumphant against superstition and conservative Protestantism in England.

Not only Christian beliefs, but religious beliefs as such, were, before the Reformation, either superstitious and polytheistic; religious enthusiasm is another uniquely modern phenomenon. Catholic superstition is, for Hume, defined by its ability to insinuate itself into and distort common sensibilities, and its rituals have a greater effect on the mind and on one's way of life. Enthusiasm, in contrast, is "chiefly spiritual" and "resembles more a system of metaphysics." The "reformers, obliged to dispute on every occasion, and inflamed to a degree of enthusiasm by novelty and persecution, had strongly attached themselves to their tenets; and were ready to sacrifice their fortunes and even their lives, in support of their speculative and abstract principles" (IV.14).[36] Catholicism had so distorted common life that enthusiasts fled common sensibilities altogether; enthusiasts left the grounded world of ritual and tradition for a world of abstraction, spiritualism, and innovation. This would have enormous, initially violent, ultimately beneficial political effects on the English Constitution.

Enthusiasts resisted established rituals, forms, and ceremonies that had restrained their "rapturous flights, extasies, visions, [and] inspirations" (IV.123; also E 74). The psychology of enthusiasm favored freedom, equality, and grand reforms. Nearly all England was infused with such a spirit of liberty. Protestant churches served as models for authority that believers would consider legitimate in politics. Anglican and Catholic hierarchies shrouded religious authority and kept it distant from the people; these forms supported the absolute, arbitrary rule of the Tudor monarchs. Demystifying and leveling clerical authority, as the Reformation and enthusiasm did, fostered a critical attitude toward political authority and encouraged a belief in equality that gave rise to a desire for civil liberty. Religious and political hierarchy was associated with England's discredited ancient superstition, and the embrace of enthusiasm infused all of England with the republican spirit of liberty (V.179, 394). The same "bold and daring spirit, which accompanied" enthusiasts "in their addresses to the divinity, appeared in their political speculations; and the principles of civil liberty... had been strongly adopted by this new sect" of Puritans. Puritans "made themselves considerable in England" in 1569 during Elizabeth's reign (IV.123–4; also IV.22–3, 140 and V.558–9),[37] but her moral authority and prestige was such that Puritans did not challenge her ecclesiastical or political prerogatives.[38] Even when Puritans constituted a majority in the commons, they were so cowed by her authority that they refrained from introducing bills to reform the religious establishment (IV.206). Despite these early setbacks, the Puritans were "actuated by that zeal which belongs to innovators, and by that courage which enthusiasm inspires." Hume continues: "They hazarded the utmost indignation of their sovereign; and employing all their industry to be elected into parliament... they first acquired a majority in that assembly, and then obtained an ascendant over the church and monarchy" (IV.146).[39] In less than a generation these "noble principles of liberty" would become "fashionable among the people" (IV.368; see also V.179). Absolute, arbitrary authority would not and could not withstand this fundamental change in public opinion; the Stuarts to their great misfortune reaped what Henry and the spirit of the times sowed.[40] In a statement that echoes several others, Hume contends that the "minds of men" began to undergo "a general, but insensible revolution" as James I ascended to the throne in 1603 (V.18).

Hume's praise of the Puritans, given his disdain for their fanaticism, is a singular example of philosophical equanimity. It is to "the puritans alone," he writes, "whose principles appear so frivolous and habits so ridiculous, that the English owe the whole freedom of their constitution" (IV.146). Royal prerogatives in ecclesiastical matters came under increasing attack during the reign of James I when "the house contained a mixture of puritans, who had great authority" and who "were continually suggesting ideas more suitable to a popular than a monarchical form of government" (V.35–6). Political prerogatives corroded as well.

The rise of Protestantism coincided with the rise of a substantial middle class, the spread of commercial mores, and increases in the power of the realm. Protestantism and the desire for civil liberty among the middle class went together hand in glove. The rise of the middle class was the continuation of the revolution that began earlier when the military ethos lost its grip on English opinion. Luxurious habits "dissipated the immense fortunes of ancient barons," whose "methods of expence gave subsistence" to independent and industrious mechanics. Landed proprietors needed "money more than men" and tried to cultivate the land for profit by enclosing fields and dismissing "useless hands" that had formerly been their instruments of war against others. Cities grew in stature and population as people left the country to pursue independent occupations, and the "middle rank of men began to be rich and powerful" (IV.384). Many Tudor laws retarded the growth of trade, but the regularity of their administration and the removal of religious, cultural, and legal obstacles to regular administration loosened the governor on the natural mechanism of progress. On Elizabeth's death, a "good county in England [would have been] able to make, at least to support, a greater effort than the whole kingdom was capable of in the reign of Henry V." Such are "the effects of liberty, industry, and good government!" (IV.379).[41]

The feudal dedication to military valor and superstitious religious belief, which sustained the nobility, was dying in England. A new commercial, enthusiastic, more egalitarian, republican ethos arose. Reformers, animated by the egalitarian, individualistic, and assertive spirit of Protestantism, sought to destroy all vestiges of feudalism. From the Reformers' "democratical, enthusiastic spirit" a "total confusion of all rank and order was justly to be apprehended" (V.361). One of the more fanatical factions, the Independents, proposed a program to institute "an entire equality of rank and order, in a republic, quite free and independent" (V.443). The Levellers, a faction associated closely with Cromwell, sought to abolish the throne, "set" the nobility "aside," and level "all ranks of men" (V.513). The pervasiveness of this reforming spirit de-legitimized the nobility in the eyes of the populace and, to a degree, in nobles' own eyes. However much the aristocracy rallied to the defense of the old order during the English Civil War, its heart never seemed to be in it.[42] The aristocratic Cavaliers had, for the most part, lost faith in their cause. Their failure to resist the Roundhead Reformers with similar dedication shows that the nobles had abandoned the superstitious faith of their fathers and embraced the modern ethos to an extent. The earlier self-destruction of the nobility in the War of the Roses was not as impressive or as important in the long term as the loss of faith in feudalism and superstition.

Eventually this spiritual change made commerce honorable in places like England, the Netherlands, and Hamburg, "all free cities, and protestant cities; that is, enjoying a double liberty" (E 92), while commerce was considered "less *honourable*" under absolute monarchies such as France and Spain.

> A subordination of ranks is absolutely necessary to the support of monarchy. Birth, titles, and place, must be honoured above industry and riches. And while these notions prevail, all the considerable traders will be tempted to throw up their commerce, in order to purchase some of these employments, to which privileges and honours are annexed. (E 93)

Protestantism destroyed the intellectual foundation for England's "subordination of ranks," and its aristocracy became, as Tocqueville argued,[43] a confused, porous, industrious, rich, and loosely-organized band of public servants. England's aristocracy responsibly oversaw the Restoration of public order in the aftermath of Cromwell's republic and during the Glorious Revolution.

The spirit of liberty that improved the English Constitution may not have arisen in the absence of Protestantism, but this spirit of liberty became politically destructive because it was associated with religious enthusiasm. Enthusiasts and Republicans were inclined to destroy all England's institutions of authority, and that put England in danger of becoming an absolute, arbitrary *democracy*. Executive power was subdued by the spirit of a more civilized age, and Hume lauded the profound enlightening mechanism that was "intimately connected" (II.519) to these political changes. Parliament's actions were beneficial and necessary because the privileges asserted by previous monarchs were inconsistent with a free, humane constitution. The entire sovereign power had "in a manner" been "transferred to the commons, and the government, without any seeming violence or disorder, [was] changed, in a moment, from a monarchy almost absolute, to a pure democracy" (V.293). Hume worried that "pure" democratic rule could prove inconsistent to the humane spirit of the age too. The changes wrought by Parliament against Charles partook of too much religious zeal and anti-executive jealousy and destabilized the political order.

Parliament's attempt "of totally annihilating monarchical power" was "a very blameable extreme" (V.574) for narrowly prudential reasons and for the interests of establishing a stable government. The attack on Charles's prerogatives prompted him to draw the sword in the name of protecting some revenue, some military force, and the discretionary powers necessary to execute the laws. These actions started England swinging between extremes of excessive democracy and arbitrary monarchical rule. The English Civil War culminated in the beheading of Charles I and the institution of Oliver Cromwell's tyrannical Protectorate. The experience under Cromwell made the English "more anxious...to guard against rebellion in the subject than encroachments in the crown" (VI.174). Many of the sensible measures used to subdue kingly prerogatives were repealed by Parliament in the spirit of mutual goodwill (VI.173, 191). By making war and claiming old ecclesiastical and economic prerogatives, Charles II became an absolute king. James II, the successor of Charles II, made himself more hateful. This prompted the English to call on William of Orange to defend their lives, liberty, and religion. The Glorious Revolution began, as Hume glowingly writes,

> a new epoch in the constitution; and was probably attended with consequences more advantageous to the people, than barely freeing them from an exceptionable administration. By deciding many important questions in favour of liberty, and still more, by that great precedent of deposing one king, and establishing a new family, it gave such an ascendant to popular principles, as has put the nature of the English constitution beyond all controversy. And it may justly be affirmed, without any danger of exaggeration, that we, in this island, have ever since enjoyed, if not the best system of government, at least the most entire system of liberty, that ever was known amongst mankind. (VI.531)

The salutary rise of the commons, abetted by religious enthusiasm, did not solve all the problems in the constitution. The Glorious settlement took the constitution to a new level of perfection in the protection of liberty.

> It was there supposed, that every subject of England had entire power to dispose of his own actions, provided he did no injury to any of his fellow-subjects; and that no prerogative of the king, not power of any magistrate, nothing but the authority alone of laws, could restrain that unlimited freedom. The full prosecution of this noble principle into all its natural consequences, has at last, through many contests, produced that singular and happy government, which we enjoy at present. (V.114)

Taming executive prerogative, placing legislative power in the commons and establishing civil and personal freedom were the defining excellences of England's "singular and happy government." Hume does not always endorse England's constitution in the *Essays*, where he is quite concerned about the balance of power between the governing institutions. Its achievement of humanity and liberty makes Hume's worries about the way it also threatens humanity and liberty all the more striking.

Politics in the Modern Commercial Republic

The tension between executive prerogative and legislative power after the Glorious Revolution is endemic to constitutionalism. In the best case, only laws limit individual freedom. Every government also needs to have a reservoir of discretionary executive authority for times of emergency (V.128; E 40), yet such authority is dangerous when used without clear need. Hume sees a "perpetual intestine struggle, open or secret, between AUTHORITY and LIBERTY" (E 40).

> No government at that time, appeared in the world, nor is perhaps to be found in the records of any history, which subsisted without the mixture of some arbitrary authority, committed to some magistrate; and it might reasonably, beforehand, appear doubtful, whether human society could ever reach that state of perfection, as to support itself with no other controul than the general and rigid maxims of law and equity. But the parliament justly thought, that the king was too eminent a magistrate to be trusted with discretionary power, which he might so easily turn to the destruction of liberty. And in the event it has hitherto been found, that, though some sensible inconveniences arise from the maxim of adhering strictly to law, yet the advantages overbalance them, and should render the English grateful to the memory of their ancestors, who, after repeated contests, at last established that noble, though dangerous, principle. (V.329–30)

Consistent with the law of mixed blessings, the rule of law is a "noble," "dangerous principle" because the need for obedience to law tempts people into believing in the adequacy of law. Strict adherence to law causes occasional inconveniences; the advantage of inculcating adherence to law may overbalance but cannot eliminate those inconveniences.

Hume notices a great improvement in monarchical rule during modern times. "All kinds of government, free and absolute, seem to have undergone, in modern times, a change for the better, with regard both to foreign and domestic management." In practice, the rule of law and constraints of custom provided a civilized and civilizing security for citizens even under absolute monarchies of Hume's Europe. A civilized monarchy can now be called "*a government of Laws, not of Men*." "Private property," Hume writes, is "almost as secure in a civilized EUROPEAN monarchy, as in a republic; nor is danger much apprehended in such a government, from the violence of the sovereign; more than we commonly dread harm from thunder, or earthquakes, or any accident the most unusual and extraordinary" (E 92–4).

Hume's presentation of modernity's humane monarchies is an implied softening of Machiavelli's bloody account of executive authority. Hume opens "Of Civil Liberty" by criticizing Machiavelli, whose "reasonings especially upon monarchical government, have been found extremely defective." Almost all of Machiavelli's teachings have been "entirely refuted" by experience, Hume contends (E 88). He illustrates the problem with Machiavelli with one example (concerning how princes should receive advice). The scope of Hume's critique invites us to speculate on other criticisms. Modern princes do not find it in their interest, as Machiavelli advised, to "satisfy and stupify" people into obedience through spectacular executions.[44] Responding to Machiavelli's praise of Alexander the Great's violent "eastern policy," Hume argues that "in every respect, a gentle government is preferable, and gives greater security to the sovereign as well as the subject" (E 23–4). To be precise, civilized monarchs have learned the lessons of Machiavelli well, even as they shunned or no longer need spectacular executions. The modern prince has learned that it is in his interest, in Machiavelli's words, to "abstain from the property of his citizens and his subjects" and to encourage citizens in peaceful commercial activities.[45] Montesquieu too articulates this point. Since the advent of modern commerce, Hume's correspondent writes,

> it turned out that great acts of authority were so clumsy that experience itself has made known that only goodness of government brings prosperity...One has begun to be cured of Machiavellianism, and one will

continue to be cured of it. There must be more moderation in councils. What were formerly called *coups d'etat* would at present, apart from their horror, be only imprudences.[46]

Reasons for entering into evil fade with the spread of commerce. Commercial relations are gentle, secure, and moderate, while Machiavellian executions cause people to fear and feel uneasy in the face of government. Stupifying executions and heavy-handed arbitrary government render property insecure, discourage commerce and innovation, and could even undermine arts and sciences. Absolute, arbitrary rule cannot recreate or govern the diverse relationships seen in modern economies. Monarchs behave with greater humanity all the better to reap the public benefits of a more powerful population; gentle rule is more efficacious than coercive rule; liberty is the best policy. Modern princes are cured of Machiavellianism, but this curing is consistent with Machiavelli's democratic, productive, humane revolution in politics.

A problem lies in the success of silent, gentle executive authority. No longer sensing the need for executive prerogatives, the legislative power is tempted to assert an absolute power over the entire constitution. This was the problem facing the English Constitution as it sided dangerously with liberty against authority. "The share of power, allotted by our constitution to the house of commons, is so great, that it absolutely commands all the other parts of the government." English monarchs possessed only the "altogether subordinate" power to execute laws and a negative on laws. "How easy," Hume marvels, "would it be for that house to wrest from the crown all these powers, one after another; by making every grant conditional, and choosing their time so well, that their refusal of supply should only distress the government, without giving foreign powers any advantage over us?" (E 44). The consequence of the house of commons becoming the sole power in a popular government was enough to make Hume "wish to see an absolute monarch than a republic in this island." Pure democracy in England would be subject to "thousands" of "inconveniences," including the "tyranny of faction" and "civil war" (E 52).

Some element of restraint or control existed in the English Constitution to secure its long-term stability and moderation. Hume locates that check in the devise known as parliamentary patronage, where many members in the house owe their positions to the king. As we saw in chapter 5, these members act in the monarch's interest because they maintain their seats by doing so. Such patronage may not be viable long-term solution to the problem of aiding executive rule—it was considered invidious even in Hume's day. Without an executive means of checking and controlling parliament, Hume thought the English had reason to fear further democratic excesses. Republican government is "an obvious absurdity, if the particular checks and controuls" did not make it in "the interest, even of bad men, to act for the public good." Executive power can be tamed too much and Hume's analysis seems to point toward an executive with some independent powers.

Constitutions incorporating checks "beget order and moderation" even when the "manners and customs have instilled little humanity or justice into the tempers of men" (E 25). For Hume the Romans exemplify the possibility that a government can be better than its people with the proper balance of powers. The Romans adopted the rude, inhumane, unnatural ancient method of patriotic education (E 259), and their government could hardly be called moderate, gentle or humane by modern standards. This leads to the second, more profound way that checks and controls are related to humanity and moderation. Only a civilized country worried about securing the rule of equal laws would make enlightened efforts to control and maintain proper checks and controls. The separation of powers is an improvement in a political science that itself is a relatively late flower of civilization. It is a cultural achievement as much as a political one.

Hume as Philosophical Historian

Hume is a philosophical historian who sees history as an intellectual endeavor well suited to our middling capacities. Consistent with his philosophy of common life, Hume's approach to history incorporates natural suppositions about what history is and proceeds with investigation, seeking to inform curious readers, to provide faithful accounts and to lay the foundation for meaningful generalizations. In supposing the common sense of the matter, Hume bypasses fundamental, seemingly unanswerable controversies that occupied philosophers before him and especially after him. Hume's initial supposition about history seems to be that history is studied because "it is universally acknowledged...that human nature remains still the same, in its principles and operations." Hume has in mind here the panoply of human motives—"ambition, avarice, self-love, vanity, friendship, generosity, public spirit"—that are the "source for all action and enterprise, which have ever been observed among mankind" (EHU 83). Different ages, countries, and people may mix the motives in different ways and proportions or put them in the service of different purposes, as Hume writes in the same paragraph, yet these are the springs of human action. History reveals, on this supposition, the springs of action and notes the variety of ways those springs are given priority and manifested in practice. In this light, Hume's striking claim that we acquire no "knowledge of public affairs, or the arts of government" from the study of history before Henry VIII (H III.82) means that the previous way human beings arranged their purposes and gave priority to their natural motives is no longer relevant to guide those who must judge things in the modern world; before Henry, there was a different regime or political constitution with different ways. The first supposition then registers the constants and the changes in a comparative way.

The second natural supposition of Hume's history is the importance of "accident" that mixes with the "small ingredient of wisdom and foresight" (H II.525) that goes into determining a civilization's political constitution broadly conceived. Hume wrote about the chance-heavy mixture in the very last sentence he penned of the *History*, giving the appearance that this is a conclusion of his long treatment of the rise of liberty, not a supposition. Accident, for Hume, seems to be an apparently unrelated or unchosen cause out of the stream of a situation; for example, one's peculiar natural personality or disposition, getting struck by lightening, discovering Justinian's Pandects, or a monarch particularly displeased with his wife. Hume may overstate the case against "wisdom and foresight" in order to deprecate Whig theorists who aspire to re-mold the English Constitution according to their theories. Nevertheless, Hume's emphasis on "accident" in history is in keeping with elements of what we now call "contingency" in history—the view that things could have been different if only, to use an American example, the soldier had not disposed of his cigars with his battle orders from Robert E. Lee before Antietam. This importance of chance comports nicely with Hume's philosophy of common life and those who practice the historian's craft today sanction it with authority.

Furthermore, there need be no conflict between Hume's first and second natural suppositions. Accidental causes can change how societies arrange their motives or organize their goals. As Hume presents it, several accidental causes contribute to the eclipse of superstitious order and the emancipation of the natural mechanism of progress (law fosters security; security, curiosity; curiosity fosters industry, knowledge, and humanity). There was nothing necessary about the creation or dislocation of superstitious and martial order and it could have come about differently but for fortuitous events and people. History does not add value to human nature; it rearranges value. The first supposition about constancy and change is more analytical than the second, which is more narrative. The first rests on repeated experiments derived from the second. The first can extend to show how some motives or purposes usually appear together and what that can tell us about human nature. The second is often informed through these bundles and the story is told with some awareness of where it is headed—otherwise history would be reduced to mere chronicling. People must use the storytelling in Hume's *History* as a basis for making qualified judgments about individual and collective patterns of action and belief. Political science (to which the first supposition points) depends on history (to which the second supposition points); political science is also the goal of historical studies. Furthermore, these suppositions, when combined with the philosophical reflection that ours is a "mixed kind of life," allows Hume to make judgments about the adequacy of constitutions, civilizations or systems and to endorse commercial arrangements and the modern system of liberty.

This "system" is problematic in its assumptions about what moves history and what history reveals. These problems point, ultimately, to problems endemic to Hume's philosophy of common life. Consider first what this chapter has found in the *History*. The transition from the feudal to modern English Constitution was accomplished by the accidental removal of obstacles that had suppressed the natural mechanism of progress. Enlightenment's dawn—the most significant event in human history for Hume—appears to be a miracle. Hume's account of historical change suggests that the most important events in human history occur because of relatively insignificant events and actions; ignoble, accidental causes are out of proportion to noble, enlightened effects. The enlightening mechanism was suppressed, with a few partial exceptions, throughout human history, and it was emancipated throughout Europe at roughly the same time in history. Much is remarkable about this description of human history. It testifies to the essential weakness of nature, if nature can be suppressed by strange and violent conventions throughout almost all of history.

How can Hume know that this is chance unbound and not chance attached to something beyond chance? By emphasizing chance, Hume, to borrow a phrase, assumes that the truth of things lies on the surface of things. Observable events are just events for Hume—not indications of a Historical spirit on which events ride. Hume's philosophy of common life rules out the "distant and high" belief that there is a unique spirit working in history. I am asking whether it is legitimate, on Hume's own description of history or on the basis of common life, to rule such a claim out.

Hume's emphasis on the final causal significance of chance or accidental events (H II.525), the importance of unintended consequences in history, and his comments about the transporting difficulties involved in predicting future events (E 47) indicate that he does not think history is a rational process. More specifically, Hume views history as a series of mostly haphazard events and actions. These haphazard events and actions are not expressions of thought or, to put this differently, events and actions have an outside expression but not an inside spiritual, logical significance. Having seemingly rejected the possibility that there is logic in the historical process, Hume must also reject the claims that history has a distinct direction, *telos* or purpose and he abjures from defining that end as equality or human freedom. Hume rejects the view that history is so structured or so patterned that it could be construed as an "intelligible whole" rather than a "haphazard series of events."[47] His emphasis on chance leads him to reject Hegelian views that history can end, that the meaning of history can become clear, and that disagreements about the purposes of government would wither away. Hume's telling of history and his occupation as a philosophic historian *presume* the falsity of Hegel's synthetic philosophy of history or Tocqueville's unidirectional history of democracy, though Hume's narrative also supports the story of history as these other thinkers would relate it. Hume would counsel against assimilating such "high and distant" stories about history, but those "high and distant" treatments appear have such predictive value that disdaining them seems unreasonable. Hume's treatment does not adequately treat and explain this revolution in human affairs that he embraces and describes.

Another issue concerns what a historical treatment of human nature can reveal. Just as Hume assimilates controversial suppositions about what drives history into his account of history, his treatment of religion contains within it a particular, very controversial account of the nature and origin of religious belief. The problems in Hume's treatment of history are tied up with these issues of religion because it is through religious belief and practice that this revolution in human affairs manifests itself. We shall see that, ultimately, Hume imagines a fundamental transformation of human religious practice in modernity—one that is difficult to explain on the basis of a philosophy of common life.

CHAPTER 8

RELIGIOUS BELIEF AND HUME'S PHILOSOPHY OF COMMON LIFE

> *A correct Judgement... avoiding all distant and high enquiries, confines itself to common life, and to such subjects as fall under daily practice and experience; leaving more sublime topics to the embellishments of poets and orators, or to the arts of priests and politicians.*
>
> —Hume, *EHU*, p. 162.

A combination of agnosticism and natural suppositions sustains a philosophy of common life. Agnostic on how mechanisms of understanding function or how nature works, we can suppose *that* we adequately judge or *that* nature works steadily and continue from there. The problem Hume confronts in his conception of history arises from a conflict between his desire to be agnostic on questions about how things in history work on one hand and our need to put forth propositions about how history moves. The last chapter covered the difficulties of establishing the "common sense" principles for a study of history since every account of history presumes something about the meaning of history and what moves history. That he conceives of history as determined by accident implies an answer to the question of *how* history works and what *moves* history. As troubling, Hume's own account lends support to the view that history is animated by a spirit of progress behind accidents that are on the surface. How should or can philosophy of common life proceed if or when *non-controversial* natural suppositions are not available?

This problem appears with greatest starkness in Hume's writings on religion. How can a philosopher of common life, who leaves topics outside of "daily life and experience" to the "embellishments" of less intellectually rigorous, more popular figures, treat religion and theology? Investigating a topic requires that one first adopt a perspective inside the practice of a particular horizon or art. Attaining the proper view between the particular and the general or between engaged sentiments and detached judgment is not easy. It is necessary to adopt the perspective of a statesman if one is to begin to understand politics or to adopt the perspective of an author or a learned reader if one is to begin to understand literature. Which perspective should an investigator adopt as the starting point for a study of religion? Might it be a priest's, a pastor's, a theologian's, or a parishioner's or a scientist's or a sociologist's? Is the perspective within common life an adequate perch from which to understand religious belief? Can it treat religion without smuggling into that treatment controversial assumptions? Is the treatment of religion from a strictly human point of view, if this is what Hume's perspective implies, adequate? This chapter and the next deal with these questions.

These questions push the philosophy of common life on what counts as a perception grounded in common sense and how to distinguish common sense from a flight of fancy.[1] Hume develops criterion for this, as we have seen. Causation and continued existence are "permanent, irresistable, and universal." Concepts that "are the foundation of all our thoughts and actions, so that upon their removal human nature must immediately perish and go to ruin" are assimilated into the philosophy of common life (T 225). In contrast, constructs of philosophy such as the selfish system of morals and social contract theory (E 471) fall outside daily life and experience and are "neither unavoidable to mankind, nor necessary, or so much as useful in the conduct of life." False principles—those that cannot be reliably assimilated into a philosophy of common life—are "changeable, weak, and irregular" (T 225).

A philosophy of common life would seem friendlier to religion than the early modern philosophic method, which endorsed variations on the resolutive-compositive method, whereby scientists wipe the slate clean with doubt and then build knowledge from the ground up. Traditional, revealed religion does not withstand the "resolutive" radical doubts and rational re-composition of the world. Understanding the limits of reason, Hume's philosophy of common life assimilates belief and faith as inescapable elements of the human encounter with the world. Much like people of faith, Hume does not expect rational explanations for all phenomena, especially on important philosophic concepts such as causation and continued existence. As Hume understands it, belief, or what may resemble it, supposing, begins where the quest for knowledge is fruitless, where human beings cannot have proof of truth or falsity. Where we know that our judgment and our concepts do not have a philosophically explicable foundation, we must rest with faith in our judgment or in the reality of the concepts.

A philosophy of common life is not antithetical to religious conviction in principle, but this is not the end of the story for Hume. This chapter examines Hume's treatment of religion in light of the criteria by which he distinguishes reliable deliverances of common sense from flights of fancy. History shows that religious belief appears to be more "permanent, irresistable, and universal" than the modern constructs of philosophy, in that it is more ubiquitous and sown into human practice in most communities. Given the great variety of faiths, religious belief also appears "changeable, weak, and irregular," which suggests that any particular religion at least is not reliable enough to be assimilated into the philosophy of common life. Particular dogmas do not appear to be part of common life; the existence of dogma and what that existence tells us about human beings may be part of common life. Scholars indeed dispute how far or deep Hume's philosophy of common life or any philosophy of common life could assimilate pro-religious sentiments. Hume's rejection of religious common life suppositions is, in my view, radical and it violates the agnosticism necessary for a philosophy of common life. Religious conviction, for Hume, is a civilizational psychological disorder that might be radically cured by enlightenment.

Much is at stake in this investigation of religion and the philosophy of common life. No investigator can submit to *unfounded* dogmas of common life for fear that scientists would be duped by every delusion of the subject under investigation. Scientists also cannot dismiss a subject's self-understanding without adequate evidence. This is the inescapable tension in Hume's account of judgment and, I submit, in all accounts of judgment. Conclusions within the philosophy of common life are based on "common sense" deliverances assimilated into that philosophy. To the extent that deliverances are controversial, questionable, or partisan, while appearing to be the result of solid reasoning and research, conclusions may secretly be controversial, questionable or partisan. If the conceptual framework derived from common life is parochial, scientific objectivity is compromised.

There is, for Hume, a deep need for a confrontation with religion because religious claims "seize on the mind more strongly" than philosophic claims and affect the "conduct of our lives and actions" to a greater extent than philosophic claims; "errors in religion" are, after all, "dangerous" (T 271–2). Theological claims aligned with philosophy in medieval scholasticism, making philosophy the handmaiden to what Hume deems superstitious absurdities (E 62–3; NHR 54). Candid surveys of human history reveal that religious sects have disturbed public peace and undermined institutions of humanity more often than philosophic factions. A philosophy of common life is treading on dangerous ground as it concerns itself with religious belief, but Hume holds out hope that his philosophy can treat religion and benefit humanity.

That Hume occupied himself with religion and theology cannot be gainsaid. Not only did he write *The Natural History of Religion* and the posthumously published *Dialogues Concerning Natural Religion*, but his first *Enquiry* also treats religious topics from "Of a Particular Providence and of a Future State" (Section XI), to "Of Miracles" (Section X), to the nature of Divine will (Sections VII and VIII). Nearly every observation Hume makes in dismantling the edifice of philosophic dogma is fraught with implications for religious belief. *The History of England* also shows that religious conviction is a powerful force in human affairs. The titles of Hume's books on religion indicate (somewhat misleadingly) that he is concerned with *natural* religion, religion either as it reveals itself unassisted through nature or as it arises from natural passions incident to common life. Approaching religion within common life allows Hume to expose *philosophic* pretensions smuggled into theological arguments, and this situates Hume to clear pretentious underbrush from George Berkeley's theological apologetics. It also allows Hume to intervene on behalf of the natural, humane morality of common life against the distorting influence of religious authorities.

Berkeley's Philosophic Apologetics

Apologetics—the task of proving or refuting the existence of God, debating His attributes and nature, explaining how people relate to Providence—has fallen in disrepute because modern people have insuperable doubts about our capacity to think about high things like "natural law" or "moral truth" or "the great scheme of things." Skepticism about reason's ability to canvas such deep truths is not confined to the twentieth century. For millennia Christian apologists have shown, to varying degrees, how awareness of human limits is consistent with Christian faith. Any competent treatment of the relationship between skepticism and revelation must acknowledge that skepticism shapes theological arguments in important ways, but skepticism as such does not rule out the possibility of Christian apologetics. The particular brand of skeptical Christian apologetics that Hume concerns himself with is found in the writings of George Berkeley. Berkeley discovered many of the skeptical observations that later found their way into Hume's thought. Berkeley, however, put those observations to a different use than Hume. While I will qualify and clarify the difference, the general difference between Berkeley and Hume is this: Berkeley makes skeptical arguments to lead human beings into the arms of God, whereas Hume's debunking of philosophic pretensions is designed to lay bare our ignorance about the most important things, including God. God's constant, active, willful intervention in human affairs, according to Berkeley, reconciled the mysteries and contradictions observed by skeptical philosophers. Observations about human ignorance found in St. Augustine and Blaise Pascal suffice to show that skeptical, Christian observations are not unique to Berkeley. Ignoring these more prominent representatives of the Christian tradition, Hume seems to have considered Berkeley to be *the* example of how skeptical philosophic observations meld with Christian theology.

The turn that Berkeley gives to his skepticism is seen in his *Principles of Human Knowledge*. Berkeley's skepticism begins by noticing that the distinction between primary and secondary qualities leads to the annihilation of all matter (PHK 1.8–9). With no material substratum or primary qualities underneath the secondary qualities that we perceive, Berkeley concludes that material things are really immaterial ideas supported only by spirit or mind (PHK 1.26).[2] Ideas about the world are conveyed to people by the willful intervention of God to our minds. People may be able to move their own limbs, but "that such a motion should be attended by, or excite any idea in the mind of another, depends wholly on the will of the Creator. He alone it is who...maintains that intercourse of spirits, whereby they are able to perceive the existence of each other" (PHK 1.147). These ideas, Berkeley understands, offend common sense (PHK 1.4), in that most people think they perceive beings from nature or think their actions proceed from their free will. Other suppositions about how perception or motion works would seem to be available, to say the least.

Berkeley answers objections through an appeal to the philosophy of common life: "Nothing can be more evident to anyone that is capable of the least reflection than the existence of God, or a spirit who is intimately present to our minds, producing in them all that variety of ideas or sensations which continually affect us, on whom we have absolute and entire dependence" (PHK 1.49). Prefiguring Hume, in a sense, Berkeley contends that ideas produced by "the Author of Nature" about the real existence of external objects are "more strong, lively, and distinct than those of the [human] imagination," which are "less regular, vivid, and constant" (PHK 1.33, 30; cf. EHU 49). God's constantly intervening will fills the explanatory vacuum that Berkeley's modern skeptical principles exposes. Berkeley attacks modern skepticism from the left (toward greater skepticism) to turn modern people to the right (toward orthodoxy or at least toward belief).[3]

What is the nature of this divinity Berkeley sees reconciling human beings to this contradiction? God is the "immediate efficient cause of all things" (PHK 1.53). Every perception of the world is akin to a miracle whereby a "superior agent" intervenes as a "*free spirit*." God's will assures the constancy, steadiness, and order in nature. God "produces every effect by a *fiat*, or an act of his will" (PHK 1.57, 60). Perception would not happen without God's active intervention causing it. For Berkeley, God's will explains mysterious phenomena and the order apparent in nature, while God can also intervene miraculously in nature and human affairs. A God defined by His will can order nature with "harmony and contrivance" but can also effect "such exceptions from the general rules of nature" that can "surprise and awe men into an acknowledgement of the Divine Being" (PHK 1.63). "Extraordinary" earthquakes, gravitational pull, the rain falling, and the inexplicable concepts of common life are all equally miraculous. All movement, all perception, all that is, strictly speaking, in fact, is miraculous: God is will, on this reading.[4]

Not resting with ignorance of cause, religious philosophers such as Berkeley, in Hume's words, "think themselves obliged by reason to have recourse on all occasions, to the same principle, which the vulgar never appeal to but in cases that appear miraculous and supernatural." Religious philosophers hold a conception of God, wherein the "Supreme Being" wills all events and lends motion to all objects. God's intervention in nature explains how that which is inexplicable to "good reasoners"—things such as causation, personal identity, and perception—occur. Hume provides three examples of how this argument looks; each of Hume's accounts relates to one of the mysterious features of common life that Hume treats in detail. Instead of arguing that one billiard ball moves another by force, religious philosophers argue that the "Deity himself...by a particular volition, moves the second ball." Instead of resting with an understanding of personal identity that leaves the diversity and unity of body and soul inexplicable and mysterious, religious philosophers hold that God is the "immediate cause of the union between soul and body." Instead of accepting our ignorance and holding that the conflict between reason and imagination seen in the deconstruction of our perceptive faculties is a cause for moderation, religious philosophers think "our mental vision or conception of ideas is nothing but a revelation made to us by our Maker."[5] Such religious philosophers extend the principle of divine sovereignty to its logical conclusion in every sphere of life, arguing that "nothing exists but by his will" (EHU 69–71)[6] and nothing limits his will.

Berkeley's argument goes beyond the evidence for theism that Hume presents in other contexts. Theists infer the existence of an all-powerful creative God from the wondrous order, complexity, subtlety, and vastness of the universe, so that God's will seems to coexist with his rationality and goodness. God fixed general laws in the beginning and does not disturb the operation of those laws with acts of particular providence. This framework, while it is not the foundation for religious belief among the vulgar, seems to arise from thoughts in common life. It gives precedence to God's reasonableness over His willfulness; His rationality limits His omnipotence. Berkeley's emphasis on the continuing particular willful intervention in human affairs posits God as the principal agent of reconciliation for the contradictions that skeptical philosophy discovers. Giving precedence to omnipotent willfulness, Berkeley's God is more inscrutable than a theistic conception and leads to a more inscrutable universe.

For Hume, Berkeley's argument is philosophically presumptuous. Berkeley's conception of God, Hume argues, carries us "quite beyond the reach of our faculties, when it leads to conclusions so extraordinary, and so remote from common life and experience." Berkeley's "very unexpected circuit" takes us into a "fairy land" of unusual analogies and unjustifiable assumptions (EHU 72, 153). As in the case of modern philosophers, Berkeley's argument betrays embarrassing assumptions, though Hume does not dwell on them. The central embarrassing assumption, it seems, is this: Berkley presumes that because human beings passively receive ideas, something (a divine will or mind) must bring those ideas to the mind. This assertion must be supported by more argument, though Berkeley's argument precludes such an argument because he denies that we can know that which exceeds our ideas.[7] In contrast, Hume understands the limits of human understanding: "We are ignorant...of the manner in which bodies operate on each other: Their force or energy is entirely incomprehensible: But are we not equally ignorant of the manner or force by which a mind, even a supreme mind, operates either on itself or on body?" We live in a "profound ignorance" as to whether motion arises "from impulse" without divine will or from elsewhere (EHU 72, 73). Berkeley's explanation is no explanation at all, but rather kicks back the question another level.

Berkeley's presumptuousness poses problems for his theory from a theological perspective too. It appears to make God responsible for everything that occurs in the world, which would turn God into "the author of sin and moral turpitude" (EHU 103). Hume argues that a strict application of Berkeley's initial insight raises the fundamental problem of explaining how evil and suffering entered into the world in its most stark form. If God is God, Hume contends, he is not good. Hume draws a lesson about the limits of human understanding from this theological problem, after showing how unattractive and inhumane this view of God is.

> To reconcile the indifference and contingency of human actions with prescience; or to defend absolute decrees, and yet free the Deity from being the author of sin, has been found hitherto to exceed all the power of philosophy. Happy, if she be thence sensible of her temerity, when she pries into these sublime mysteries; and leaving a scene so full of obscurities and perplexities, return, with suitable modesty, to her true and proper province, the examination of common life; where she will find difficulties enough to employ her enquiries, without launching into so boundless an ocean of doubt, uncertainty, and contradiction! (EHU 103)

Human beings may insist on asking the question "Why me?" or "Why?" when they suffer. When such questions are pushed beyond daily experience, that question must be abandoned as unanswerable by human reason.

In this confrontation with Berkeley's argument, there is a model for how a philosopher of common life can confront theological claims. Insofar as theological claims rest on inferences of reason, other thinkers can probe the philosophical validity of those inferences. Philosophers expose unsupported assumptions, showing that they are not as obvious, reasonable or compelling as their adherents claim them to be. Neither philosophic dogmas nor Berkeley's particular theological pretension "carry conviction" (EHU 72) in such a way as to affect human action or belief. Deconstructing Berkeley is harmless, from a political point of view, because Berkeley's rational defense of God is far-fetched, sterile, and unbelievable. Few laymen bother reading Berkeley for his defense of God's existence, and it is not surprising that his peculiar defense of God's existence has few, if any, followers today. The debate between Hume and Berkeley on this matter is an abstruse academic question far from concerns arising from common life that nearly nothing depends on it. Such is not always the case with philosophic or political doctrines, as we have seen. Theological claims are also not always as academic as in this case. As Hume discovered, attempts to expose difficult theological doctrines such as the immortality of the soul, miracles, and suicide are more difficult, controversial, and dangerous. Attacking Berkeley's miraculous, willful God is one thing, but taking on *sine qua non* of Christian faith is another.

Religious Dogmas, Revelation, and Common Life

Berkeley sought to provide definitive natural (i.e., non-revealed) proof of God's existence. Hume's devastating critique of Berkeley need not lead to a total dismissal of the religious perspective: it leaves open religious belief on the basis of revelation and in the form of natural theology. Revealed truth, for instance, is of a different character and order than natural knowledge, and revelation is not, on its own terms, subject to the same criterion of evaluation as rational argument. It is revealed truth, which cannot be ascertained without the active agency of God in history. It is supernatural in origin, whereas Hume's philosophy of common life confines itself to what arises in "daily life and experience." Hume differentiates the natural from the supernatural in the *Treatise*. "If *nature* be oppos'd to miracles," Hume writes, "every event, which has ever happen'd in the world," is natural (T 474). In this section, I show that natural theology, for Hume, depends on revelation.

Hume is a proponent of faith, understood as a belief in things unseen. He believes in, but cannot rationally demonstrate the mode of, causation, continued existence, the coherence of matter, and the reality of moral distinctions. Faith in these concepts has no obvious effect on religious faith because it is removed from specifically religious doctrines or dogmas. Hume considers the reasonableness of unseen, specifically religious doctrines such as the existence of an immaterial and immortal soul, the argument from design,[8] and direct, divine interventions into nature and human affairs. As a philosopher of common life who believes in things unseen, Hume cannot dismiss unseen doctrines out of hand. Many elements of religious faith are sanctioned in common life more than Berkeley's proof of God's existence. Ancient thinkers, for instance, presumed that human beings have souls and nearly all religions and even many people today agree with the ancients. God seems rarely to reveal Himself to people, but many in history have thought that it is reasonable to think that God reveals Himself to people through His creation and that God can intervene in human affairs. How can Hume differentiate between that which is a reasonable presumption of common life and that which is not?

Consider the soul, which Hume treats while discussing personal identity in the *Treatise*. As we saw in chapter 3, previous philosophers assert that our diverse impulses are "in effect the same, however interrupted and variable." They rationalize "some new and unintelligible principle that connects the object together, and prevents their interruption." "The notion of a *soul*" is such a construct (T 254). The idea of the soul pleases our imagination, which wants to transcend the ephemeral, empirical and particular, but it offends reason, which shows us that impressions are interrupted, fleeting, and variable. Such an analysis might have led him to posit that the soul is a permanent, universal, *but inexplicable* feature of human nature.[9] Hume also doubts reasoning that purports to explain the "*local conjunction*" of soul and matter or that tries to establish the existence of an immaterial soul (T 232–51; E 590–7). Ideas of immaterial souls melding with matter are incomprehensible in part because we do not understand what matter is and in part because we do not know what an immaterial thing could be. Our ignorance on these matters leads Hume to "condemn even the question itself."[10] Yet he need not dismiss the notion of an immaterial soul—he could treat the notion of a soul as unconfirmed and unconfirmable data from common life and assimilate it into his common life philosophy.[11]

Why is the idea of an immaterial (and immortal)[12] soul different from an idea of causation or continued existence? Hume makes two moves that show that he does not think idea of a soul is a reliable concept of common life. First, he presents the moral and political implications of a belief in the soul and argues that such a belief can be avoided and is harmful to the conduct of life. Human beings can limit the scope of their concerns to "the present life" which has obvious "steddiness and efficacy," while concern for one's soul is "so floating an idea, and the most doubtful persuasion of any matter of fact, that occurs in common life." Man's "whole time, his whole capacity, activity, courage, passion, find sufficient employment, in fencing against the miseries of his present condition." In a passage to which I will return, the idea that we have immaterial, immortal souls "would quickly vanish, were they not artificially fostered by precept and education" (E 592, 593). For Hume, the idea of a soul is not universal, permanent or irresistible and human nature would not perish were human beings to abandon it (using criteria from T 225). Hume greets the waning of religious conviction as a boon to philosophy and moral practice.[13] Belief in soul perverts our moral judgments and must be a curse from an evil, unjust god (E 594–5). Otherworldly or theological virtues point away from the virtues of humanity that could govern our sensible, common life together. This is Hume's second move. Unlike causation, ultimately our knowledge of an immaterial soul within us depends on a "new interposition of the supreme cause" [i.e., on revelation] (E 592; also 597–8).

Hume follows the same method in his deconstruction of the argument from design. Though Hume sometimes seems to endorse the argument from design as a reasonable inference from the order in nature,[14] he also shows that there are insuperable difficulties in this reasoning. He doubts "whether it is possible for a cause to be known only by its effect" and whether we can assign a cause to an effect "of so singular and particular a nature as to have no parallel and no similarity with any other cause or object." Creation, Hume elliptically observes, is such a miraculous event

(EHU 148).¹⁵ The way Hume shows that the soul and the argument from design are contrary to common life raises the stakes for Hume's treatment of miracles, since, in the end, both ideas rest, for Hume, on particular revelation.

One of Hume's most controversial and perplexing essays, "Of Miracles,"¹⁶ concerns the status of revealed knowledge. Does common life sanction belief in miracles or a view of the universe consistent with miracles?¹⁷ The vulgar seem to suppose that miracles happen, that the normal rules of natural necessity can be suspended through acts of particular providence. That the views are vulgar need not trouble Hume: he often assimilates vulgar views into his philosophy of common life. In this case, Hume, seeing contradictions between what the vulgar (sometimes) claim to believe about the divine and the basis of their own actions, which presumes a regularity in nature, resolves this case against the vulgar view. In fact, the natural supposition is that there are hidden *natural* causes behind everything that happens.

> Even when these contrary experiments are entirely equal, we remove not the notion of causes and necessity; but *supposing* that the usual contrariety proceeds from the operation of contrary and conceal'd causes, we conclude, that the chance or indifference lies only in our judgment on account of our imperfect knowledge, not in the things themselves, which are in every case equally necessary, tho' to appearance not equally constant or certain. (T 403–4; emphasis supplied)

Hume repeats the same sentiment in the first *Enquiry*. "There is contained a vast variety of springs and principles, which are hid, by reason of their minuteness or remoteness." People believe that it "is at least possible the contrariety of events may not proceed from any contingency in the cause, but from the secret operation of contrary causes." This mere "possibility is converted into certainty by farther observation." (This is one of the rare occasions where Hume invokes a standard of certainty in natural philosophy.) We may not be able to make the operation of natural necessity intelligible in that we cannot explain how causes cause effects, but the existence of natural necessity is a certain, natural supposition for Hume. Natural necessity constitutes for philosophers "a maxim that the connexion between all causes and effects is equally necessary."¹⁸ It resolves the vulgar's indeterminacy between miracles and necessity in favor of necessity without seeming to take a stand on how nature works. Belief in natural necessity is, for the most part, "permanent, irresistable, and universal" and constitutes "the foundation of all our thoughts and actions, and so that upon [its] removal human nature must immediately perish and go to ruin" (T 225). This conception seems to compromise human freedom as such and may, in the end, clash with Hume's vision of history (which entertains the import of accident)[19]; it also rules out miracles.

I use Hume's examples to illustrate the assumption of natural necessity. Suppose there is universal agreement that the earth went dark during the first eight days of 1600. This would be "extraordinary," for Hume, but not miraculous. We learn "by so many analogies" about "the decay, corruption, and dissolution of nature" and we "ought to search for the causes whence it might be derived." Such an "extraordinary" occurrence could be explained by profound investigations into nature. This "extraordinary" example contrasts to the "miraculous" example of Queen Elizabeth returning to rule England after being dead for a month. Even if this event were as well attested to as any in history, Hume would "not have the least inclination to believe so miraculous event" (EHU 127–8). Such an event—suggestive of Christ's Resurrection, the central miracle of Christian revelation—cannot be explained by natural phenomenon. Consider also Hume's skeptical treatment of Joan of Arc in *The History of England*, where he distinguishes between "the *miraculous* and the *marvelous*": the "business of history" is "to reject the first in all narrations merely profane and human; to doubt the second" (H.II, 398).[20] The task of the historian is to "reject" supernatural explanations of things, some of which, like the episode surrounding Joan of Arc, concern miraculous events.

Probing Hume's examples of Joan of Arc and a resurrection brings to light a second element of Hume's common life treatment of religion, for the strictly philosophic assertion of natural necessity hardly suffices since it presumes an answer to the issue at stake. According to Hume, miracles are for most people "the sole arguments" for believing in the existence of God (NHR 41) and in the doctrines of any particular church. Christianity, for instance, is nothing without the assumption that God enters into human history.[21] Historical religions such as Judaism, Christianity and Islam appeal to miraculous events as verification for their truth foundations and for bringing the truth about God to the people. These religions qualify belief in natural necessity with belief that a creating or loving God could create a world in which He could or must intervene. Belief in miracles sits at the foundation of the greatest world religions and these religions are, if not universal in practice, universal in aspiration and very widely believed. If natural necessity is the truth about nature, what explains the persistent, widely held belief in miracles?

This is where Hume's philosophy of common life provides a psychology of religion that grounds an alternative explanation for where the belief in miracles comes from. Hume often takes the existence of something in common life to be a tip-off to the way things really are; he often seeks the wisdom in common opinion as he corrects common opinion. Credulous observers swallow opinions from religious leaders who claim to have had special insights in order to gain a flock and achieve a this worldly glory and power. The philosopher of common life, in this instance, locates the passions, aspirations, and interests that prompt people to believe in miracles. Instead of putting God in the dock as he did when treating natural necessity and miracles, Hume puts those who claim to witness miracles on trial to show that their testimony cannot be trusted (EHU 127). The critical methodology that Hume suggests to future historians is this: Weigh the probability that a miracle happened (upsetting the experience of mankind and established laws of nature) against the probability that the person who observes the miracle is a liar, mistake-prone, ambitious, tyrannical or deluded and those who trust the person who claims access to God's will are credulous, desperate, fearful, or needy (EHU 115–6).[22]

This manner of solving the philosophic problem of miracles uses what is observable (individual psychology) to inform our judgments about what is not nearly as observable (divine interventions in nature). Hume concludes that religious believers and fanatical priests and prophets manifest a deluded codependent psychology. Ambitious, greedy, duplicitous, and self-aggrandizing human beings want to see themselves as vehicles for God's intervention in the world. They find others wanting to believe such delusions. Human beings have a "passion of *surprise* and *wonder*, arising from miracles," even if they are only experienced vicariously (EHU 117). Hume's treatment of Joan of Arc's visions is again illustrative. With the French throne in peril, Joan "mistook impulses of passion for heavenly inspirations." As she challenged the English, Hume dismisses all prospects of her having a "divine mission" and contends that "the wiser commanders prompted her in all her measures" and used her divine pretensions to impress the credulous vulgar, whom she "captivate[d]" with her "undoubted and supernatural" pronouncements (H.II, 398–407).[23]

Resolving the issue of miracles depends on Hume's psychology of religion or, more precisely, Hume's views about what the presence of widespread religious belief suggests about human nature. Hume provides a systematic treatment of how religious belief establishes itself in human nature in his *Natural History of Religion*. This treatment is crucial for understanding Hume's disposition toward religion and thus for evaluating his philosophy of common life.

Miracles, Common Life, and the Psychology of Religion

I elaborate Hume's psychology of religion to complete this discussion of miracles and to locate the assumptions assimilated into his philosophy of common life. I am treating a philosophic dilemma: What can unassisted reason reveal about religion or about the place of religion in human nature? To what extent can reason testify to the ultimate validity, nature, and sources of religious belief? These questions take us to the limits of Hume's philosophy of common life and to the limits of human reason as such. The previous section introduced Hume's account of acute psychological codependence that tempts the ambitious and credulous alike to believe in miracles. This section investigates the extent to which Hume's account of the codependence is a presupposition assimilated into his philosophy of common life or is the strict result of historical investigation and experience. At stake is the very possibility of there being a philosophic treatment of religion, agnostic on thorny philosophic issues, within Hume's philosophy of common life and within philosophies of common life as such.

Religious belief is nearly universal, according to Hume, but no single specific religious belief gains adherence from all. Religious preconceptions spring "not from an original instinct or primary impression of nature, such as gives rise to self-love... since every instinct of this kind has been found absolutely universal in all nations and ages" (NHR 21). Religious belief differs from reliable beliefs in causation and continued existence, which deliver roughly the same idea (so to speak) to everyone. Religious "principles must be secondary," Hume continues, since they "may easily be perverted by various accidents and causes" and their operation "may, by an extraordinary concurrences of circumstances, be altogether prevented" (ibid.). As a further sign of how tenuous religion's hold on the mind is, recall developments in *The History*. When religious authority was removed, English Christians were forced to make up their own minds about the meaning of Christian doctrines. Once people are free to judge for themselves, almost no religious consensus can be established because religious belief is so far removed from common life (H III.355).

People must have the same desires, hopes, and fears and they must be willing to listen to the same religious stories or the same religious authorities in order for a religious consensus to be established. The nature of religious beliefs, and perhaps the existence of religious beliefs, is determined by first-level psychological traits or "original instincts" shared by all human beings. Hume's philosophy or sociology of religion involves demarcating bridges between original psychological characteristics and religious beliefs. We must revisit some of the issues canvassed in chapter 5. The "first ideas of religion arose...from a concern with regard to the events of life, and from the incessant hopes and fears, which actuate the human mind." Blind to "the true springs and causes of every event," powerless in the face of manifest ills, and hanging between "life and death, health and sickness, and plenty and want," we impute power to *"unknown causes"* that become "the constant object of our hope and fear; and while the passions are kept in perpetual alarm by an anxious expectation of the events, the imagination is equally employed in forming ideas of those powers, on which we have so entire a dependance" (NHR 27–9).[24] Like Hobbes, Hume believes that religious passions are expressions of fundamental fears, human ignorance, desperation, psychological disorder, and powerlessness. Insofar as a "man's course of life is governed by accident," Hume expects that we "always find, that he encreases in superstition" (30).[25]

In response to these passions, barbarians tend to embrace superstitious stories in which different gods control different parts of nature and human beings are their playthings (NHR 30, 34). Polytheist stories are so unbelievable that they sit "easy and light" on barbaric minds and make no "deep impression on the affections and understanding" (65). Relatively tolerant, if not scientifically fruitful, polytheist belief dissolves because of natural tendencies in human psychology are exacerbated by priestly schemes. Priests lead people from polytheism to theism by exaggerating the powers of limited deities until those powers reach "infinity itself" (43). Belief in one intelligent, invisible power giving life to the entire universe seems to be a reasonable inference from the order and beauty we observe in nature (26, 42, and 53). Were early human beings capable of resting with or even understanding the theistic inference they might have lived together in peace. However, "since the vulgar, in nations, which have embraced the doctrine of theism, still build it upon irrational and superstitious principles, they are never led into that opinion by any process of argument, but by a certain train of thinking, more suitable to their genius and capacity" (42). Theistic superstition is built on a belief in particular providence, a belief that God intervenes in nature and human affairs, a belief in miracles (41). Here the distorting psychological codependence between the vulgar and the priest or prophet—and the profound inequality characteristic of pre-modern times—comes to the fore. Great disorders impress upon ignorant people "the strongest sentiments of religion" and those vulgar sorts obey those who seem to be impressed with the stamp of God's approval (NHR 42). Misery, dread, and melancholy throw people to their knees and into the arms of scheming clergy because human beings are ignorant of how the natural world operates. The seemingly natural fear of death adds urgency to devotion (E 580, 588) as human beings attempt to comfort themselves with stories of the afterlife. That these have been almost universally felt passions in human history is the result of the ignorance and poverty experienced by most human beings (NHR 75).

Human beings are haunted with terror and anxiety about their suffering, misery, and mortality,[26] and scheming zealots exploit these infirmities (NHR 73).[27] Allaying these fears requires, Hume's priests teach, direct and "immediate service of the supreme Being." Such services bear as little relationship to the ordinary duties of life as possible because no one wants to risk mixing selfish motives with "more purely religious" motives. Fasting or subjecting oneself to a "sound whipping" have been revealed by zealots as having "direct reference... to the service of God" precisely because they are of no use in common life. Strict regimens suggest to the devout a superiority over infidels and allow all devout to participate in priestly superiority (NHR 70–1). An unbeliever's refusal to join in a religious cause is an indication of almost subhuman viciousness, an affront the presumed superiority of the orthodox. What results is a drive for orthodoxy, which, according to Hume, is the "origin of all religious wars and divisions" (E 61; also 60). Devotion, persecution, fighting faiths, and the propagation of monkish virtues follow from this aspiration to orthodoxy fostered by priestly ambition. As Hume asks in summarizing "Of Miracles," "What greater temptation than to appear a missionary, a prophet, an ambassador from heaven?... Or if, by the help of vanity and a heated imagination, a man has first made a convert of himself, and entered seriously into the delusion; who ever scruples to make use of pious frauds, in support of so holy and meritorious a cause?" In such cases "the smallest spark" kindles "into the greatest flame; because the materials are always prepared for it" (EHU 125–6).

Miracles are, in fact, a tip-off to reality for Hume—a reality of delusion and ubiquitous human unscrupulousness. Given these difficulties, probabilistic reasoning, for Hume, suggests that it would be irrational ever to believe in miracles. He believes he has delivered a proof against miracles "as entire as any argument from experience can possibly be imagined" (EHU 114). His analysis "with regard to all popular religions, amounts to an entire annihilation; and therefore we may establish it as a maxim, that no human testimony can have such force as to prove a miracle, and make it a just foundation for any such system of religion" (EHU 127).[28]

Many commentators have criticized Hume's circular reasoning in the argument from natural necessity. He addresses the question of whether miracles could ever occur by asking if nature is governed by natural necessity. This is not philosophically adequate because, as C. S. Lewis argues, Hume "gets the answer to one form of the question by assuming the answer to another form of the same question."[29] Not only is Hume's "that" proposition controversial in this case, it also involves violating agnosticism on a "how" question. As important for the purpose of exploring the limits of Hume's philosophy of common life is the circular reasoning involved in his account of the psychology of religion and the probabilistic reasoning that leads to the dismissal of miracles. Hume's characterization of religionists as credulous, weak and deluded *rests on* the assumption that miracles never happen; only if belief in miracles is always unreasonable can the religious life always be defined by ignorance and psychological exploitation. At the same time, Hume's argument against miracles *rests on* the contention that religionists are credulous, deluded and fanatical. The glow from the oft-observed circularity in Hume's argument from necessity prevents many from seeing this deeper circularity. Hume's psychology of religion is open to no other possibility than that that religionists are weak-minded (T 225), deluded, credulous, and power-hungry. His hope to encourage active rejection of miracles goes beyond the sophisticated, philosophic agnosticism or mitigated skepticism that is a defensible implication of a philosophy grounded in common life. Hume's goals in the essay are more political and rhetorical in checking "all kinds of superstitious delusion" (EHU 110) than they are philosophical.

This speaks to what I take to be a pre-philosophic commitment smuggled into Hume's philosophy of common life. The priority Hume gives to "original instincts" such as fear for the future and powerlessness over "secondary" religious beliefs—the assumption that "original instincts" cause and shape religious belief—is a controversial premise. It cannot be proved by reason and it assumes answers to the questions at stake. All sides grant that people are fearful and restless. The philosophic question conjured by this reality concerns the causes of this fear and restlessness. Christian philosophers such as Pascal argue that the fear and restlessness are caused by estrangement from God or by living in a fallen world. Tocqueville, adopting a Pascalian view, argues that religion relies on the "sentiments, instincts, and passions that one sees reproduced in the same manner in all periods of history." These "sentiments, instincts, and passions" are "a natural disgust for existence and an immense desire to exist", human beings "scorn[] life and fear[] nothingness."[30] This description of human nature gives causal priority (or is open to giving causal priority) to a religious disposition over merely human passions. These conceptions of where religious belief comes from are as reasonable as Hume's—and friendlier to religious belief as well. The selection criteria for distinguishing reliable presuppositions of common life from flights of fancy does not allow for a selection between Hume's conception and Tocqueville's, though there may be ways of working this out in practice perhaps.

Hume assumes that fear and restlessness are caused by material paucity, scientific ignorance, and the political instability characteristic of pre-modern times. In fact, Hume adopts the Enlightened trajectory, if not the form, seen in modern state of nature theorists such as Hobbes and Locke, who predict that the dark violence and ignorance characteristic of the pre-civil state of nature will be succeeded by a more civil, enlightened, secular future once effective institutions are established. "In proportion as any man's course of life is governed by accident, we always find, that he encreases in superstition." Superstition and narrow-minded patriotism rule only "before the institution of order and good government" (NHR 30).[31] Reversing the Christian view, the Enlightenment view explains religious psychology in light of merely human passions and human ignorance. Christianity differs from Hume's analysis on what it means to be a human being, or how human nature is structured, or what the observable passions in human nature reveal about human nature. Hume differs from other philosophers on this matter as well. These are not questions that can be by-passed when dealing with the psychology of religion or with the philosophy of religion.

Hume's abject failure (to use John Earman's phrase) in treating miracles, his secretly controversial assumptions about the priority of human over religious passions, and his secretly controversial way of treating history raise fundamental questions: Can reason unassisted treat questions about what human nature means or what history reveals without presuming answers to controversial questions? Is dogmatism necessarily a feature of philosophies of common life as such? Is a nonfoundational philosophy of common life possible?[32]

Questions about Hume and the Enlightenment

Much is at stake in how we resolve these problems. Cognizant of their inability to refute religion directly and philosophically, Locke, Hobbes, Descartes and other Enlightenment thinkers hoped reason guided by science could illuminate clear and distinct ideas, the fundamentals of precise knowledge. From these fundamentals, they hoped to reconstruct human experience such that no irrational opinions (i.e., revealed religious beliefs) would survive. The modern "refutation" of religious orthodoxy requires, as one commentator suggests, "the success of a system. Man had to establish himself theoretically and practically as master of the world and master of his life." Modern thinkers sought to refute the Christian tradition indirectly by showing that the world was perfectly intelligible without the assumptions of orthodoxy.[33] This Enlightenment optimism has, for the most part, collapsed in the face of Rousseau's questions about the desirability of civilization, Nietzsche's questions about the possibility of civilization, and Hume's questions about the possibility of such a precise, systematic science. Investigating human faculties, Hume shows that our contradictory and limited faculties prevent us from grasping fundamentals (see chapter 3) and rationally re-constructing the world (see chapter 5).

What is the status of religious orthodoxy in Hume's thought given his apparent opposition to Enlightenment hopefulness? Does Hume provide a tenable, philosophic method of treating religious orthodoxy distinct from Enlightenment orthodoxy? Early returns on Hume's philosophy of common life canvassed in this chapter—his secretly controversial assumptions about miracles and circular argument about religious psychology—are not encouraging about *Hume's* philosophy of common life as it treats religion. Only Hume's dialogues—Section XI of the first *Enquiry* and *Dialogues Concerning Natural Religion*—reveal whether Hume's philosophy of common life is adequate because only in dialogues does he discuss arguments that make a third way—a way other than Enlightenment dogmatism and the embrace of an utterly inscrutable God—possible.

His life-long preoccupation with the philosophy of religion and his frequent treatment of religion in a dialectical framework suggests that we take seriously the possibility that he entertained questions about the assumptions of his own argument. As Pamphilius (the narrator of Hume's *Dialogues*) intimates, "any question of philosophy...which is so *obscure* and *uncertain* that human reason can reach no fixed determination with regard to it—if it should be treated at all—seems to lead us naturally into the style of dialogue and conversation" (D 1). Dialogues investigate controversial issues, encourage the exploration of alternative readings of phenomenon under investigation, expose hidden dogmatisms, and develop implications of plausible alternative interpretations without necessarily reaching firm conclusions. Socratic dialogues are famous (or infamous) for the philosophic *aporia* in which they leave readers. Dialogic exercises could explore what is "taken for granted" in a philosophy of common life. Perhaps Hume's own dialogues concerning religion explore alternative suppositions arising from common life about religious matters.

CHAPTER 9

HUMANITY AND THEOLOGY IN HUME'S
RELIGIOUS DIALOGUES

Hume's philosophy of common life is an attractive approach to achieving human knowledge and a plausible ground for the gentle, humane virtues. Oriented by our "mixed kind of life" and aware of the depths that lay beyond reason, philosophy submits to reasonable, universal, permanent, and irresistible presuppositions from common life. Awareness of human limits cultivates a spirit of modesty and humility in scientific inquirers and a spirit of gentle humanity in social relations. Emphasis on the non-rational, non-scientific elements of human nature distances Hume from his Enlightenment forbearers who vainly sought a scientific explanation for everything in an effort to disprove, overcome, or outflank Christian orthodoxy. The last chapter ended with questions about whether Hume is not in deeper agreement with Enlightenment thinkers on the issues of why human beings turn to God (the psychology of religion) and whether human beings inhabit a disenchanted world (where no miracles happen). These questions implicate Hume's philosophy of common life at its core by raising the unavoidable, embarrassing question of what counts as a deliverance of common life. Hume's philosophy of common life is not "nonfoundational" if it takes a (secretly dogmatic) position on controversial, "pre-rational" issues such as history, miracles, or the psychology of religion.

The persistence of "value-laden" assumptions in common life pushes Hume's philosophy of common life past its limits. In fact, Hume's thought forces us to confront the theological-political problem or the conflict between Edinburgh and Geneva. Does *Hume's* common life philosophy exacerbate, obscure, or helpfully frame the problem? Hume's problem is not an easily avoided, logical problem or necessarily reflective of a personal animus against religious belief. His writings imply a view on a core issue and all such views are ultimately (perhaps) contestable. If Hume's view is dogmatic, perhaps *Hume's* philosophy of common life could be improved upon with a more philosophic philosophy of common life.

Consider Hume's difficult and ambiguous position. Enlightenment thinkers such as Hobbes and Locke used two somewhat inconsistent weapons against religious orthodoxy: science and mockery. Hume rejected the extravagant hopes earlier thinkers had placed in science, but he still offered pseudo-psychological, pseudo-scientific, moral "criticisms" of religious faith as a means of moving beyond religion. Ignorance, poverty, and the original passions surrounding terror could be removed or given more natural outlets than they had heretofore, allowing for the emergence of a new humanity. This formulation seems extreme. Denying that "the cave" could be "Enlightened," how could the somewhat conservative, skeptical Hume align himself with the Enlightenment radicalism in denying that human beings need God?

To answer these questions I turn to Hume's two dialogues on religious matters (Section XI of the first *Enquiry* and *Dialogues*). These dialogues place arguments about God in an explicitly political, educational, and moral context. Discussing things religious in such a context seems to rehabilitate the ancient patrician view toward civil religion against the more or less ostentatious atheism gaining ground among modern thinkers. Alas, things are not so simple, because, against ancient patricians and consistent with modern enquirers, Hume questions the very political utility of religion and the durability of religious belief. Hume's arguments about the nature of Divine Being are situated within a broader political horizon between the ancient patrician view that the city needs God or gods and the modern view that man does not need God or gods. In fact, against those who emphasize religion as an essential feature of common life,[1] Hume, in my judgment, follows the Enlightened trajectory of previous thinkers further in the direction of a secular future than any had. Ultimately, that is, Hume's writings on religion culminate in questioning the utility of religion and in a critical analysis of the elements in human nature through which religion is born.

Religious Dialogue in the first *Enquiry*

Section XI comes down to us with the title "Of Particular Providence and of a Future State." Originally it was named "Of the Particular Consequences of Natural Religion."[2] The original title emphasized the analysis of revealed doctrines from the perspective of natural religion and how natural religion differs from revealed religion. Particular providence and a future state (a revealed doctrine implying life after death or the immortality of the soul) are fundamentals of the Christian religion in particular, fundamentals that assume there is more to life than meets the eye.[3] The new title is somewhat more offensive to Christian belief because it emphasizes the doctrines that go more to the core of Christian belief. None of the essay's substance was changed.[4]

In "Of Miracles" (EHU, Section X), Hume undermines confidence in historical religions such as Christianity because miraculous revelations are contrary to (Hume's) common sense philosophy and humane politics. Can the spirit of religion be doused too much though? Moralists worry that undermining religious belief risks undermining the foundations for public morality and civic peace. Unconcerned about whether religion is true or convinced that it is not, those adopting this perspective care about whether and, perhaps, how much and what kind of religion is necessary to sustain public morality. "Miracles" leads into "Particular Providence,"[5] which analyzes the relationships among religion, political health, and philosophy.[6] "Particular Providence" asks whether doctrines beyond daily life and experience support political morality and treats the problematic assumptions in arguments for theistic natural theology.

"Particular Providence" is the only dialogue in the first *Enquiry*. This dialogue is suggestive of Hume's *Dialogues* in several ways. I begin by considering Hume's discussion from the *Dialogues* about why and when a writer should write dialogues. According to Pamphilus, the narrator, dialogues are appropriate either when entertaining the reader while teaching obvious and important truths or treating questions of philosophy that are "so obscure and uncertain that human reason can reach no fixed determination with regard" to them (D 1–2).[7] Both questions of "Particular Providence" are in the second category—both the political usefulness of religion and God's very Being are shrouded in obscurity.

There is a crucial difference in the characters from Hume's dialogues on natural religion. In "Particular Providence," Hume and an anonymous friend (Hume's second mind, perhaps) discuss the issues, while several fictional characters, including an impressionable youth, a religious fanatic, and two philosophical personages, discuss matters in the *Dialogues*. The more intimate, sympathetic setting in "Particular Providence" allows for a greater degree of candor (akin to the "unreserved intimacy" between Philo and Cleanthes display in Section XII of the *Dialogues*). "Particular Providence" presents Hume's unnamed friend's apology for philosophy in front of a philosophical Athenian crowd and presents the range of acceptable opinion on the topics of religion's usefulness and natural theology. I do not present all the dialogue's action. Many of the puzzling themes developed in the *Dialogues* are prefigured in "Particular Providence," though the *Dialogues* is more perplexing and complicated still.

Let us turn to "Particular Providence." Hume begins the conversation by reflecting on the singular good fortune of philosophy to have begun in an age and country (Athens) where it was "never cramped" by "any creeds, confessions, or penal statutes" (132).[8] Hume cites Epicurus to prove his case and explains away the banishment of Protagoras and the death of Socrates as neither examples of his own age's "bigoted jealousy" against philosophy. This beginning has allowed philosophy to thrive even amid the "inclemency" of Hume's day.

Hume's friend responds with his own history of philosophy. Pre-Christian religious beliefs were founded on tradition[9] instead of "argument and disputation." After initial alarm over the questioning of traditional beliefs (i.e., Socrates and Protagoras), chastened philosophers lived in "harmony with the established superstition." Philosophers and political communities made a "fair partition" that allowed them to coexist. Philosophers would live in outward harmony with established religions and abide by the city's interests as long as they could be "learned and wise" in private. This bargain collapsed when philosophy was forced to align itself with superstition. The new alliance forced philosophers to accept creeds that limited the freedom of thought essential to philosophy because philosophy was called on to justify supra-rational religious claims about the nature of God.

Hume responds. Not quarrelling with this new reading of history, he worries that the friend's response "leaves politics entirely out of the question." His friend wrongly supposes that philosophy never corrupts politics. Hume illustrates this with the curious example of Epicurus, who denied the existence of "a providence and a future state." This denial seems "to loosen in a great measure, the ties of morality" and may be inimical "to the peace of civil society" (133–4). The friend had emphasized how superstition posed dangers to philosophy, and Hume emphasizes how philosophy may pose dangers to politics by posing dangers to religion. Hume mentioned Epicurus in his first speech as the example of an atheistic philosopher who lived a long life in "peace and tranquility" (132). Hume's second speech suggests that a "wise magistrate" might have "justly" (133) made Epicurus' life less peaceful.

This response about the politically dangerous effects of philosophy sets the dialogue in motion. The friend suggests that Epicurus could have "proved his [atheistic] principles of philosophy to be as salutary as those of his adversaries." Earlier philosophers need not have bargained with political communities because philosophic teachings are too abstruse to be dangerous. Hume challenges the friend to stand for Epicurus and make a speech to satisfy a "philosophical" Athenian audience. The friend promises to deliver a "harangue as will fill all the urn with white beans"

(134). He obtrusively (four times) protests that he will not "dispute concerning the origin and government of worlds," but will confine himself to the question of "how far such questions concern the public interest." His speech puts the lie to this disclaimer.

The friend begins with an argument about public interest. Human beings do not act as if denying the existence of particular providence and a future state affects the foundation of society. The "present order of things" shows that virtue is greeted "with more peace of mind than vice" and more public approval. Friendships, moderation and good character bring their own rewards as well. Pious reasoners may take the current system of rewards for virtue—that God orders things so that virtue brings its own rewards—as evidence of benevolent divine ordering. This conclusion presumes the philosophic issue at stake (140–1): we know the goodness of revelation in common life only by examining its effects on common life, so why exceed common life? Nature can take care of herself better without distortions from superstition. Even if religion is an inducement to good behavior, we have seen that its inducements often lead to inhumane behavior too. Religion is either superfluous or pernicious.

After arguing that civil religion is hardly useful for public morality, the friend treads on the argument from design despite his promises to refrain from it. The usefulness of religion is related to its truthfulness. The question is whether Hume is more concerned about the usefulness or the truth of religion, or whether he reads arguments about religious truth in light of questions of religion's utility.

The argument from design proceeds as follows. (1) The universe exhibits order and regularity; (2) such order could only be the product of a powerful, intelligent designer; and (3) therefore, a powerful, intelligent designer created the world. The friend offers several arguments against the second move. He argues that we can only grasp the qualities of the cause from the effects we see. The friend relates two illustrations. We see a scale with a ten ounce weight on it begin to rise. This proves that the weight on the other side exceeds ten ounces; we cannot infer that the weight is eleven ounces or a hundred pounds. Much the same is true for people. We cannot infer from the sight of a great painter that he is also a great sculptor. We can only know his talents from the works that we have seen or heard of. The same rules apply to observations about nature. Allowing "the gods to be the authors of the existence or order of the universe; it follows, that they possess that precise degree of power, intelligence, and benevolence, which appears in their workmanship; but nothing farther can ever be proved" (136–7).

The friend's argument proceeds on two levels. First, he calls into question God's goodness *assuming that God has authored the universe*. Supposing attributes other than those inferred from observable effects is not proper reasoning. Such suppositions are flights of the imagination producing "something greater and more perfect than the present scene of things, which is so full of ill and disorder." Inferences about God's "superlative intelligence and benevolence" or divine justice are not proportioned to the evidence before us (137). This disorderly vale of tears does not allow us to infer that there is a benevolent, order-producing Governor of the world. The world appears neither to be just nor good nor governed by intelligence (139–40, 141–2).

Hume interrupts his friend on behalf of the mere assumption that God exists. He tells his friend to imagine that the world is like an incomplete building moving toward completion. Can we not infer that the perfect builder will complete a perfect building? Can we not infer the existence of a God-Builder from the existence of our Earth-Home?[10] The friend responds with an argument to which Hume does not object, and this response illustrates the second level of the friend's argument. The analogy of building is imperfect because it is founded on a different species of experience. We see homes built everyday and every home has a builder and a plan. Our inference that there is a builder is based on an inference from the observed past to the future. We never see God in the same way we see houses built, however. Neither God's goodness nor God's existence are consistent with rigorous inferences from common experience (142–6). This conclusion is never challenged in "Particular Providence"; it is only deepened by Hume's subsequent intervention.

Hume makes a *political* objection to the friend's critique of the argument from design. He is dissatisfied with his friend's argument about philosophy's political effects. Because religious arguments and beliefs *"ought* to have no influence" does not mean that they *"can* have no influence." Men "draw consequences" from belief "that the Deity will inflict punishments on vice, and bestow rewards on virtue" or belief that God acts contrary to "the ordinary course of nature." These doctrines—belief in the immortality of the soul or in miracles—depend on revealed knowledge and point to the revealed doctrines after which Hume names the essay. Hume in this context indicates that the usefulness of religion depends on belief in doctrines that Hume, in other contexts, rakes over the philosophic coals. By placing these doctrines within his discussion of natural theology Hume indicates that the reliability of natural theology lends credence to revealed theology and that natural theology itself does not serve political purposes overmuch.[11] Revealed beliefs are "one restraint" on the disorderly passions of men and make the infringement of society's laws "in one respect" less likely. Those who destroy revealed religious arguments and beliefs may be a "good reasoners," but Hume cannot call them "good citizens and politicians" (147).[12] Nature gets a little help from religion, whether it needs help or not.

Hume hesitates upon reaching this conclusion. He "may, perhaps, agree" with his friend's "general conclusion in favour of liberty, though upon different premises." Instead of arguing that philosophy does political communities a favor in bringing about a more natural morality, Hume now argues that philosophy has no effect on political communities. Returning to his friend's earlier argument, Hume now argues that every principle of philosophy should be "tolerated" because no government has ever suffered "in its political interests by such indulgence." True philosophers are not prone to dangerous enthusiastic flights of fancy that lead to persecution. The vulgar do not find philosophic doctrines "very alluring." Public indifference for philosophy and philosophic indifference for the public serve the interests of each.

Hume immediately amends this co-incidence, which depends on philosophers exercising self-restraint. Philosophers conduct investigations dangerous to the public when prompted by "persecution or oppression" (147); they can be dangerous when disturbed from their natural diffidence or self-restraint. They may seek to upset common doctrines insofar as they are able. Hume considered his own time—a time when philosophy was subjected to "harsh winds of calumny and persecution" (133)—to be a time when philosophers must touch on points where human beings are "more deeply interested and concerned" in order to protect themselves. If this reading is correct, Hume concedes that philosophers *can* affect how people hold their religious beliefs. This puts a more radical construction on Hume's statement at the beginning of "Of Miracles," where he promises that his argument concerning miracles will prove "useful" for the "wise and learned" for "as long as the world endures" (110). The wise can learn how to fend off religious persecution by undermining religious doctrines. They may have to moderate religious fervor by mocking the evidence on which religious conviction rests and by presenting a semblance of reasoning when they do so.

Herein lies the interpretive dilemma. In "Particular Providence," Hume (the character) asserts that revealed doctrines can be useful for a political community. In Hume's other works—notably, "Of Miracles" and "Of the Immortality of the Soul"—he argues that belief in such doctrines is irrational and *detrimental* to humane, moderate politics and morals. Hume's criticisms of religion are so unmistakable that his ambiguous, friendly comments toward religion cannot appear as politic bows to prevailing religious beliefs; his plain criticisms are more prominent than his subtle, perhaps friendly comments. If Hume is friendly, albeit in an understated way, toward religion, whence his decisive criticisms of its intellectual foundations and political utility?

Religious Belief and Natural Obscurity: Hume's *Dialogues*

The main theme of Hume's directly philosophical works—how ignorance about fundamental matters orients our scientific aspirations and encourages scientific modesty—manifests itself "destructively" in "Particular Providence." Neither Hume's friend nor Hume argues that religious doctrines of particular providence, a future state, and natural theology can be depended upon given the "strange infirmities of human understanding." Such a position is not, and, in any event, need not be, a devastating critique of Christianity. There was before Hume a long history of philosophic treatments of human ignorance,[13] and these treatments are located within the Christian intellectual tradition. St. Augustine, Blaise Pascal, and even St. Thomas Aquinas embrace varieties of skepticism about the adequacy of human reason in their Christian apologetics. These apologists question the competence of reason in accounting for human nature itself and for our ability to apprehend the world; they enlist this skepticism to serve Christianity as the key that unlocks the contradictions that define our condition. Only in the *Dialogues* does Hume evaluate the possibility that human ignorance could come to the aid of religion. What is most revealing is that the Christian of the *Dialogues*, Demea, insists *against* the sufficiency of the argument from design.[14] Of what benefit is the *Dialogues's* famous argument against the argument from design if the Christian of the *Dialogues* does not insist on it? The answer to this (seldom-asked) question is found by paying close attention to the importance of revealed religion in this work ostensibly about natural religion.

The *Dialogues* is Hume's most dramatic, artful, and literary work.[15] Scholars have sought to identify Hume's mouthpiece in the work by measuring Hume's statements from his other works with statements from characters in the *Dialogues*. This approach, while not unreasonable, underplays the literary context in which the arguments are found, and it undervalues the educational context in which the *Dialogues* are set. More reasonable is what Keith Yandell calls "the safest assumption; namely that it is the *Dialogues* itself which serves as Hume's spokesman."[16] This view is ascendant.[17] The book concerns more than Hume's critique of the argument from design or of the *a priori* argument for God's existence; he did not write *Dialogues Concerning Natural Theology*. He was concerned with *religion*, which is a more comprehensive concept encompassing theology, piety, conventions such as liturgy, and proper conduct and with the political implications of religious belief. In this Hume adopts the form, if not the substance, of the philosophic treatments characteristic of ancient thinkers.[18] What follows is not a comprehensive reading of the *Dialogues*. The work is interesting for our purposes because it asks: How and whether human ignorance can be assimilated into religious belief? Whether belief in God has the status of common sense in Hume's thought? And whether natural or revealed religions have an unmovable foundation in human nature? These questions are raised in a conversation, narrated in twelve parts by a young eager auditor, Pamphilus. The conversation is among three characters: Demea (a man of faith); Philo (a skeptic); and Cleanthes (a common sense skeptic).

The book begins with Demea praising Cleanthes for the care he takes educating his youthful ward Pamphilus. Demea takes the opportunity to relate his own theory of education, because he assumes Cleanthes follows traditional educational approaches. The emphasis on education shows that the dialogue's abstruse theoretical or theological points have implications for morality. Demea's educational theory relies on a rather Humean critique of reason's sufficiency. Demea exposes his children to the "science of natural theology" at the end of their education because their minds must be seasoned "with early piety" if they are to come to the proper conclusions amidst all the controversies among theologians. While teaching his children, Demea emphasizes "the uncertainty of each part, the eternal disputations of men, the obscurity of all philosophy, and the strange, ridiculous conclusions which some of the greatest geniuses have derived from the principles of mere human reason." These topics open their minds to "the greatest mysteries of religion" and humble the "assuming arrogance of philosophy" (D 3–4). Demea seems to tap into the Christian skeptical tradition by showing the reasonableness of a life of faith in an incomprehensible world.[19] If one can succeed in getting people to mind human limits—both an intellectual and a moral endeavor—Christianity appears to be an attractive or even a compelling way of life.

Philo seizes on Demea's remarks in a spirit of "raillery or artificial malice" that the insensible Demea does not notice. Philo appears to put Demea's well-founded skepticism in the service of religious belief.

> Let DEMEA's principles be improved and cultivated: Let us become thoroughly sensible of the weakness, blindness, and narrow limits of human reason: Let us duly consider its uncertainty and needless contrarieties, even in subjects of common life and practice: Let the errors and deceits of our very senses be set before us; the insuperable difficulties, which attend first principles in all systems; the contradictions, which adhere to the very ideas of matter, cause and effect, extension, space, time, motion... When these topics are displayed in their full light, as they are by some philosophers and

almost all divines; who can retain such confidence in this frail faculty of reason as to pay any regard to its determinations in points so sublime, so abstruse, so remote from common life and experience? (D 4)

In response to a criticism from Cleanthes, Philo commends awareness of human limits on topics beyond "human affairs and the properties of surrounding bodies" to include speculations of "the two eternities," creation, and spirits living in a realm "quite beyond the reach of our faculties" (D 7). Theology is so remote from common life that people cannot reason about it. This exchange raises two questions: Is this skepticism an accurate description of what reason can tell us about God? If so, can religious faith be constructed on the edifice of philosophic skepticism?

Throughout parts one through eight, Demea and Philo seem to agree that God's nature is incomprehensible to human reason and that this view supports the life of faith. In this context Philo (with assent from Demea) subjects the argument from design to a searching criticism. These criticisms, surveyed in Parts II and III, are similar to those in "Particular Providence," so we need not detain ourselves with them. Most telling for our present purposes is Cleanthes' reaction to the skepticism in arguments denying the analogy between human and divine designs. He contends that the evidence for the argument from design is pre-rational. Observing the astounding functions of the eye and the fortuitous compatibility between male and female sex organs, among other things, strikes a "reasonable skeptic" with "so full a force that he cannot, without the greatest violence, prevent" his nature from assenting to belief in an intelligent designer. Cleanthes challenges Philo to consult his feelings. "Survey [nature's] structure and contrivance, and tell me, *from your own feeling*, if the idea of a contriver does not immediately flow in upon you with a force like that of a sensation" (D 25, emphasis supplied). Even "if the argument for theism" contradicts the "principles of logic" its "*universal*, its *irresistible* influence proves clearly that there may be arguments of a like irregular nature" testifying to its validity (D 25–6, emphasis supplied). Cleanthes holds that Philo's "too luxuriant a fertility" of thought suppresses his "natural good sense" with cavils, scruples and objections (D 26).

The language Cleanthes uses to describe the feeling that overcomes people who observe order in nature and infer the existence of an Author of Nature is reminiscent of Hume's description of reliable deliverances of common sense. Belief in theism, according to Cleanthes, is "universal," "irresistible" (D 25) and "incontesible" (D 26).[20] Lively, forceful feelings in favor of the inference overwhelm the devastating arguments against this inference. The argument from design appears to be as intrinsic to common life as causation and continued existence.[21] Philo's reaction to Cleanthes's challenge confirms this conclusion. At this important hinge in the conversation, Pamphilus intervenes to describe how "PHILO was a little embarrassed and confounded" by this appeal to experience and common sense (D 26). Philo's embarrassment and silence seem to indicate that there is no argument against the forceful appeal to feeling and sense. Philo's decisive arguments about the limits of reason, when applied to the theological matters that he reiterates and deepens in the subsequent five sections, appear to lack the force of conviction. This exchange prefigures one of the curious incidents of the *Dialogues*, where Philo seems to confess adherence to theism (D 77). These philosophical friends seem to support the conclusion of the Psalter, who thought "the heavens declare the glory of God and the firmament shows his handiwork," while the Christian, Demea, does not.

This conclusion is curious.[22] As I argued in the previous section, there is little room for this conclusion in "Particular Providence," where Hume and his friend poke holes in the argument from design without rehabilitating it. More fundamentally, it is not clear that the belief in design is "the foundation of all our thoughts and actions, so that upon [its] removal human nature must immediately perish and go to ruin" (T 225). Hume deconstructs philosophic explanations for the deliverances of common sense in an effort to expose the limits of human understanding: Locke's idea of power or the scholastic division of form and matter do not have the explanatory power that they purport to have. Hume aims to show that concepts such as causation and continued existence are unexplainable but indispensable to human reason; the alternatives—a loose universe without causation or a Heraclitean universe where nothing has a stable existence—are destructive of science and life. Criticisms of natural theology cut in a different direction because, as Philo establishes, there are reasonable alternative explanations to the argument from design. He shows that other explanations such as one that "ascribes and eternal, inherent principle of order to the world" (D 42–3) are at least as plausible as the argument from design. In fact, Philo twice (at the ends of Part VI and Part VIII) argues against Cleanthes that the "no system ought ever to be embraced with regard to such subjects" and a "total suspense of judgment is here our only reasonable resource" (D 53; see also 43). Cleanthes even supports Philo's criticisms of the argument from design in Part IX (D 55–6).[23] Hume never argues for a "total suspense of judgment" about the *existence* of causation or continued existence. The argument from design, it seems, is not a deliverance of common sense because, unlike causation and continued existence, alternatives to the argument from design are reasonable, sustainable, and constructive. The *Dialogue's* attempt to assimilate the argument for design into the philosophy of common life may, perhaps, be grounded in politics, but not in philosophy.

Demea is silent and supportive as Philo destroys the argument from design because he thinks that the analogy between human design and Divine Design wreaks of "anthropomorphism" (D 28–32). Demea concludes that God's nature does not resemble human nature, that God's making does not resemble human making, that God's intelligence does not resemble human intelligence, and that God's goodness does not resemble human goodness. God's footprint is on earth *only by revelation*. God is the All-Powerful Author of everything that happens on earth, though God's otherness makes it impossible for people to comprehend His ways (D 65–6). Demea's is a Calvinist understanding of a pure, mysterious, willful, completely other God, a totally depraved man, and a belief that *only by revelation* shall the twain meet. This was the theology typical of the largely Presbyterian Scotland of Hume's time.

The uneasy alliance between Demea and Philo continues even as Demea announces his understanding that our knowledge is in a state of "imbecility and misery" (Part X). Demea and Philo alternate wallowing in human misery, exchanging stories about bad things happening to good people, about the eternal transience of all human things, and about the triumph of injustice. Reflecting a distorted, somewhat superstitious variation on a Christian theme, these observations lead Demea to "look forward and endeavor, by prayers, adoration, and sacrifice, to appease those unknown powers whom we find, by experience, so able to afflict and oppress us" (D 58). Demea's God is one of vengeance and appeasement, without the Christian emphasis on grace. Philo endorses the observations, but not the conclusion: the alliance is about to break on the question of how God's goodness relates to His power.

Assertions of God's power and goodness raise what Philo calls the old question of Epicurus: "Is [God] willing to prevent evil, but not able? Then he is impotent. Is he able, but not willing? Then he is malevolent. Is he both able and willing? Whence then is evil?" (D 63). Cleanthes smiles at the raising of this question because he knows that Philo's feigned alliance with Demea is about to dissolve. Demea is not perturbed by these "most innocent" and "most generally received" questions (D 64). They have been raised "amongst the religious and devout themselves" and answered by "pious divines and preachers." His very philosophic, almost stoical representation of the Christian tradition is as follows:

> The world is but a point in comparison of the universe; this life but a moment in comparison with eternity. The present evil phenomena, therefore, are rectified in other regions, in some future period of existence.

And the eyes of men, being then opened to larger views of things, see the whole connection of general laws, and trace, with adoration, the benevolence and rectitude of the Deity through all the mazes and intricacies of providence. (D 64)[24]

Demea's answer depends on the revealed knowledge not only of a future state, but of God's goodness—precisely the issues in the first *Enquiry's* "Of Particular Providence."

The meaning of the *Dialogues* turns in part on the reaction to Demea's beliefs. Demea's crucial beliefs do *not* center on the argument from design. Christianity does not stand or fall on the argument from design, but it does stand or fall on the truth of doctrines revealed through miracles such as the incarnation and resurrection. It is striking that the normally gentle, even-tempered Cleanthes passionately and decisively responds to Demea's reliance on revealed knowledge. Cleanthes finds in Demea's confidence a series of "arbitrary suppositions" that "can never be admitted contrary to matter of fact, visible and uncontroverted" (ibid.). Cleanthes emphatically ("No!...No!" he begins) denies the possibility of revealed, miraculous knowledge. He reacts to the way Demea, with Philo's help, has emphasized the ubiquity of human misery. Denying original sin and the need for redemption, he embraces "divine benevolence" and denies "absolutely the misery and wickedness of man" (ibid.).

Demea radicalizes the problem of evil by denying the existence of human responsibility in evil. Philo could perhaps assert the existence of free will and deny that God is responsible for the evil in the world. Perhaps Philo could admit Demea's somewhat traditional reliance on revealed knowledge by asserting the reliability of the Christian miracles—especially the crucifixion and resurrection, which reveal God's goodness and mercy to human beings. Either path could maintain Philo's alliance with Demea because each would be suggestive of fundamental sympathy. Or Philo could implicate either God's goodness or His power and/or derogate the possibility of revealed knowledge of God's ways. That Philo takes the last of these paths is illustrated by the fact that Demea, feeling betrayed and disappointed, storms out after Philo's extensive speech about the divine culpability in moral and natural evil (D 67–75).

What does Demea's departure tell us about the fundamental questions of the *Dialogues*? The assimilation of human ignorance to religious belief depends on the willingness to acknowledge the possibility of miracles; the philosophic souls in the *Dialogues* follow Hume's "Of Miracles." This suggests that Hume was not intending a serious confrontation with the skeptical Christian tradition in the *Dialogues*. By aligning Demea's character—his confident piety, his intolerance for Cleanthes, his vehemence—with a belief in miracles Hume further illustrates the psychological infirmities he associates with believers. The argument from design, while it makes belief in particular providence and a future state more plausible, is not the crux of the difference between religious believers and the philosophic skeptics of the *Dialogues*. Demea himself endorses the destruction of the argument from design. Only when philosophy threatens the life of faith (i.e., when miracles are called into question) does Demea depart. Demea's departure illustrates the tension between faith and reason.

The other remarkable feature of the *Dialogues* through Part XI is the unevenness of the arguments. Philo dominates the discussion[25] and he announces the powerful arguments against belief in the argument from design and in favor of human limits and misery. Cleanthes' reaction to Philo in all these cases is to deny that reason is the proper judge of the matter: Sentiment and feeling force us to believe in an Author of the Universe; and he "feel[s] little or nothing" of human misery himself and "hope[s] that it is not so common as [they] represent it" (D 62). These are hardly adequate responses *from the standpoint of reason* to Philo's pile of arguments and observations. Cleanthes appears diffident in these arguments because he rejects the standard implied by arguing. One of the central questions of the *Dialogues* concerns the status of Cleanthes' differences from Philo on this score. Is feeling a sufficient resource to combat Philo's arguments? How grounded are the purported feelings that counteract Philo's arguments? How can we take Cleanthes' feelings seriously when there are powerful evidences against them? These questions raise the issue of religion's status in common life. Only when this issue comes to a head is Cleanthes roused to make decisive arguments or assertions against Demea and he, in short order, contradicts those arguments or assertions.

Section XII resolves these philosophic issues, insofar as they are resolved in the *Dialogues*. The section begins with Philo appearing to recant both the power of argument and his own arguments against design. He is "less cautious" in disputes about natural religion than in disputes on any other topic because he does not think that he can "corrupt the principles of any man of common sense" and because no person of "common sense will ever mistake [his] intentions" (D 77). He then admits, consistent with his earlier confusion and embarrassment and with Cleanthes' feelings, that the commitment to natural religion is pre-rational.[26] Or is the commitment to natural religion political and moral? They each endorse an attenuated theism as the system best suited for a humane politics[27] and for one such as the youthful, eager (perhaps over-eager?) Pamphilus. As Cleanthes remarks after Philo's confession, human beings embrace systems of belief and it is best to structure one's arguments to suit this trait in human nature (D 79). Hume's argument seems to be as follows. It is best to emphasize that the natural features of God resemble human attributes such as creativity, skill, goodness, and workmanship. Some people will emulate His attributes. Theism unadorned by superstitious beliefs helps to avoid the servility, factiousness, ignorance, and barbarity associated with superstition by reinforcing the common sense, humane, commercial ethic. Theism, not true in the strict sense, reinforces our humanity; it is natural and humane in its effects. Hume judges religious practices and religious doctrines by a social ethic independent of religion.

This tentative agreement between Cleanthes and Philo leads to the most remarkable exchange of the work—an exchange that raises the issue of whether religious belief itself is necessary. After Philo admits that he takes pleasure in destroying fervently held religious principles, Cleanthes demurs in much the same way the character Hume did near the beginning of "Particular Providence":

> Religion, however corrupted, is still better than no religion at all. The doctrine of a future state is so strong and necessary a security to morals that we never ought to abandon or neglect it. For if the finite and temporary rewards and punishments have so great an effect, as we daily find: How much greater must be expected from such as are infinite and eternal? (D 82; cf. EHU 133–4)

After Philo's response, Cleanthes describes the theology most conducive to moral health.

> Forfeit not this principle, the chief, the only great comfort in life and our principal support amidst all the attacks of adverse fortune. The most agreeable reflection which it is possible for human imagination to suggest is that of genuine theism, which represents us as the workmanship of a Being perfectly good, wise, and powerful; who created us for happiness; and who, having implanted in us immeasurable desires for good, will prolong our existence to all eternity, and will transfer us into an infinite variety of scenes, in order to satisfy those desires and render our felicity complete and durable. (D 86)

Lay aside how Hume calls these observations into question in treatises and essays and, to a large degree, in "Particular Providence." What is striking about these comments is that they contradict each other and contradict Cleanthes's earlier argument, where he labeled Demea's belief "in some future period of existence" an unsupportable "arbitrary supposition[] ' (D 64). Can Cleanthes mean that the most abject superstition is preferable to "no religion at all" while endorsing only a happy, follow-your-feelings religion of humanity? Why would Cleanthes passionately take the lead in chasing Demea away on the very issue that he makes central to his own veneration for true religion?[28] Why does he praise the "consolation" (D 86) people find in religion when he earlier, in precipitating Demea's departure, denied the misery of mankind? What Cleanthes takes away with one hand he gives back with the other. Distracted by Philo's transparent *volte face* on natural theology, Cleanthes' more important one has gone unnoticed.

Cleanthes elaborates on his discussion of true religion in his next speech, where he argues that the "proper office of religion is to regulate the hearts of men, humanize their conduct, infuse the spirit of temperance, order and obedience; and, as its operation is silent and only enforces the motives of morality and justice, it is in danger of being overlooked and confounded with these other motives" (D 82). Religion serves as "a cover to faction and ambition" when it is separate from such motives (ibid.). Clenathes' theology is purely functional or mercenary, in that "true religion" is defined by the contribution it makes toward the ethic of humanity. There is no talk of eternal damnation because fear of punishment disrupts a cheerful, quiet sleep. There are no strenuous demands of piety, only a cheerful, quiet demand that people be amused and happy. There are no trials, tribulations, or tests, only comfort and support from a good guardian. Cleanthes' theological agility serves the cause of ease, diffidence, cheerfulness, humanity, and gentleness. His cheerful theology—an afterlife without terrors and a God who endorses our happiest impulses—cultivates an untroubled attitude. Cleanthes opposes Demea's theology of terror and fear because it tends to upset an easy, humane existence and to trigger the destructive psychological dynamic discussed in *The Natural History of Religion*. Consistent with Hume's threats in "Particular Providence," philosophic equanimity is disturbed only by doctrines hostile to society and philosophy. Cleanthes advocates and represents the unperturbedness amidst contradictions and human limits that is the proper moral reaction of a philosopher.

After Cleanthes' remarkable speech, Philo offers a series of arguments from history—about the weakness of religious motives, about the terror-stricken way that they corrupt morality when they do operate, and about how such religions distort common sense (D 82–6, 86–8). Cleanthes never speaks again in the dialogue, leaving the impression that the "true religion" he would like to see people embrace has, as Philo argues, "never" been a "popular religion" anywhere in history (D 87). But there is a pregnant possibility. Can progress be made on this front?

Can history bring such a revolution in human psychology that makes Cleanthes' cheerful religion possible?

Philo's speech deepens these questions by arguing that the unsteadiness of human nature renders the emergence of a cheerful theology unlikely. Passions of hope and fear "enter into religion because both these passions, at different times, agitate the human mind, and each of them forms a species of divinity suitable to itself" (D 87). People with a "cheerful disposition" are "fit for business, or company, or entertainment of any kind" and "naturally" apply themselves "to these and think[] not of religion." Cleanthes' theology is superfluous because happy people do not think about God (see NHR 31). Such cheer, while desirable, is, unfortunately, all too fleeting. Fear, melancholy, dejection, misery, and affection re-appear to engrave "religious opinions" into people's "thought and imagination." In fact, "terror is the primary principle of religion, it is the passion which always predominates in it, and admits but of short intervals of pleasure" (D 87). Philo characterizes religions founded on fear as follows: "It is contrary to common sense to entertain apprehensions or terrors upon account of any opinion whatsoever, or to imagine that we run any risk here after, by the freest use of our reason" (D 88). The pregnant possibility of the *Dialogues* concerns the viability of such a "cheerful" religion of "common sense." Must future religious practice and belief resemble the past's? Is there no way to remove human nature from the see-saw between good cheer and dejected terror? The next section concerns these questions.

What do the *Dialogues* reveal about Hume's philosophy of common life? First, Hume's approach to common life presupposes a moral and philosophic dismissal of revealed religion. Those who see a steady agnosticism in Hume's religious writings argue that he reveals "the futility of...theological argument" in order "to show that the only sensible course is to abandon such topics for what he calls 'the examination of common life.'" If "the question of natural theology is unanswerable," it follows that "religious agnosticism is the only tenable solution."[29] I am arguing that Hume's agnosticism or suspense of judgment or nonfoundationalism is subordinate to his Enlightenment commitments on religious matters. Hume's philosophy of common life sometimes hides its anti-religious premises under the guise of agnosticism, reasonableness and philosophic impotence. This is most obvious on the issue of miracles and on the psychology of religion, where Hume presumes contested premises not sympathetic to religion. Given the natural suppositions at the ground of Hume's philosophy of common life, anti-religious conclusions are inescapable. The *Dialogues*, presented in a form that could mitigate this problem, extends the problem to the issue of religion's usefulness.

Philo's apparently spectacular *volte face* on natural religion does nothing to amend this fundamental problem.

Second, the unanswered question concerning the future of religious practice illustrates another conflict between philosophic agnosticism and Enlightenment. As we will see in the next section, Hume suggests that an unprecedented and promising earthquake has shaken the religious landscape. The deepening attachment to the modern politics of humanity coincides with a psychological and moral revolution that has profound implications for the future of religious practice. Hume greeted this revolution with unqualified support. The problem this poses cuts quite deep into Hume's views on human nature. In this context the Enlightenment commitments evident in his religious writings intrude on his political teaching. His commitment to a particular psychology of religion tempted him, in my judgment, to indulge in uncharacteristically radical hopes for the future.

Hume's Enlightenment and the Sufficiency of Humanity

Because religious passions are not fundamental in common life, the structure of Hume's psychology of religion holds out the possibility that religious outlets for original or fundamental passions can be closed or forgotten or transcended.[30] Enlightenment science cannot explain away God and mockery does not lead people from God unless the scientific project offers a more compelling explanation for phenomena. Enlightenment strategies for amending religious practice presume the continued existence of the psychological dynamic between fear or terror and common sense. Neither Enlightenment science or enlightenment strategies would be successful in turning people from God because human life is, as Hume shows, shrouded in mystery, contradictions, and ignorance. Any revolution in religious practice and belief must render God obsolete, superfluous, or benign on a basis different than apodictic Enlightenment certainty. The humane revolution in politics and morals appears to do just that. It holds out the possibility of Cleanthes' cheerful religious practice. The ethic of humanity coincides with that cheerful ease and scientific progress that combine to confine the imagination to this-worldly concerns. God is not explained away or overcome so much as He is forgotten in the fun, frolic, plenty, and ease of the commercial regime. Hume is enticed by the progressive Enlightenment, wherein history slowly transforms human beings toward a happy, secular future without the need for God.

The action of "Particular Providence" and the *Dialogues* shows that Hume leaves open the possibility that an age's ethos can be devoid of meaningful religious faith. Hume's apparently definitive statements about the durability of faith are qualified and ambiguous. "Belief of invisible, intelligent power has been very generally diffused over the human race, in all places and in all ages; but it has... [not] been so universal to admit of no exception." He continues: "Some nations have been discovered, who entertained no sentiments of Religion." In fact, he hesitates in suggesting that the operation of religious principles "in some ages, may, by an extraordinary concurrence of circumstances, be altogether prevented" (NHR 21). *The Natural History of Religion* shows how the secondary religious passions spring from more powerful, original passions.[31] In so doing, it suggests a map for how original passions may be channeled away from religion. I must re-open questions about the nature of humanity, begun in chapter 6, if we are to understand the latent radicalism of Hume's religious writings.

Virtues of humanity displace the less than natural religious passions and satisfy the original passions that lead human beings to religion. The original passions that lead human beings to religious belief are "a concern with regard to the events of life, and from the incessant hopes and fears, which actuate the human mind" (NHR 27). More specifically, it is our uncertainty about our future—the uncertain satisfaction of our needs and our ignorance about life after death—that agitates people to embrace God. Affliction is connected to a "due sense of religion" (NHR 31). Hume connects the psychology of fear and anxiety on the one hand and our inability to know nature on the other in *NHR*, Parts II and III. Part II is entitled "Origin of Polytheism," and, because polytheism is the first religion, it concerns the foundation of religious beliefs as such. Polytheism has its origins in an agitated, fearful, anxious, and terrified "dread of future misery" (NHR 28). Part III is entitled "The Same Subject Continued," the only such chapter title in the book (see T Book I, Part II, Chapter V for the only other such title in Hume's corpus). In what sense does Part III continue the topic of Part II? Part III emphasizes how ignorance of causes leads people to embrace gods as the hidden causes of everything: "While the passions are kept in perpetual alarm by an anxious expectation of the events, the imagination is equally employed forming ideas of those powers, on which we have an entire dependance" (NHR 29). Hume is more direct in the subsequent paragraph.

> No wonder, then, that mankind, being placed in such an absolute ignorance of causes, and being at the same time so anxious concerning their future fortune, should immediately acknowledge a dependence on invisible powers, possessed of sentiment and intelligence. (NHR 30)

Parts II and III show that fear is related to ignorance, to the lack of developed scientific investigations into natural causes, and to our inability to control nature.

Both our ignorance of causes and our lack of control over nature are channels for religious belief. As I related earlier, "in proportion as any man's course of life is governed by accident, we always find, that he encreases in superstition." Superstition and narrow-minded patriotism rule only "before the institution of order and good government" (NHR 30). Ancient, feudal, and barbarous people lived in "continual alarm" (E 259) over war and rumors of war with neighbors, and Hume connects uncertain fortunes of war with the belief that gods "have an influence in every affair" as well (NHR 30). Hume continues, "Every disastrous accident alarms us, and sets us on enquiries concerning the principles where it arose: Apprehensions spring with regard to futurity. And the mind sunk into diffidence, terror, and melancholy, has recourse to every method of appeasing those secret intelligent powers." Suffering, affliction, and apprehension throw people "on their knees" more often than agreeable passions do (NHR 31). Accidents occur where people have not built dams and dikes to control the violent, raging river, to use Machiavelli's image.

This description of human psychology implies two secularizing avenues: either fear can be given less superstitious outlets or fear can be drowned in a flood of prosperity. Improving human life by controlling nature especially undermines superstition by making belief in particular providence superfluous. Human beings can learn to provide for themselves. This pride in human self-sufficiency is another aspect of the virtue of humanity. The very word humanity suggests a human world defined by our basic "humane" nature without the imposition from divine beings. Proud self-sufficiency begets competent scientific action, and successful action begets the conditions for cheerfulness. The scientific revolution that undergirds the humane revolution leads to forgetfulness about the Divine. "Prosperity is easily received as our due, and few questions are asked concerning its cause or author. It begets cheerfulness and activity and alacrity and a lively enjoyment of every social and sensual pleasure: And during this state of mind, men have little leisure or inclination to think of the unknown invisible regions" (NHR 31). Humane "confidence and sensuality" make people "forgetful of a divine providence" (ibid.). Can this state of mind last? Can human beings remove themselves from the see-saw of fear and cheer?

Hume reveals the anti-transcendent implications of the scientific revolution in his presentation of commerce and humanity. Recall Hume's account of commercial motivations from chapter 6: People engage in commerce from a complex mixture of selfish concerns, curiosity, and a desire for distraction. Hume's belief in the centrality of the desire for distraction is nearly unique among political thinkers, and it appears more remarkable in the shadow of his religious writings.

> There is no craving or demand of the human mind more constant or insatiable than that for exercise and employment; and this desire seems the foundation of most of our passions and pursuits. Deprive a man of all business and serious occupation, he runs restless from one amusement to another. (E 300) [32]

The industriousness borne of commerce, trade and manufacturing "satisfies" the mind's "natural appetites, and prevents the growth of unnatural ones, which commonly spring up, when nourished by ease and idleness." Exercise and employment borne of commerce keep psychologically disordering terrors from arising to the mind, and commercial people will not consider questions of human destiny in their time of rest and recreation. In fact, most people find relaxation intolerable and debilitating. Exercise and employment have the virtue of taking "a man from himself," of immersing people in activity while obscuring their self-consciousness. The ethic of humanity implies sufficiency and comfort in an entirely human world (E 270). It is a world united in enjoyment, and amusement, where chance has been controlled and technological progress is the aim. As the "dismal dress" of monkish and ancient austerities "falls off," Hume foresees a time when "nothing appears but gentleness, humanity, beneficence, affability; nay even at proper intervals, play, frolic, and gaiety" (EPM 279).

The sufficiency of Enlightenment for Hume is seen in his comments about mortality. Hume does not promise, like Descartes,[33] to free human beings from death's inevitable knock on the door, but he does suggest that we can stop thinking about it. In much the same fashion as Rousseau, Hume seems to believe that concerns about "futurity" or life after death would "quickly vanish, were they not artificially fostered by precept and education" (E 592–3).[34] Immersion in everyday life turns people away from consciousness about finitude. This is in keeping with his argument that those reconciled to the ethic of humanity do not worry about "unknown invisible regions" and do not waste time in self-conscious personal reflection about such things—commerce takes "a man from himself." Consciousness of mortality puts a certain, sobering limit on Enlightenment aspirations and our desire for an easy-going happiness. Such concerns are associated with the old "dismal dress." As long as people are troubled by their imperfections when compared to perfect creatures or people think that there is a distinction between this world and the next, they remain (to a degree) restless in this world and susceptible to the machinations of priests and patriots. The ethic of humanity, for Hume, coincides with forgetfulness of "dismal" questions and speculative answers. No longer existentially troubled, the human being can be understood as he emerges comfortable and at home in the world. To repeat, "*nothing* appears but gentleness, humanity, beneficence, affability; nay even at proper intervals, play, frolic, and gaiety" (emphasis supplied). Hume's philosophy of common life presumes that we are no longer disturbed by death, or think about it.

Hume's several proposals for amending religious establishment aim to cultivate a spirit of religious indifference. In "Idea of a Perfect Commonwealth," Hume argues that the "dependence of the clergy on the civil magistrate" is essential to the "security or stability" of "any free government" (E 525). Such dependence, as Hume argues in more detail in the *History*, is designed to prevent the "interested diligence of the clergy." "In order to render himself more precious and sacred in the eyes of his retainers," an interested priest instills a "most violent abhorrence of all other sects" and endeavors "to excite the languid devotion of his audience." Parishioners are, in effect, "customers," who are drawn to preachers by invective, bombastic rhetoric, intolerance, and inhumanity. Placing clergy on the public dole would "bribe their indolence" and render "active," unsettling self-promotion "superfluous." Indifferent, lazy clergy will not evoke the fear and misery that can lead to superstitious or enthusiastic religious beliefs. Without such interested prompting, religious beliefs would wither on the vine. This redounds to the "political interests of society" (H III.135–6). Hume also praises the Romans, who prevented "the strong effect of the priestly character" by prohibiting people under 50 years old from holding "sacerdotal office" (E 201n). The policy was successful in promoting religious indifference because older people are too accustomed to profane life to become interested in cultivating stringent piety. These cynical suggestions reveal Hume's fundamental optimism about the possibility of extinguishing religious belief. The conductors of religious belief can be short-circuited.

Hume believes "it is much to be hoped" that "the progress of reason will, by degrees abate" religious "acrimony" and cultivate a "spirit of moderation" throughout Europe. Hume does not think this new spirit can be "entirely trusted" yet in his day (E 510). At other times, he suggests that there is the historical changes afoot throughout Europe give reason for indulging such hope. Hume sees decline in religious sentiment from superstition to enthusiast Protestantism. As Hume writes in "Of National Characters, "Our ancestors, a few centuries ago, were sunk in the most abject superstition, last century they were inflamed with the most furious enthusiasm, and are now settled into the most cool indifference with regard to religious matters, that is to be found in any nation of the world" (E 206). Enthusiasm, while violent when ascendant, soon exhausts itself and leads its adherents "naturally" to "sink into the greatest remissness and coolness in sacred matters" (E 77). Religion itself becomes *"more gentle and moderate"* (E 76) as time progresses in modernity. The revolution in politics parallels the revolution in religious belief. If the singular English Constitution and its culture of humanity can arise (EPM 256), so also can a humane culture that tranquilizes and extinguishes religious devotion. Modernity's humane revolution in politics and morals may be the "extraordinary concurrence of circumstances" (NHR 21) needed to extinguish religious belief.[35]

Hume's is neither the ancient understanding of a citizen's virtue nor the Christian understanding of piety, both of which see self-abnegation and adherence to law in the service of something above the individual. Hume's endorsement of humanity debunks the very notion of "something above the individual" or a "higher perfection of soul."[36] Such "sublime topics" topics distract and disorder people. "Modern education" is more humane and moderate than the ancient (E 94) because modern peoples are more commercial and more secular or agnostic than ancient peoples—moderns have humane, "narrow souls" (EPM 256). Commerce behaves like Christianity on any number of levels, but without the negative effects of fanaticism and dividing authority between heaven and earth. Commerce transcends nations, eludes the control of sovereigns, renders priests and organized religion less relevant, discourages fanaticism, is universal and imperial (E 202, 206–7) and cannot be united under a single head. It is almost as if Hume presages the ascension of a new man in modernity, albeit a new man that, paradoxically, perhaps, has always existed beneath the surface. Humanity emphasizes the horizontal and debunks as dangerous the vertical. Emphasis on keeping human beings satisfied in the humane, horizontal plane marks Hume as among the most consistent non-teleological thinkers. Restricting philosophy to daily life and experience presumes a barrier between heaven and earth, a barrier that humanizes and tranquilizes the soul.

CHAPTER 10

TOWARD A MORE PHILOSOPHICAL PHILOSOPHY OF COMMON LIFE

It should be clear that I oppose the very old, vulgar view that Hume abandoned philosophy for the study of history and for the pursuit of literary fame. Hume's philosophic achievement lies in an articulation of the "mixed kind of life" to which human beings are consigned. The human condition is defined by inescapable oppositions between reasonableness and sentimentality, reason and the imagination, the need for action and the need for rest, the particular and the universal, sociality and individuality, and history and nature, among others. The proper political and ethical reaction to the paradoxes and contradictions defining human nature is best found in modern commercial republics, where the virtues of humanity, gentle political authority, and an easy-going tolerance find a home. Modern arrangements provide freedom for people to work out the contradictions in their nature in a manner consistent with their own character and inclinations. Hume has, to a large degree, brought about a de-mystified, disenchanted, moderately skeptical, humanist *ethos*. The philosophy of common life arises almost of itself in the modern commercial republic, though it sometimes needs to be maintained and restored by humanizing philosophers when excessively rationalist or excessively mystical ways of thinking emerge.

Also interesting and persuasive about Hume's philosophy of common life is its recognition of the law of mixed blessings (as I call it) as it applies to life. All human institutions and social arrangements partake of both good and evil. Though Hume often accentuates the positive when it comes to modern commercial republics more than he emphasizes the negatives, it takes just a little digging to understand Hume's rhetorical reasons for this and to see that he often has worries about what the commercial republic will hold. Further, it is consistent with his thought that these evils or problems will reveal themselves only in time or after the establishment of the order. Ours is a mixed condition defined by mixed blessings—this teaching qualifies and stands in tension with Hume's sometimes extravagant praise of modern commerce, the virtues of humanity, and the middling element that normally arises with it. Perhaps this is another ultimate antinomy in Hume's thought: the sometimes extravagant hopes for progress and humanity on the one hand and the recognition that "progress" is a rearranging of the world's goods and evils on the other hand.

Hume's philosophy of common life is diagnostic, prophylactic, and salubrious. It is diagnostic, in that it identifies the natural psychological tensions that give rise to diseases of the mind, such as partisanship, enthusiasm, and philosophical error, when they are carried too far. It also shows that we begin to view our world with a disposition of trust in the senses, in the regularity of nature, in the reality of moral distinctions and other natural or inescapable suppositions. It is prophylactic, in that it subjects those errors to rigorous, skeptical philosophical analysis and historical testing in an effort to protect the humanity and moderation already existing in common life. Skeptical arguments help to destroy pretentious, potentially disrupting doctrines in religion, politics, and morality—and thereby lend protection to more solid reasoning. It is salubrious because it is designed to make us respect and enjoy the unique historical achievements of modernity armed with a proper self-understanding.

Hume's thought seeks to insulate common life from excessive rationalism, superstition, enthusiasm, and a corrosive skepticism or relativism while injecting a proper understanding of philosophy into common life as part of a project to reconcile human beings to their mixed conditions of mixed blessings. Hume would intervene in common life to protect common life and the principles of his philosophy necessary to accomplish philosophy in this prophylactic and reconciliationist mode. Yet one cannot help but worry that certain elements of Hume's thought—most prominently, his contentions that the imagination constructs our ideas of nature and good and bad and that human beings make moral and aesthetic distinctions—could, in the hands of vulgar followers, devolve into skepticism or an expressive relativism. Perhaps even more reticence in the philosophy of common life is necessary in our time, when skepticism about the ability of reason to account for the world around us abounds.

However such issues of prudence may be, Hume's project of reconciliation is not without serious difficulties. As it defends the eclipse of enchantment and sees modern commerce as an activity that distracts human beings from the intractable contradictions of human nature, it may be as narcotic as it is salubrious. The salubriousness of Hume's philosophy of common life may be a narcotic in its attempt to make people comfortable with (and perhaps to ignore) the contradictions that define our condition or in his counseling against looking for deeper truths about our condition in those contradictions. Furthermore, Hume's philosophic agnosticism is not necessarily a tenable strategy for dealing with our ignorance, in that some of the suppositions in his philosophy of common life are inherently controversial and prone to foster a misreading of the phenomena under consideration. I developed the two most prominent examples of this problem in Hume's thought. First, I argued in chapter 7 that Hume's conception of history opposes Enlightenment rationalism, progressive or providential history, and historicism, but that Hume's opposition to these positions is moral and political instead of philosophic; it is a component of his effort to articulate a way of reading history consistent with what he regards as the moral demands of our "mixed kind of life." Hume does not make an argument for the governance of accident and chance in history; instead, he presumes that governance because he finds the moral implications of that way of reading history most propitious, in that it combats the active sovereignty characteristic of early modern thinking. Beliefs in the cunning of reason through history (as in Hegel) or in the providential achievement of equality of conditions (as in Tocqueville) are both consistent with the historical facts that Hume relates; both Hegel and Tocqueville could use Hume's narrative to support their treatments of where history was tending. Hume's politically and morally sensible desire to deny the existence of abstractions or Ideas in history may lead him to embrace a conception of history at odds with historical reality and with the story as he tells it. The moral and political duties of the historian, which entail reconciling human beings to a humane reaction to "our mixed kind of life," are not as consistent with the philosophic duties of the historian as Hume seems to suggest. In any event, it is difficult to know what Hume's argument against historicism would be or could be, especially since so much in his narrative supports such a reading of things.

Second, I argued in chapters 8 and 9 that Hume assimilates controversial, pre-rational, anti-religious suppositions into his philosophy of common life. As we saw in chapter 3, Hume denies that we know of a unified and unifying soul or mind at the heart of personal identity; "successive perceptions only...constitute the mind," as Hume writes in the *Treatise* (T 253). Hume seems to presume that human beings are not possessed of a permanent spiritual nature or mind. In the same breath, Hume argues that the nature of human being remains obscure to people: we must be able to articulate how thought could inhere in body in order to know what human being is, but this is beyond human ken. Hume's conclusions about the obscurity of human knowledge and of human being preclude his conclusion that the human mind is constituted only by successive perceptions. The evidence needed for the conclusion about human mind requires of Hume the deepest knowledge of what constitutes a human being, but such "high" enquiries about the nature of human being are beyond the scope of his philosophy of common life. This pattern repeats itself on several philosophic doctrines related directly and indirectly to issues of religious belief. Hume's belief that commercial activity will distract people from "dismal" questions about death and his belief that concern with life after death would "quickly vanish" without the machinations of priests are based on the contestable view that human nature can be transformed by historical forces. His characterization of religious passions as following from anxiety about material deprivation and fear due to our lack of control over nature presumes his denial of soul and a natural concern for immortality or a natural concern for righteousness and justice in the world. Fear and anxiety, as Hume conceives of them, are, relative to the Christian interpretation of these passions, easy to relieve. Once prosperity spreads, the well of religious conviction dries up and God is rendered obsolete because there is no permanently restless soul, for Hume, grounding transcendent longings and religious passions. Hume's teaching on these matters is all of a piece and follows from his hope to show the sufficiency of humanity.

That Hume's teaching on these matters forms a logical circle, however, does not mean that his teaching is the only one available to a philosophy of common life—his teaching may be a castle in the air. Reaching conclusions about the soul or the nature of religious longing requires of Hume the embellishment of a poet. If human discontent (broadly speaking) has deeper, more ineradicable roots than Hume thinks; if, that is, human discontent follows from our unquenchable desire to know answers to the deepest metaphysical issues or from an existential anguish in the face of finitude or a deep human longing for justice to be done, then there is reason to doubt the sufficiency of humanity as Hume conceives of it.

This difficulty in Hume's treatment of religion raises fundamental moral and philosophic issues. Hume lays bare the nature of our intractably contradictory, mysterious, and obscure faculties as a means of achieving a state of easy-going *ataraxia* (unperturbedness). We must press the issue here: Is this state of *ataraxia* desirable? Why does Hume consider it to be normative and controlling? From other intelligible perspectives (e.g., Pascal's and Nietzsche's), a distracted *ataraxia* in the face of deep contradictions and unsolvable mysteries is bafflingly de-humanizing. On a Pascalian reading, for instance, a philosophic awareness of human contradictions and about the incomprehensible nature of our self promotes a legitimate, noble, anguished sense of existential longing. How can we adjudicate this conflict between Edinburgh and Rome?

The disagreement between Hume and Pascal turns on the meaning and proper use of skeptical arguments and the moral status of *ataraxia*. For Hume, skeptical arguments destroy false philosophic and religious certainty in order to make us easy in our "mixed" condition. For Pascal, skeptical observations prod us from our easy-going, de-humanizing, distracted self-satisfaction and make us thirst for God's grace. For Hume, philosophy articulates the character of the human mix and moral philosophy infers the proper moral reaction to that mix, but philosophy exceeds its bounds when it attempts to go "underneath" this mix and tell us where the mix comes from or what that mix might mean about human destiny. Pascal tries to get underneath the mix, believing that Christianity is the key to explaining it; no responsible moral philosophy, in Pascal's judgment, can proceed unconcerned about getting underneath our common experience because the "underneath" questions must be resolved in order to direct people to the proper way of life. While Hume describes our mixed condition, Pascal presses to discover what that mixed condition could mean and where that mixed condition could have come from.

All hands agree that there is more to the world than meets the eye. Hume's trust in natural suppositions and Pascal's Christian faith place both, in some measure, outside the empiricist camp. Hume's philosophy proceeds with the sober acknowledgement that our "knowledge" of the world is enmeshed with true opinions about the world—the dividing line between knowledge and opinion is anything but bright. In doing so, Hume exposes the failure of modern philosophers to acknowledge their dependence on natural suppositions and he would have them recognize their dependence on an uncritically held belief at the foundation of their aspirations to know. Knowledge is inseparable from belief, despite the efforts of previous modern philosophers to achieve knowledge by making it. Belief in natural suppositions precedes the modern making of knowledge and makes that making possible. This dependence on the unexplainable adds mystery to our observations about the world—the mystery does not affect our practical knowledge of causes, but rather it suggests that there is a plane of meaning on which our observable world rests. These two realms—the realm of practical, made knowledge and the realm of meaning in which we explain belief—are independent; our inability to explain the inexplicable leaves us with questions about the meaning of the inexplicable, though it does not leave us wondering about the practical operation of nature. Hume's philosophy of common life attempts to seal these realms from one another and to take the question of meaning off of the table. The decisive questions, in my judgment, are these: can human beings act and live well without understanding their lives to be shot through with meaning? And, is there a perspective on the practical realm that is not already shot through with meaning? I hope to have shown that there is not a neutral perspective on the latter question and therefore that the decisive question about how one should live one's life turns on the former question—but that at that level Hume's philosophy of common life insists on silence.

This problem can be framed in a different way. As we have seen in Hume's theory of judgment, Hume trusts that people can know the facts about their world, can discover causal relationships among things, and can achieve reasonable judgments about the relative merits of different virtues and artistic performances, among other things. Another decisive question for Hume (and for those interested in evaluating Hume's philosophy of common life) revolves around distinguishing proper, reasonable trust from improper, unreasonable faith. Hume tries to explain this difference several times in his writings, and his answer, as we have seen, refers, among other things, to the force and vivacity of feelings conjured in the spectator. This is not altogether dissimilar to the Platonic view that people have a natural capacity for hitting the mark, an internal, somewhat untrained, somewhat trainable sense for sifting the falsehood out of the truth. Perhaps human beings cannot improve on this no doubt unsatisfactory description of how we attain knowledge.

Yet Hume's thought is plagued with this problem—what is "common" sense? How can we know whether common sense is a tip off to a deeper reality (whether it is Aristotelian philosophy or Christian theology)? We may be able to describe our mixed condition on the basis of Hume's philosophy of common life, but we also need to know why ours is a mixed condition and what our mixed condition means for us. These questions lead me to conclude that Hume's rendering of the philosophy of common life is, in places, subject to many of the same criticisms he makes of other thinkers. Hume's philosophy of common life smuggles premises about the nature of human life and the *cosmos* that are not justified by reason and are not the only available, reasonable or "common" suppositions on the matter. Perhaps this is why the philosophy of common life, despite its virtues, has not swept the field in the sciences or humanities and was seen as unsatisfactory by subsequent philosophers. It is not merely the thirst for wisdom that induces people to search for answers about the nature of the reality that eludes our eye. Knowing the nature of the reality underneath common life is important (and perhaps indispensable) for understanding political and moral, and indeed all, things.

Because Hume's philosophy of common life denies the philosophical relevance of "distant and high enquiries" and "confines itself to common life" (EHU 162), it often distances itself from the most important human concerns. Beginning philosophy in common life and *confining* philosophy to common life are two very different things. The confinement of philosophy to common life partakes a bit too much of the social scientific attitude so prevalent today, in that it admits only the common surface and that which is beneath the surface into the study of human things. Confining philosophy to common life begets a stunted humanism that cannot, in practice, withstand the reductionism typical of the modern science it opposes. What I am suggesting is a philosophy of common life open to seeing the human as part of a larger, more meaningful whole if it is to resist the moves characteristic of social science. Humanism requires something above common life—at least an openness to a universe of meaning above common life. Ancient, Medieval, and Christian philosophers before Hume and Historical philosophers such as Hegel after him agreed with his critique of corrosive skepticism, but none accepted Hume's confinement of philosophy to common life. Many ancient philosophers agreed that philosophy must begin in common life, but none (so far as I am aware) confined philosophy to common life. There is a pressing philosophic need—borne of the demands of common life, the thirst for wisdom, and the demands of wisdom—to ask, "what is common life hiding?" or "what does our mixed kind of life mean?" or "where do human things fit within the whole of which man is a part?" Ancient, Christian and Historical thinkers had, in different ways, argued that common life hid an ordered world, that high and distant enquiries revealed the human; these traditions generally held that common life or common sense must be defended theoretically from outside common life, and that some accounts (Aristotle's, for instance) of that which lies beyond common life make more sense than others. Such poetic accounts are problematic when they reach the level of philosophic dogma; Hume's skeptical treatment of such dogma is helpful at this point, for it helps deflate dogmatism. Anti-dogmatic skepticism and the excessive confinement of philosophy to common life, however, can turn into dogmatisms too. It seems that the prevalence of dogmatisms religious and philosophic in Hume's day tempted him to embrace a philosophy too confined to common life. Today we in the West are more comfortably distant from political dangers posed by revealed religion; therefore, we are afforded the luxury to view religion more philosophically and perhaps with greater sympathy. There is a pressing need, once again, to be open to seeing the human things in light of a larger universe of meaning. Today we are more threatened by the emerging thoughtlessness and incuriosity about the meaning of common life. There is less danger from entertaining high and distant inquiries and more need to cultivate wonderment.

Hume's strategy for dealing with such observations beyond common life is to deny the validity of the question, to confine human speculation to common life, and to maintain a studied agnosticism on classical metaphysical, ontological, and epistemological debates. As an initial strategy, this seems plausible and reasonable and perhaps even necessary. In the final analysis, such agnosticism is possible, as I have argued, on certain issues. Let me present what I take to be most telling example of the problem. For Hume, the imagination is the ultimate source for our ideas about the world, with the implication being that human beings (somehow) are responsible for constructing our "reality" because it is not immediately comprehensible to us. Hume's assumptions about our estrangement from Nature, the utterly impenetrable nature of God, and our lack of provision with respect to a well-formed natural conscience are debatable. Hume's rendering of the philosophy of common life is tenable only if these are the only tenable assumptions. On Hume's own account of our ignorance, however, it is impossible to endorse these assumptions without slipping into a species of dogmatism about matters on which philosophy must remain silent. This is what I believe happens in Hume's theory of history and in his religious writings.

Toward a More Philosophic Philosophy of Common Life

Is there a way to save the philosophy of common life from the occasional misuse of it by its most sophisticated advocate? What I suggest is that it is legitimate, in the spirit of Human analysis, to pluralize, in a sense, Hume's philosophy of common life. Pluralizing the philosophy of common life would have two chief elements. First, it would give reasonable alternative natural suppositions their due by building several alternative systems of common life on the basis of alternative starting points. On the question of history, for instance, a system of common life based on the assumption that history is determined mostly by accident and chance would resemble Hume's thought for the most part without as much discussion of the spirit of the times giving rise to new thoughts at the same time in different places. Alternative systems about the meaning of history—one resembling Hegel's, perhaps, or Tocqueville's—could be constructed, based on the assumption that History is a process governed by an abstract Idea. These systems would emphasize the seemingly universal, almost providential character of history or put forward alternative views about what moves History. Each system could be elaborated upon, worked out in its implications, associated with a substantially related system of morality, and then compared to the world for plausibility.

This pluralizing, on the surface, nudges the philosophy of common life in a more postmodern direction. This conclusion derives from the fact that there may be several serious systems of explanation (as per Hume's theory of judgment). Pluralizing the assumptions on which systems of common life rest makes allowance for legitimate intellectual difference and for our limited knowledge. It recognizes a truth found in postmodernism and in Hume's theory of judgment, namely that *at the highest levels* judgments about better and worse are not easy and natural suppositions can be controversial as we confront the world of human diversity in morals, politics, religion, literature, and history. Yet this perspective demands neither relativism nor postmodern nihilism: "If we cannot decide which of two mountains whose peaks are hidden by clouds is higher than the other, cannot we decide that a mountain is higher than a molehill? If we cannot decide, regarding a war between two neighboring nations which have been fighting each other for centuries, which nation's cause is more just, cannot we decide that Jezebel's actions against Naboth [were] inexcusable?"[1] By pluralizing starting points or pointing to a range of acceptable opinion (underneath the clouds), a more philosophical philosophy of common life allows us to make judgments about the plausibility of theories about what is underneath common life. Some systems of historical interpretation (the Marxist theory of economic determinism, for instance) are found wanting when they confront the world; other theories of history survive, though they may in time lose their plausiblity as they are measured against the world. Some revealed religions would seem more plausible than others because their fault-lines and mysteries best mirror natural fault-lines and mysteries. A religion, for example, would seem less than reasonable in promising a fundamental transformation of human nature or the world in time. A more philosophic philosophy of common life must, with charity, be ready to enter into, elaborate, clarify, and test assumptions about the nature of historical reality and religion.

Much the same can be said about the suppositions about religion and religious psychology at the foundation of Hume's thought. Perhaps, as Hume suggests in the vein of the Enlightenment, religion comes from human fears of material deprivation and ignorance of causes and we could conclude that such "passions" and ignorance could be relieved given the right mix of circumstances. That is one legitimate view of religious belief (though it seems to take on the form of the religious view it seeks to displace, in that it promises a progress beyond the messy reality of life heretofore). However, if religion comes from other, less relievable passions (such as the passion for justice or righteousness) or from uneasiness in the face of human mortality or from other features of human life, religion would take much different forms and would prove a more lasting feature of human life. Tocqueville, for instance, considers religion mostly from a human point of view, though he links religion to permanent human hopes for a better life and anguish at our short existence and this leads him to treat beliefs about the afterlife as a permanent feature of human life. Linking religious conviction to particular human passions seems a reasonable way of starting a psychology of religion, but finding a "neutral" or natural starting point for that treatment seems fruitless. Again, it might make more sense to "pluralize" the philosophy of common life in this case, so that several systems of philosophy could be entertained and tested from these different starting points. This, it seems to me, is at least part of how the ancient philosophers understood religion.

These examples also illustrate the second feature of a more philosophic philosophy of common life. There is less reason to be closed to explanations of where common life or "mixed kind of life" comes from; such a search would not declare attempts to get underneath common life out of bounds. Philosophic openness consists in a willingness to hear out those who seek to explain where our mixed kind of life comes from and the alternative moral messages of this mixed kind of life. It would be open to hearing, in the spirit of ancients, perhaps, what must be true of the world for natural suppositions about identity, continued existence, and causation (for instance) to be true. It would open philosophy up to deeper speculation and wonder, elements eclipsed by Hume's confinement of philosophy to common life. It would be based on the recognition that classical metaphysical, ontological, and epistemological positions represent serious attempts to explain our world. This approach is inseparable from a less dogmatic or a friendlier treatment of religious beliefs. Perhaps Hume's worries about "high and distant" inquiries being more likely to resemble the embellishments of poets made the most sense in his day, when modern rationalism used "high and distant" principles to combat the "high and distant" principles of Christian religion and (some features of) ancient thought. In our particular situation, where confidence in reason is at its lowest ebb, perhaps it is necessary to dust off the mostly ignored, dual nature of Hume's teaching and discuss the formation of judgment and the need to ascend from the particular to a more universal evaluation of morals, politics, and literature or works of art and to entertain systems of explanation based, in part, on speculation about what the first things are. This is especially true since today errors Hume only dimly anticipated have become elements of common life, including the idea that artistic or literary beauty is merely in the eye of the beholder or that moral distinctions are, strictly speaking, relative to one's time and place. We think that there is less to common life than even Hume thought—and any solution to this must start with a confidence that there is more to common life than there at first appears to be.

A more philosophic philosophy of common life probably means that we would not be able to reach the firm conclusions Hume does about the superiority of the modern commercial republic or the ridiculousness of Christian faith. At the same time, a more philosophic philosophy of common life would restrain elements of the postmodern abandonment of reason, clarify what would have to be true about the world in order for controversial suppositions to be true, and outline the range of legitimate moral and political disagreements. (For those interested, I have sought to provide such a more philosophic philosophy of common life in the conclusion to my earlier book on the idea of marriage in modern political thought.) A more philosophic philosophy of common life may modestly continue a search for "pluralized" meaning that Hume abandons and it might lay out the fundamental, insolvable dilemmas at the root of institutions that we think we know. Instead of positing one natural assumption, it entertains reasonable assumptions about the matter and seeks to show how our practice needs to integrate or assimilate these reasonable assumptions. The spirit of Hume's philosophy of common life can live on, even if the letter of Hume's thought must be, in several cases, supplemented and revised.

NOTES

1 David Hume's Philosophy of Common Life

1. Leo Strauss, "Social Science and Humanism," in *The Rebirth of Classical Rationalism*, edited by Thomas L. Pangle (Chicago: The University of Chicago Press, 1989), pp. 3–12.
2. James Ceaser, *Liberal Democracy and Political Science* (Baltimore: The Johns Hopkins University Press, 1990); Thomas L. Pangle, *Leo Strauss: An Introduction to His Thought and Intellectual Legacy* (Baltimore: The Johns Hopkins University Press, 2006), Chapter 4.
3. See most recently Christopher Findlay, *Hume's Social Philosophy: Human Nature and Commercial Sociability in a Treatise on Human Nature* (London: Continuum, 2007); Galen Strawson, *The Secret Connexion: Causation, Realism, and David Hume*, Revised Edition (Oxford: Oxford University Press, 2014).
4. Scott Yenor, "Between Rationalism and Postmodernism: David Hume's Political Science of 'Our Mixed Condition.'" *Political Research Quarterly* 55 (2002).

2 "Nothing but Sophistry and Illusion": Metaphysical Speculation before Hume

1. St. Thomas Aquinas, *Summa Theologica*, Q 84; Article 1, following Aristotle, characterizes Heraclitean position in the following manner: "It should be said in order to elucidate this question, that the early philosophers, who inquired into the natures of things, thought there was nothing in the world save bodies. And because they observed that all bodies are mobile, and considered them to be ever in a state of flux, they were of opinion that we can have no certain knowledge of the true nature of things. For what is in a continual state of flux, cannot be grasped with any degree of certitude, for it passes away ere the mind can form a judgment thereon: according to the saying of Heraclitus, that 'it is not possible twice to touch a drop of water in a passing torrent.'"

2. They cannot explain how the matter got there in the first place or what is present when a thing is being generated or destroyed, for instance (1010a18 and 999b5–9).
3. 987a29–b14. This characterization is borrowed from St. Thomas Aquinas, *Commentary on Aristotle's Metaphysics* (South Bend: Dumb Ox Books, 1995), 153. See also *Summa Theologica*, Q 84; Article 1.
4. Aquinas, *Summa Theologica*, Q 84; Article 1 summarizes Aristotle's objection as follows: "It seems ridiculous, when we seek for knowledge of things which are to us manifest, to introduce other beings, which cannot be the substance of those others, since they differ from them essentially: so that granted that we have a knowledge of those separate substances, we cannot for that reason claim to form a judgment concerning these sensible things."
5. Aquinas, *Summa Theologica*, Q 84; Article 1 summarizes Aristotle's objection as follows: "Since those species are immaterial and immovable, knowledge of movement and matter would be excluded from science (which knowledge is proper to natural science), and likewise all demonstration through moving and material causes."
6. Thucydides appears to be one taken with Heraclitean metaphysics, and this leads him to doubt the naturalness of justice and to assert the primacy of warfare (*stasis*) or motion in human affairs. The Heraclitean view of nature leads into the sophistic view that justice is the advantage of the stronger.
7. "If this is not clear, it is not possible to define anything; for definition has to do with the general and with forms; so that as long as it is not evident what sort of parts are material and what sorts not, it is impossible to have a clear idea of anything" (103626–31).
8. Recourse to imagination is part of Aristotle's argument against Plato; no imagination would be needed if the intellect were simply to contemplate the Ideas that exist apart from bodies. Consider St. Thomas, *Summa Theologica*, Q. 84; Article 6.
9. One possible solution—the solution imputed to the Schoolmen by modern thinkers—is the doctrine of innate ideas. Aristotle unequivocally rejects the idea that there might be innate ideas of forms already in the mind (*De Anima* 430a1). Socrates claims that a science conversant with universals is derived from the memory and that teaching a person merely means awakening in her the remembrance of what she used to know suggests that he understood some variation on the theme that universals are innate. Consider *Meno* 82b–85c and Adam Smith, "The History of Ancient Logic and Metaphysics," in *Essays on Philosophical Subjects*, edited by W. P. D. Wightman and J. C. Bryce (Indianapolis: Liberty Fund, 1982), 124–5.
10. Aquinas, *Summa Theologica*, Q. 85; Article 1; Reply to Objection 2: "The intellect...abstracts the species of a natural thing from the individual sensible matter, but not from the common sensible matter; for example, it abstracts the species of man from 'this flesh and these bones,' which do

not belong to the species as such, but to the individual (Metaph. vii, Dic. vi, 10), and need not be considered in the species: whereas the species of man cannot be abstracted by the intellect form 'flesh and bones.'"

11. Smith, "Ancient Logic and Metaphysics," in Essays on Philosophical Subjects (Indianapolis: Liberty Fund, 1982) 126, believes that these "elusive" and "altogether incomprehensible" doctrines pass "easily enough, through the indolent imagination, accustomed to substitute words in the room of ideas' so long as they are "not much rested upon" or "particularly and distinctly explained." This suggests that ancient metaphysics are, for Smith, if not for Hume, a species of common sense more than a philosophical construction.

12. Frederick Copleston, *Aquinas* (Baltimore: Penguin, 1955), 81.

13. Hume's treatment of ancient philosophy makes no distinction between Aristotelean, scholastic and peripatetic philosophy. All branches of ancient philosophy, fundamentally resembling modern philosophy, in Hume's presentation, begin with a skepticism of the senses, an imaginative attempt to overcome the skepticism by announcing dualistic philosophic doctrines, and continued wrangling over the proper interpretation of the system (T 221–4).

14. "The opinions of the ancient philosophers, their fictions of substance and accident, and their reasonings concerning substantial forms and occult qualities, are like the spectres in the dark, and are deriv'd from principles, which, however common, are neither universal nor unavoidable in human nature" (T 226).

15. Locke typifies modern philosophy as Hume understands it, though I make reference to other modern thinkers in the text and in footnotes. Locke, following Hobbes, Descartes and Bacon, presents the modern system with sufficient clarity for my purposes. He also begins to come to grips with the contradictions in the modern system that prompted Hume's re-evaluation of it.

16. Consider also Thomas Hobbes, *Leviathan*, edited by Richard Tuck (New York: Cambridge University Press, 1991) 461 (Chapter 46): "The naturall Philosophy of those [Greek] Schools, was rather a Dream than Science, and set forth in senselesse and insignificant Language; which cannot be avoided by those that teach Philosophy... I beleeve that scarce any thing can be more absurdly said in naturall Philosophy, that that which now is called Aristotles Metaphysiques."

17. René Descartes, "Optics," in *Selected Philosophical Writings*, translated by John Cottingham, Robert Stoothoff, and Dugald Murdoch (Cambridge: Cambridge University Press, 1988), p. 62 (Discourse 5).

18. Consider Descartes' promise to doubt even "our revered theology" in "Discourse on the Method" in *Selected Philosophical Writings*, 23 (Part 1); Hobbes' account "Of Darkness from Vain Philosophy, and Fabulous Traditions," for instance, in *Leviathan*, 458ff. (Chapter 46); and Locke, ECHU 1.2.24 and 4.20.4.

19. René Descartes, "Principles of Philosophy," in *Selected Philosophical Writings*, 187 (# 74) makes much the same point: "The thoughts of almost all people are more concerned with words than with things; and as a result

people very often give their assent to words they do not understand." Cf. James Gibson, *Locke's Theory of Knowledge and Its Historical Relations* (Cambridge: Cambridge University Press, 1917), 190, who believes that Locke simply "takes for granted the validity of the [scholastic] categories which were fundamental for the thought of his age, and their adequacy for the interpretation of reality."
20. Hobbes, *Leviathan*, 14 (Chapter 1). See also Descartes' explanation of the five senses in "Principles of Philosophy," 203–4 (# 191–5).
21. Descartes makes precisely the same distinction in "Principles of Philosophy" (185–6; # 70–1) and he thinks, like Locke, that the chief error human beings make lies in assuming that imputing an existence outside the mind to sensed secondary qualities. Consider: "It is clear, then, that when we say that we perceive colours in objects, this is really just the same as saying that we perceive something in the objects whose nature we do not know, but which produces in us a certain very clear and vivid sensation which we call the sensation of colour... As long as we merely judge that there is in the objects (that is, in the things, whatever they may turn out to be, which are the source of our sensations) something whose nature we do not know, then we avoid error... But it is quite different when we suppose that we perceive colours in objects. Of course, we do not really know what it is that we are calling a colour; and we cannot find any intelligible resemblance between the colour which we suppose to be in the objects and that which we experience in our sensations... [The body is stimulated by] what we call the sensations of taste, smells, sounds, heat, cold, light, colours, and so on—sensations which do not represent anything located outside our thought."
22. In *Of the Conduct of the Understanding*, Locke argues that notions of the schoolmen signify nothing: "To one that can form no determined ideas of what they stand for, they signify nothing at all; and all that he thinks he knows about them is to him so much knowledge about nothing, and amounts at most but to a learned ignorance" (Para. 29).
23. Hobbes, *Leviathan*, 463 (Chapter 46). See also Descartes, "Principles of Philosophy" (206; # 198–9): "There is no way of understanding how these attributes (size, shape, and motion) can produce something else whose nature is quite different from their own—like the substantial forms and real qualities which many philosophers suppose to inhere in things; and we cannot understand how these qualities or forms could have the power subsequently to produce local motion in other bodies."
24. This tart formulation comes from Michael P. Zuckert, "Fools and Knaves: Reflections on Locke's Theory of Philosophic Discourse." *The Review of Politics* 36 (1974), 562–63. See also Maurice Mandelbaum, *Philosophy, Science, and Sense Perception* (Baltimore: The Johns Hopkins University Press, 1964), 23.
25. The skepticism of the senses inherent in this view—its radical doubt about the adequacy of common experience and pre-scientific reasoning

(which Hobbes calls mere prudence)—is almost never linked to the modern critique of scholasticism because we have lost sight of how the scholastic view attempted to defense the natural harmony between nature and human mind.

26. Eugene Miller, "Locke on the Meaning of Political Language." *The Political Science Reviewer* 9 (1979), 178n, 175, 176. Michael Ayers, *Locke*, vol. 2 (London: Routledge, 1991), 75, reduces Locke's central contention to its most essential elements in wondering how Locke "could have thought that things may deserve to be sorted one way rather than another, and yet deny that there is a right way to sort them determined by objective boundaries between kinds."
27. G. W. F. Hegel, *Natural Law*, translated by T. M. Knox (Philadelphia University of Pennsylvania Press, 1975), 64.
28. G. W. F. Hegel, *Lectures in the History of Philosophy*, vol. 3, translated by E S. Haldane and Frances H. Simson (London: Routledge & Kegan Paul 1986), 307.
29. Leo Strauss, *Natural Right and History* (Chicago: The University of Chicago Press, 1953) 175, writes: "Man can guarantee the actualization of wisdom, since wisdom is identical with free construction. But wisdom cannot be free construction if the universe is intelligible. Man can guarantee the actualization of wisdom, not in spite of, but because of, the fact that the universe is unintelligible."
30. Francis Bacon, *New Organon*, 1.129. Neal Wood, *The Politics of Locke's Philosophy* (Berkeley: University of California Press, 1983), 65–93, esp. 78–9, also recognizes Locke's kinship with Bacon, but fails for the most part to trace their kinship to their deepest assumptions about science.
31. Strauss, *Natural Right and History*, 174.
32. Hobbes, *Leviathan*, 47 (Chapter 7).
33. Peter C. Myers, *Only Star and Compass* (Lanham: Rowman & Littlefield, 1999), 75ff, raises provocative questions concerning "the limits of Locke's conventionalism."
34. Myers, *Only Star and Compass*, 81–5.

3   Active Sovereignty in Natural and Moral Philosophy

1. Thomas Reid, *An Inquiry into the Human Mind* (Chicago: University of Chicago Press, 1970) 14, 18 (Introduction, Sections V and VII). See also T. H. Green, *Hume and Locke* (New York: Thomas Y. Crowell, 1968) 133, 161ff.
2. Cited in Norman Kemp Smith, *The Philosophy of David Hume* (London: Macmillan, 1941), 4.
3. Smith, *The Philosophy of David Hume*, p. 447, also pp. 449–58. Others assenting to the "naturalistic" interpretation offered by Smith in at least a qualified manner include John W. Danford, *David Hume and the Problem of Reason* (New Haven: Yale University Press, 1990), 77; Donald

W. Livingston, *Hume's Philosophy of Common Life* (Chicago:University of Chicago, 1984), 27; Barry Stroud, *Hume* (London: Routledge & Kegan Paul, 1977), xi, 14, 68, 76–7, 222–4, 247–8; Anthony Flew, *Hume's Philosophy of Belief: A Study of His First Inquiry* (South Bend: St. Augustine Press, 1997), 272–3. Instead of "naturalism," some prefer to call Hume's combination of skeptical thinking and dependence on the natural deliverances of the senses and on the natural registering of human feelings a version of "classical scepticism." See Terence Penelhum, *David Hume: An Introduction to His Philosophical System* (West Lafayette: Purdue University Press, 1992), 22; Richard H. Popkin, *The High Road to Pyrrhonism* (San Diego: Austin Hill Press, 1980), 125–32. David Fate Norton, *David Hume: Common Sense Moralist, Sceptical Metaphysician* (Princeton: Princeton University Press, 1982), 6, 17, suggestively calls naturalism the "subordination thesis," in which reason is always subordinated to some form of passion or belief.

4. Livingston, *Hume's Philosophy of Common Life*, 27 and Nicholas Capaldi, *David Hume: The Newtonian Philosopher* (Boston: Twayne Publishers, 1975), 198. Comprehensive critiques of the "naturalistic" school are found in Norton, *David Hume: Common Sense Moralist, Sceptical Metaphysician*, 227–38 and Frederick G. Whelan, *Order and Artifice in Hume's Political Philosophy* (Princeton: Princeton University Press, 1985), 67ff.

5. Norton, *David Hume: Common Sense Moralist, Sceptical Metaphysician*, 235.

6. Danford, *David Hume and the Problem of Reason*, 77; Livingston, *Hume's Philosophy of Common Life*, 2: "In the last ten years or so there has been a growing tendency to view Hume's philosophical works as of a piece and to interpret him as the pioneer in moral philosophy that he set out to be." Also Robert A. Manzer, "Hume's Constitutionalism and the Identity of Democratic Constitutionalism," *The American Political Science Review*, Vol. 90, No. 3 (September 1996), 488–96.

7. It is characteristic of Hume to name no names in relaying this account, presumably because he wants to call attention to the permanence of the problem that he is discussing.

8. Nor is the sense of sight the only one subject to these difficulties. Taste too shows that "we are influenc'd by two principles directly contrary to each other, *viz*. that inclination of our fancy by which we are determin'd to incorporate the taste with the extended object, and our reason, which shows us the impossibility of such an union" (T 238).

9. Livingston, *Hume's Philosophy of Common Life*, 20–33, also views Hume as criticizing both ancient and modern forms of rationalism on this point. In contrast, Danford, *David Hume and the Problem of Reason*, 40–61, sees Hume reacting to Descartes, Hobbes, and Locke or, more generally, to modern forms of rationalism.

10. Conventionally, the criticism of modern and ancient attempts to reconcile reason and the senses is seen as a critique of "metaphysics" or

"rationalism" leading to a species of "naturalism." See, for example, John Passmore, *Hume's Intentions* (London: Gerald Duckworth, 1968), 70–2; Smith, *The Philosophy of David Hume*, 543–7. A growing number of scholars have noticed the literary character of Hume's presentation. Most suggestively, Livingston, *Hume's Philosophy of Common Life*, 11–15 and 44–5C, argues that Hume should be read as a "dialectical thinker," in that he begins with a common intuition or observation, subjects the common to critical inquiry, transcends the common view, subjects the new view to scrutiny, and so on. This "dialectic" is a dramatic unfolding of the philosophic issues surrounding, in this case, the matter of perception by examining and transcending contradictions in our experience. See also Donald W. Livingston, *Philosophical Melancholy and Delirium* (Chicago: University of Chicago, 1998), 13–16. Robert J. Fogelin, *Hume's Skepticism in the Treatise of Human Nature* (London: Routledge & Kegan Paul, 1985), 80–92, similarly explains Hume's literary narrative as a "natural history of philosophy," in which successive philosophic positions on perception arise and undergo transformations from a mixture of natural causes (the conflict between custom and reason) and contingent beliefs (philosophic systems) identifiable to the mind; the process of unfolding the common and philosophic perspectives leads to a natural privileging of common life. Consider also Annette Baier, *The Progress of Sentiments: Reflections on Hume's Treatise* (Cambridge: Harvard University Press, 1991), 27, who sees the *Treatise* as a "dramatic work" with the qualities of a "dialectic."

11. Cf. Livingston, *Philosophical Melancholy and Delirium*, 120, who writes that "Hume has more sympathy with the ancients than with the moderns" on this very point.
12. John Yolton, *John Locke and the Way of Ideas* (Oxford: Clarendon Press, 1970), 126.
13. Hume states the same case in the first *Enquiry*: "Bereave matter of all its intelligible qualities, both primary and secondary, you in a manner annihilate it, and leave only a certain unknown, inexplicable something, as the cause of our perceptions" (EHU 155).
14. Some Locke commentators dispute this. See Maurice Mandelbaum, *Philosophy, Science, and Sense Perception* (Baltimore: The Johns Hopkins University Press, 1964), 18–30; Yolton, *John Locke and the Way of Ideas*, 126–37. Michael Ayers, *Locke*, vol. 2 (London: Routledge, 1991), 46, and many others claim that "his onslaught on the Lockean version of [natural philosophy]" is "justified." See, for example, Livingston, *Philosophical Melancholy and Delirium*, 120; Danford, *David Hume and the Problem of Reason*, 46; Antony Flew, *Hume's Philosophy of Belief* (South Bend: St. Augustine Press,1997), 252–4.
15. See ECHU 2.23.*passim* and 4.11.3 for assertions of this supposition. Cf. T 187.
16. Earlier in the *Treatise* Hume contends that this "new system may esteem'd," but that "it contains all the difficulties of the vulgar system" (T 211).

17. Hume continues: "Nothing can be more inexplicable than the manner, in which body should so operate upon mind as ever to convey an image of itself to a substance, supposed of so different, and even contrary a nature" (EHU 153). Also T 84.
18. Nor does this opinion change from the *Treatise* to the first *Enquiry*, where Hume writes that we are "necessitated by reasoning to contradict or depart from the primary instincts of nature, and embrace a new system with regard to the evidence of our senses" (EHU 152). See also EHU 155; T 266ff.
19. The relationship between the treatment of personal identity in the body of the *Treatise* and that in the appendix has been a cause of much controversy. Some follow Wade L. Robison, "Hume on Personal Identity." *Journal of the History of Philosophy* 12 (1974), 182, in arguing that "Hume clearly thinks his former opinions a philosophical disaster—not just false, but inconsistent." See also Livingston, *Philosophical Melancholy and Delirium*, 14; Fogelin, *Hume's Skepticism*, 100–8; Garrett, "Hume's Self-Doubts about Personal Identity." *The Philosophical Review* 90 (1981), 337–58; Passmore, *Hume's Intentions*, 77–83; and Smith, *The Philosophy of David Hume*, 555–8. Against this view, I conceive of Hume's appendix as demonstrating that previous philosophic accounts of personal identity are incoherent and that the difficulties Hume identifies in the appendix follow from the limits of human understanding. The clearest palliative to the former view is found in Swain, "Being Sure of One's Self," *Hume Studies* 17 (1991), 108–12.
20. This dilemma prompts Hume to apply the problem of primary and secondary qualities to the sense of taste: The quotations in the text are drawn from the following longer discussion (T 238).
21. See also the following: "But tho' in this view of things we cannot refuse to condemn the materialists, who conjoin all thought with extension; yet a little reflection will show us equal reason for blaming their antagonists, who conjoin all thought with a simple and indivisible substance" (T 239).
22. See, for example, Fogelin, *Hume's Skepticism*, 38–52; Beauchamp and Rosenberg, *Hume and the Problem of Causation* (New York: Oxford University Press, 1981); and Smith, *The Philosophy of David Hume*, 365–403.
23. Also Danford, *David Hume and the Problem of Reason*, 67.
24. Consider Locke's most extensive account of cause-effect relationships: "In the notice, that our senses take of the constant vicissitude of things, we cannot but observe, that several particular, both qualities and substances, begin to exist; and that they receive their existence from the due application and operation of some other being. From this observation, we get our ideas of *cause* and *effect*. *That which produces any simple or complex idea*, we denote by the general name, *cause*; and *that which is produced, effect*." (ECHU 2.26.1)

25. Quoted in Matthew Rose, "The Disconsolate Philosopher." *First Things* (January 2003), 48.
26. John P. Wright, "Hume's Academic Scepticism." *Canadian Journal of Philosophy* 16 (1986), 414–5, "Hume identified certain *suppositions* which originate in that faculty of mind which he calls imagination; in fact, we would be closer to the roots of Hume's own skeptical problem if we spoke of his theory of natural suppositions rather than (as is commonly done) of his theory of natural beliefs... Hume thinks that they have some claim to give us a genuine account of reality."
27. Consider, for instance, E 111–2, 254–5, 295–6, 303, 378–80.
28. For other instance of Hume's use of "fiction" in just such contexts, see T 16, 200–1, 205, 208, 209, 263.
29. Consider the following examples: "We suppose that there is some connexion between [cause and effect]" (EHU 75); "If flame or snow be presented anew to the senses, the mind is carried by custom to expect heat or cold, and to *believe* that such a quality does exist, and will discover itself upon nearer approach" (46); and "The supposition of such a connection is... without any foundation in reasoning" (153).
30. Consider, for instance, T 16, 57, 92, 190, 199, 208, 213, 255, 259. Cf Wright, *The Sceptical Reason of David Hume* (Minneapolis: University of Minnesota Press, 1983), 55–6, who believes that natural suppositions are indeed false.
31. Hence the prevalent and not unreasonable contention that Hume abandons questions of philosophy for questions of psychology. Passmore *Hume's Intentions*, 60, for instance, quips that "in the end... psychology triumphs." See also Shirley Robin Letwin, *The Pursuit of Certainty* (Indianapolis: Liberty Fund, 1998), 46; Fogelin, *Hume's Skepticism*, 65 and Smith, *The Philosophy of David Hume*, 92–3. The fact that Hume switches the terms of the debate frustrates many commentators Beauchamp and Rosenberg, *Hume and the Problem of Causation*, 9, write "As Hume fully realizes, his description of the ordinary use of the term fails to answer the important philosophical question—no doubt recondite to the common user—wherein the necessity lies." Identifying what is frustrating about Hume's procedure, Smith, *The Philosophy of David Hume*, p. 93, contends that Hume's analysis "affords no *insight* into the nature of causation."
32. A person "*feels*" certain "events to be *connected* in his imagination" (EHU 75–6).
33. See also T 103. Letwin, *The Pursuit of Certainty*, 55, argues that Hume undermines the traditional distinction between reason and passions and sees only different kinds of passion. For Hume, she writes, "man is not then a divided nature but all one, and he is moved, not by two opposing principles, but by a variety of sensations."
34. I am indebted to Charles L. Griswold's, *Adam Smith and the Virtues of Enlightenment* (Cambridge: Cambridge University Press, 1999), 339–41.

lucid discussion of the role of the imagination in the thought of Hume and Smith. Baier, *The Progress of Sentiments*, 1–27, places Griswold's discussion in its proper context within Hume's dramatic presentation of the imagination. Fogelin, *Hume's Skepticism*, 62, too notices that "a dialectical conflict" emerges in Hume's treatment of the imagination: "The imagination underlies all our causal reasoning, yet, at the same time, it can generate beliefs in opposition to causal reasoning." See also Whelan, *Order and Artifice*, 97, 99–100.

35. See also the discussion of how philosophy provides no remedy for one who is callous to moral distinctions in "The Sceptic" (E 169–70).
36. Locke's moral science posits that science can provide principles "as incontestible as those in mathematics" (ECHU 4.3.18) and build systems from those principles.
37. According to Hume in "Of the Dignity or Meanness of Human Nature," these theorists say "All is self-love... Were the idea of self removed, nothing would affect you. You would be altogether unactive and insensible: Or, if you ever gave ourself any movement, it would only be from vanity, and a desire of fame and reputation to this same self" (E 85). Smith, *The Theory of Moral Sentiments* (Indianapolis: Liberty Fund, 1985), 315–17 (VII.iii.1), develops much the same critique of "those systems which deduce the principle of approbation from self-love," but without a reference to Locke.
38. Consider also the statement of "The Sceptic" (E 159–60). Smith, *The Theory of Moral Sentiments*, 299 (VII.ii.2.14), also observes the tendency of philosophers to "account for all appearances from as few principles as possible." Taking Hume's analysis a step further, Smith connects the "love of system" or the desire for simplicity to the love of beauty which modern philosophy for the most part ignores as a topic of philosophic reflection. One is tempted to see the "love of system" as a distorting deflection of the irrepressible love of beauty. See Griswold, *Adam Smith and the Virtues of Enlightenment*, 148–55 and 330–6, on the connection between the love of system and the love of beauty.

4 "Mitigated Scepticism" and Our "Mixed Kind of Life": The Philosophic Modesty of Hume's Science of Common Life

1. Thomas Reid, "Essays on the Active Powers," in *Inquiry and Essays*, edited by Keith Lehrer and Ronald E. Beanblossom (Indianapolis: Bobbs-Merrill, 1975), 360–8 (Essay V, Chapter VII). Pierre Manent, *City of Man*, translated by Marc A. LePain (Princeton: Princeton University Press, 1998), 144, similarly sees Hume's elevation of sentiment as culminating in "a dogmatism of the common occurrences of life." German romantics turned to Hume for inspiration because he was seen as a proponent of sentiment and feeling. See Isaiah Berlin,

"Hume and the Sources of German Anti-Rationalism," in *David Hume: Bicentenary Papers*, edited by G. P. Morice (Austin: University of Texas Press, 1977), 93–116.
2. Norman Kemp Smith, *The Philosophy of David Hume* (London: Macmillan, 1941), p. 447.
3. Donald W. Livingston, *Hume's Philosophy of Common Life* (Chicago: University of Chicago Press, 1984), p. 27 and Nicholas Capaldi, *David Hume: A Newtonian Philosopher* (Boston: Twayne, 1975), p. 198. See the beginning of chapter 3 for a more elaborate discussion of Hume's naturalism and its limits.
4. Charles L. Griswold, *Adam Smith and the Virtues of Enlightenment* (Cambridge: Cambridge University Press, 1999), p. 163. Consider the staged dialogue between Hume and an unnamed person who believes moral distinctions are founded on reason, where Hume criticizes his interlocutor for his "abstruse hypothesis" and claims that "there needs nothing more to give a strong presumption of falsehood" than a recourse to "metaphysics" (EPM 298). Wright's, "Hume's Academic Scepticism,' pp. 415–6, comments about the limits of Hume's agnosticism are well taken. Hume's agnosticism about *how* nature functions "does not mean that he is *agnostic* regarding our fundamental ontological suppositions."
5. Griswold, *Adam Smith and the Virtues of Enlightenment*, p. 165.
6. In his wonderfully suggestive examination of the context in which Hume's thought must be understood, David Fate Norton, *David Hume: Common-Sense Moralist, Sceptical Metaphysician* (Princeton: Princeton University Press, 1982), p. 9, sees Hume responding to "two quite distinguishable crises, a speculative crisis and a moral crisis." In the formulation of his subtitle, Norton sees Hume as a "common-sense moralist" in response to the moral crisis and a "sceptical metaphyscian" in response to the philosophic crisis. While I do not endorse the details of Norton's formulation, his observation that Hume is fighting, in effect, a two-front war parallels my formulation.
7. For a more detailed discussion of Hume's philosophical moods in the *Treatise*, see Annette Baier, *The Progress of Sentiments: Reflections on Hume's Treatise* (Cambridge: Harvard University Press, 1991), pp. 21–7.
8. Hume's essay on "Of Superstition and Enthusiasm" is placed between essays "Of the Parties of Great Britain," which concerns the influence of Lockean political thought on the ideological character of British parties, and "Of the Dignity or Meanness of Human Nature," which concerns in part Locke's treatment of human nature. This arrangement may suggest that Locke's teaching partakes of the superstition against which Locke himself argued.
9. We must be aware of the dramatic location of Hume's words in the conclusion of the first book of the *Treatise*. This statement is drawn from the portion of the conclusion after the nadir of his "philosophical melancholy and delirium" (T 269).
10. Consider John W. Danford, *David Hume and the Problem of Reason* (New Haven:Yale University Press, 1990), pp. 85, 109–10. See also Steven

Salkever, "'Cool Reflexion' and the Criticism of Values: Is, Ought, and Objectivity in Hume's Social Science," *American Political Science Review* 74 (1980), p. 72, who agrues that "in general, my reading of Hume suggests that his account of practical reasoning (though certainly not its content) is much closer to Aristotle's than most (including Hume) have thought."

11. Frank D. Balog, "The Scottish Enlightenment and the Liberal Political Tradition," in *Confronting the Constitution*, edited by Allan Bloom (Washington DC: AEI Press, 1990), p. 206. See also Constant Noble Stockton, "Economics and the Mechanism of Historical Progress in Hume's History," in *Hume: A Re-evaluation*, edited by Donald W. Livingston and James T. King (New York: Fordham University Press, 1976), p. 296.

12. Danford, *David Hume and the Problem of Reason*, pp. 36–7 and 89–90, on the centrality of imagination and nature respectively. See also Frederick Whelan, *Order and Artifice in Hume's Political Philosophy* (Princeton: Princeton University Press, 1985), pp. 94, 97–9.

13. One might see in the somewhat impervious character of common opinion in the matter of moral luck another instance of the tension between nature and reason. Smith, in his discussions of the influence of fortune on the sentiments and of moral corruption, makes explicit what is implicit in Hume's analysis. See Adam Smith, *The Theory of Moral Sentiments* (Indianapolis: Liberty Fund, 1985), pp. 61–2 and 92–108 (I.iii.2.I and II.iii). Hume concludes his discussion of moral luck with the following. "A man who has cured himself of all ridiculous prepossessions, and is fully, sincerely, and steadily convinced, from experience as well as philosophy, that the difference of fortune makes less difference in happiness than is vulgarly imagined; such a one does not measure out degrees of esteem according to the rent-rolls of his acquaintance" (EPM 248). The philosophic perspective, it seems, is able to correct the judgments of even relatively astute moral judges, and therefore represents a horizon beyond "mere" moral judgment.

14. Hill, "David Hume" in *The History of Political Philosophy*, edited by Leo Strauss and Joseph Cropsey (Chicago: University of Chicago Press, 1972), p. 521.

15. Similarly Smith, *The Theory of Moral Sentiments*, p. 265 (VII.I.1) begins his most philosophic book by announcing that his theory accomplishes a reconciliation of previous philosophic accounts of moral judgment. "If we examine the most celebrated and remarkable of the different theories which have been given concerning the nature and origin of our moral sentiments, we shall find that almost all of them coincide with some part or other of that which I have been endeavouring to give an account of; and that if every thing which has already been said be fully considered, we shall be at no loss to explain what was the view or aspect of nature which led each particular author to form his particular system. From someone or other of those principles which I have been endeavouring to unfold, every system of morality that ever had any reputation in the

world has, perhaps, ultimately been derived. As they are all of them, in this respect, founded upon natural principles, they are all of them in some measure in the right. But as many of them are derived from a partial and imperfect view of nature, there are many of them too in some respects in the wrong."

16. We presume that judgment is like the imagination, one fits constituent parts, in this respect. The imagination is "a magical faculty in the soul" and "inexplicable by the utmost efforts of human understanding" (T 24).
17. *Federalist 37*, pp. 195–6.
18. As Madison drew some of his reflections from Hume's "Of the Idea of a Perfect Commonwealth," this deep similarity is suggested by Douglass Adair, "'That Politics May be Reduced to a Science,'" in *Fame and the Founding Fathers*, edited by Trevor Colbourn (Indianapolis: Liberty Fund, 1974).
19. *Federalist 70*, pp. 394–5.
20. Hume's allusion to a philosopher's closet (see also E 52) is seen in Madison's discussion of epistemology, where Madison defends the Constitution against criticisms made from the perspective of "an ingenious theorist" who might plan a Constitution "in his closet or in his imagination." See *Federalist 37*, p. 198.
21. "Of the Standard of Taste" first appeared in the *Four Dissertations* of 1757 and was incorporated into the *Essays* a year later. "Of Delicacy of Taste and Passion" appeared in the first edition of the *Essays* in 1741.
22. Danford, *David Hume and the Problem of Reason*, p. 94, finds this "an extraordinarily prescient account of the sort of relativism which dominates contemporary social science of the positivist variety." The prescience consists in the fact that "Hume anticipates exactly the formulations of Ayer or Stevenson, which place moral judgments in the realm of personal preference (affective judgments) and divide them sharply from factual statements, which are verifiable by reference to the empirical world." It may be that Hume put this "species of philosophy" forth in anticipation of a misreading of his own account of moral sentiments. Many commentators have seen Hume endorsing precisely this radical divorce between sentiment and judgment. Consider for example, Flew, "On the Interpretation of Hume," in *The Is-Ought Question*, edited by W. D. Hudson (New York: St. Martin's, 1969), p. 67 and Stevenson, *Ethics and Language* (New Haven: Yale University Press, 1944), pp. 273–6. For a direct rejoinder to this misreading, see Steven Salkever, "'Cool Reflexion' and the Criticism of Values: Is, Ought, and Objectivity in Hume's Social Science," *American Political Science Review*, Vol. 74 (1980).
23. Hume describes what we must come to know before we can make moral evaluations: "No new fact to be ascertained; no new relation to be discovered. All the circumstances of the case are supposed to be laid before us, ere we can fix any sentence of blame or approbation. If any material

circumstance be yet unknown or doubtful, we must suspend for a time all moral decision or sentiment" (EPM 290).

24. Reid notices this parallel. Moral judgment, for Hume, Thomas Reid, *Essays on the Active Powers of the Human Mind* (Cambridge: MIT Press, 1969), pp. 360–8 (V.VII) writes, "has no other foundation but an arbitrary structure and fabric in the constitution of the human mind: so that, by a change in our structure, what is immoral might become moral, virtue might be turned into vice, and vice into virtue. And beings of a different structure, according to the variety of their feelings, may have different, nay opposite measures of moral good and evil." It is not clear that Hume would disagree with this and he might ask Reid in response: "Do you expect a change in human beings? Where else would you propose to put the standard?"

25. Raising this objection resurrects the position of the "species of philosophy" against which Hume is arguing. This is another example of how Hume's presentation is dialectical. Hume responds that we answer a "bad critic" when "we show him an avowed principle of art; when we illustrate this principle by examples, whose operation, from his own particular taste, he acknowledges to be conformable to the principle; when we prove that the same principle may be applied to the present case, where he did not perceive or feel its influence: he must conclude, upon the whole, that the fault lies in himself, and that he wants the delicacy which is requisite to make him sensible of every beauty and every blemish" (E 241). See Peter Jones, "Cause, Reason, and Objectivity in Hume's Aesthetics," in *Hume: A Re-evaluation,* edited by Donald W. Livingston and James T. King (New York: Fordham University Press, 1976), pp. 323–42, for an analysis of Hume's aesthetic judgment.

26. For other such statements consider the following characterizations of human faculties and the human condition: "mix'd and heterogeneous nature" (T 84); and "the intermediate situation of the mind" (T 216).

27. Compare "'Tis this principle [the imagination], which makes us reason from causes and effects; and 'tis the same principle, which convinces us of the continu'd existence of external objects" (T 266) with "Nothing is more dangerous to reason than the flights of the imagination" (T 267).

28. John Locke, *First Treatise*, Paragraph 58.

5 The Liberal Imagination and the Problem of Abstract Speculative Principles in Politics

1. Frederick G. Whelan, *Order and Artifice in Hume's Political Philosophy* (Princeton: Princeton University Press, 1985), p. 30. Others who see Hume as *the* conservative modern philosopher include Pierre Manent, *The City of Man* (Princeton: Princeton University Press, 2000), pp. 140–6; Donald W. Livingston, *Hume's Philosophy of Common Life* (Chicago: University of Chicago Press, 1984), pp. 306–10; David Miller, *Philosophy and Ideology in*

Hume's Political Thought (Oxford: Oxford University Press, 1981), pp. 2, 15, 96–7, 159, 161–2, 193–6, 200; Duncan Forbes, *Hume's Philosophical Politics* (Cambridge: Cambridge University Press, 1975), p. x; and Sheldon S. Wolin, "Hume and Conservatism," *American Political Science Review* 48 (1954).
2. See Douglas Wilson, "Jefferson vs. Hume," p. 53 and throughout.
3. John B. Stewart, *Opinion and Reform in Hume's Political Philosophy* (Princeton: Princeton University Press, 1992), pp. 6, 9. Also seeing Hume as, in many decisive respects, a classical liberal Robert A. Manzer, "Hume's Constitutionalism and the Identity of Democratic Constitutionalism," *The American Political Science Review*, Vol. 90, No. 3 (Sept., 1996), p. 493; Paul Rahe, *Republics Ancient and Modern, Inventions of Prudence: Constituting the American Regime* (Chapel Hill: University of North Carolina Press,1994)., pp. 307–10; Frank D. Balog, "The Scottish Enlightenment and the Liberal Political Tradition," In *Confronting the Constitution*, Edited by Allan Bloom (Washington DC: American Enterprise Institute, 1990), pp. 207–8; John W. Danford, *David Hume and the Problem of Reason* (New Haven: Yale University Press, 1990), pp. 138–63; Ralph Lerner, *The Thinking Revolutionary*, pp. 195–6, 204–7; and Albert O. Hirschman, *The Passions and the Interests* (Princeton: Princeton University Press, 1987).
4. Wolin, "Hume and Conservatism," p. 999.
5. Wolin, "Hume and Conservatism," p. 1016; Miller, *Philosophy and Ideology in Hume's Political Thought*, pp. 193–4; and Forbes, *Hume's Philosophical Politics*, p. x.
6. Manent, *The City of Man*, p. 144. Also Donald W. Livingston, *Philosophical Melancholy and Delirium* (Chicago: Chicago Press, 1998), pp. 333–44, for an account of emphasizing Hume's opposition to what Livingston regards as the abstractions of modern political life.
7. After all, as George Grant, *Lament for a Nation: The Defeat of Canadian Nationalism* (Toronto: McClelland and Stewart, 1965), p. 96, writes, "if one cannot be sure about the answer to the most important questions, then tradition is the best basis for the practical life."
8. Donald Livingston, "Hume's Historical Conception of Liberty," in *Liberty in Hume's History of England*, edited by Donald W. Livingston and Nicholas Capaldi (The Netherlands: Kluwer Academic Publishers, 1990), p 140, points out that "Hume's criticism of the contract theory is well known, but most commentators have failed to appreciate the depth of the criticism. The contract theory is a form of false philosophy." See also Livingston, *Philosophical Melancholy and Delerium*, pp. 127–9 and *Hume's Philosophy of Common Life*, pp. 277, 325.
9. The essays from the last edition that I do not consider "political" are as follows: "Of the Delicacy of Taste and Passion"; "Of Superstition and Enthusiasm"; "Of Eloquence"; "The Epicurean"; "The Stoic"; "The Platonist"; "The Sceptic"; "Of Polygamy and Divorce"; "Of Simplicity and Refinement in Writing"; "Of Tragedy"; and "Of the Standard of Taste.

10. Madison's analysis of faction in *Federalist 10* bears a strong resemblance to Hume's account in "Of Parties in General." See Adair, " 'That Politics May be Reduced to a Science,'" pp. 140, 146–50. Madison does not express worries about parties or even mention parties founded on abstract speculative principle. Also Rahe, *Republics*, vol. 3, p. 309, emphasis is in original.
11. For Locke, the problem of partisanship emerges in what can be seen as a two step psychological process. First, a state of unease practically forces individuals to embrace unexamined propositions so that they have "*some* foundation or principle to rest their thoughts on" (ECHU 1.2.24). Second, reverenced propositions are provided by conniving elites who seek to enslave the minds of men; men willingly and thankfully oblige the opinion elites who supply unthinking followers with principles on which to settle their uneasy minds. These swallowers of opinions from others "of all men, hold their opinions with the greatest stiffness" (4.16.3). According to Locke, this unthinking mental enslavement is "the foundation of the greatest, I had almost said all the errors in the world" and certainly the "most dangerous" ones (2.33.18).
12. See Manzer, "Hume's Constitutionalism," p. 489.
13. See, for example, Edmund Burke, *Reflections on the Revolution in France* (Indianapolis: Hackett Publishing, 1987), pp. 51–7. Also Livingston, "Hume's Historical Conception of Liberty," pp. 142 and *Hume's Philosophy of Common Life*, pp. 315, 323–4; Miller, *Philosophy and Ideology in Hume's Political Thought*, pp. 196–204; Wolin, "Hume and Conservatism," pp. 1008–9. Cf. Shirley Robin Letwin, *The Pursuit of Certainty* (Indianapolis: Liberty Fund, 1998), pp. 123–7 and Whelan, *Order and Artifice*, pp. 321–2, who see Burke as a rationalist enamored of abstract, divine conceptions of natural law.
14. See Alexis de Tocqueville, *The Old Regime and the Revolution*, translated by Alan S. Kahan, eds. Francois Furet and Francoise Melonio (Chicago: University of Chicago Press, 1998), pp. 99–101 and 195–209 (1.3 and 3.1).
15. Cf. Manzer, "Hume's Constitutionalism," pp. 489–90.
16. Consider Hume's discussions of what appears to be saint-worship in his treatment of how theism arises from polytheism. "The principles of polytheism, founded in human nature" show human beings anxious about happiness and misery, and "our anxious concern endeavours to attain a determinate idea of them; and finds no better expedient than to represent them as intelligent voluntary agents, like ourselves, only somewhat superior in power and wisdom" (NHR 40). In fact, Hume thinks the "heroes in paganism correspond exactly to the saints in popery" (NHR 52). See also NHR 43–4, 47–8.
17. Hume offers the same account in the *Essays*. "Religions, that arise in ages totally ignorant and barbarous, consist mostly of traditional tales and fictions, which may be different in every sect, without being contrary to each other; and even when they are contrary, every one adheres to the traditions of his own sect, without much reasoning or disputation" (E 62).

18. See also Tocqueville, *The Old Regime and the Revolution*, pp. 99–101 (1.3).
19. Consider the following characterizations of Catholic England from the *History of England*, Volume 1: "profound ignorance and superstition" (237); "nothing can be a stronger proof of the miserable ignorance in which that people were then plunged, than that a man... who subsisted by absurdities and nonsense, should think himself intitled to threat them as barbarians" (267); "the English of that age were still a rude and barbarous people" (272); "profound ignorance" (335); "barbarous and violent" (359); and "vulgar superstition" (370).
20. Religious and secular variations share the same "moral spirit" in that they both emphasize "man's affinity to God" or impute to man "a rational faculty linking him to God," according to Letwin, *The Pursuit of Certainty*, pp. 21, 37.
21. See Leo Strauss, *Philosophy and Law*, Translated by Eve Adler (Albany: SUNY Press, 1995), pp. 29–32, for an account of how modern political thought became enamored of system as it attempted to replace the system of Christianity. Modern philosophy aimed to replace divine sovereignty with human sovereignty in an effort to displace and discredit revelation.
22. As Letwin, *The Pursuit of Certainty*, p. 96, observes, "in later times, when idealism was no longer linked to God, and the danger was not of religious enthusiasm, Hume would have spoken against its modern equivalents—faith in the master race, the class struggle, progress or equality. For they, too, have inspired men to 'disclaim all control by human law, reason, or authority' in the name of a higher glory."
23. Hume paraphrases these thoughts near the end of "Of the Original Contract."
24. Livingston, "Hume's Historical Conception of Liberty," p. 117, writes, "Hume rejected the main thesis of the individualistic Whig tradition as taught by such thinkers as Sidney and Locke, and followers such as Price and Macaulay which forged a conceptual connection between representative government and liberty as the rule of law."
25. See Michael Zuckert, *The Natural Rights Republic* (South Bend: Notre Dame University Press, 1996), pp. 16–40.
26. See also Burke, *Reflections on the Revolution in France*, p. 68, "Kings will be tyrants from policy when subjects are rebels from principle."
27. *Federalist 49*, p. 283.
28. See Manent, *The City of Man*, p. 143, and Burke's critique of "barbarous" and "mechanic philosophy" in *Reflections*, pp. 68, generally 49–60.
29. Letwin, *The Pursuit of Certainty*, pp. 115–23; Livingston, *Philosophical Melancholy and Delirium*, pp. 256–89; "Hume's Historical Conception of Liberty," pp. 80–1; *Hume's Philosophy of Common Life*, pp. 323–9; Stewart *Opinion and Reform*, pp. 302–6; and Forbes, *Hume's Philosophical Politics*, pp. 187–9 recognizes that Hume's theoretical fears about modern rationalism were realized by the Wilkes Rebellion. The first manifestation of the deleterious effect of "abstract speculative principle" in politics,

according to Hume, was seen in the events surrounding the English Civil War. See Letwin, *The Pursuit of Certainty*, pp. 94–113.
30. Livingston, *Philosophical Melancholy and Delirium*, pp. 256–7, recounts how Hume's friend and publisher, William Strahan, urged Adam Smith to publish these thoughts, but Smith declined as per Hume's wishes.
31. The story of the Wilkes Riots is derived from Ian R. Christie, *Wilkes, Wyvill and Reform* (London: Macmillan, 1962), pp. 25–38 and Peter D. G. Thomas, *John Wilkes: A Friend to Liberty* (Oxford: Clarendon Press, 1996), pp. 27–108.
32. These words are drawn from various letters characterizing the Wilkes and Liberty Riots and the prevalent British reaction, see *Letters* II.182, 208, 269, 310. See also *Letters* II.218, 226, 245, 261, 306.
33. Livingston, "Hume's Historical Conception of Liberty," p. 80.
34. Livingston, *Philosophical Melancholy and Delirium*, pp. 285, 309, 312–13, links the "revolution ideology" surrounding the Wilkes and Liberty crisis to the cast of mind of the English Revolution and the American Revolution.
35. Tocqueville, *The Old Regime and the Revolution*, pp. 197–200 (3.1).

6 Humanity and Commerce

1. "The glory of the nation has spread itself all over EUROPE; derived equally from our progress in the arts of peace, and from valour and success in war. So long and so glorious a period no nation almost can boast of: Nor is there another instance in the whole history of mankind, that so many millions of people have, during the space of time, been held together, in a manner so free, so rational, and so suitable to the dignity of human nature" (E 508). See also E 382–3.
2. Leo Strauss, *Natural Right and History*, p. 18, calls this "fundamentally the classical view." This also appears to be the orthodox Christian view, as stated by Herbert Butterfield, *Christianity and History* (New York: Schribners, 1950), pp. 9–25.
3. Aristotle, *The Poetics*, translated by Theodore Buckley (Buffalo, New York: Prometheus Books, 1992), pp. 17–18 (Chap. IX).
4. Butterfield, *Christianity and History*, p. 18.
5. Hume exchanged several letters with Montesquieu at the end of the Frenchman's life, although these letters have yet to be translated (Letters I.133–8; April 10, 1749). As Ernest Campbell Mossner, *Life of Hume*, p. 229, relates, "to the great Montesquieu, it would appear, belongs the credit for having been the first distinguished thinker to recognize the genius of Hume. Having read the 1748 edition of *Essays Moral and Political*, Montesquieu was so taken with it that he sent the author his own *E'Spirit des Lois*, which Hume had already read at Turin."
6. For Montesquieu's discussion of ancient virtue, see *The Spirit of the Laws*, Book 4, Chapters 6–8 and Book 7, Chapter 5, and of monastic virtues, see Book 5, Chapter 2.

7. Pierre Manent, *The City of Man*, translated by Marc A. LePain (Princeton: Princeton University Press, 1998), p. 31, "The Christian and Greek ideas of virtue overlap a good deal. For both the philosophers and the Christians, virtue is the subjection of passions to reason, of the soul's lower to its higher parts, an ordering and an order wrought by the soul."
8. Montesquieu, *The Spirit of the Laws*, IV.6, 7, also observes the "singularity" of Sparta's republican institutions.
9. Montesquieu, *The Spirit of the Laws*, IV.5.
10. "Our modern convents are, no doubt, bad institutions: But there is reason to suspect, that anciently every great family in ITALY, and probably in other parts of the world, was a species of convent... We have reason to condemn all those popish institutions, as nurseries of superstition, burthensome to the public, and oppressive to poor prisoners" (E 398).
11. Montesquieu, *The Spirit of the Laws*, V.2, "The less we can satisfy our particular passions, the more we give ourselves up to passions for the general order. Why do monks love their order? Their love comes from the same thing that makes their order intolerable to them. Their rule deprives them of everything upon which ordinary passions rest; what remains, therefore, is the passion for the very rule that afflicts them. The more austere it is, that is, the more it curtails their inclinations, the more force it gives to those that remain."
12. Hume's *History* is replete with examples of how Christianity contradicts the dictates of common morality and common sense, consider H 1.139 308ff., 333, and 434.
13. Consider Montesquieu, *The Spirit of the Laws*, IV.8: "In the Greek republics, one was... in a very awkward position. One did not want citizens to work in commerce, agriculture, or the arts; nor did one want them to be idle. They found an occupation in the exercises derived from gymnastics and those related to war. The institutions gave them no others. One must regard the Greeks as a society of athletes and fighters."
14. *Federalist 9*, p. 39.
15. "Our modern education and customs instill more humanity and moderation than the ancient" (E 94). Also EPM 257.
16. Hume also begins "Of Refinement in the Arts" by summarizing the objection that luxury leads to various forms of personal vice (E 268–9).
17. Several different phrases reference the natural (i.e., original) disposition of the passions and mind for Hume. Consider the "original fabric and formation" (EPM 172) "simple, original instinct in the human breast" (201), the "original constitution of nature" (213), "original constitution of the mind" (214), "original passion" (297), "original frame of our temper" (302), and "natural inclinations" (NHR 72).
18. See Hume's treatment of the "selfish system of morals" endorsed by Thomas Hobbes and John Locke, EPM 296ff.
19. Consider also the following: "There is a very remarkable resemblance, which preserves itself amidst all their variety; and this resemblance must

very much contribute to make us enter into the sentiments of others, and embrace them with facility and pleasure" (T 318). What Hume refers to as sympathy in the *Treatise* is not altered by him using the word humanity in his other works; in fact, this change, by emphasizing more the commonality among all human beings, brings greater clarity to the presentation. See Nicholas Capaldi, *Hume's Place in Moral Philosophy* (New York: Peter Lang International Academic Publishers, 1992), pp. 241ff. It is revealing that, for Hume, the "laws of humanity" and the "restraints" of humanity are binding on human beings in their interactions with one another even when the "restraint of justice" is not. Justice is an artificial virtue, for Hume, tailored more or less to the particular circumstances of a nation, but "laws of humanity" are natural and binding on all rational creatures (EPM 190–1).

20. Hume's characterization of the difference between ancient and modern modes at times looks like a rough translation of Montesquieu. Consider the following from Montesquieu, *The Spirit of the Laws*, in light of this passage: "Most of the ancient peoples lived in governments that had virtue for their principle, and when that virtue was in full force, things were done in those governments that we no longer see and that astonish our small souls" (IV.4); "The spirit of commerce brings with it the spirit of frugality, economy, moderation, work, wisdom, tranquility, order and rule" (V.6).

21. See also Robert S. Hill, "David Hume" in *History of Political Philosophy* (Chicago: University of Chicago Press, 1963), p. 518.

22. See also Alexis de Tocqueville, *Democracy in America*, translated by Harvey Mansfield (Chicago: University of Chicago Press, 2002), 2.4.17 (p. 588).

23. On Rousseau's "natural pity," which he sees as "a disposition that is appropriate to beings as weak and subject to as many ills as we are; a virtue all the more universal and useful to man because it precedes in him the use of all reflection," see *Second Discourse*, pp. 130–1.

24. Locke, ECHU, 2.21.passim emphasizes the psychological paramouncy of unease, while Hobbes, *Leviathan*, p. 74 (Chapter 11) sees anxiety for the future as the mother of curiosity and ambition.

25. Adam Smith, *Wealth of Nations* (Indianapolis: Liberty Fund, 1982), Book I, Chapter 2, notices "the propensity to truck, barter, and exchange one thing for another" one "of those original principles in human nature."

26. The feudal order had not yet come to experience the "commerce" can bind "together the most distant nations in so close a chain" (H I.296).

27. "We ought perhaps to deem their acquaintance with foreigners rather an advantage; as it tended to enlarge their views, and to cure them of those illiberal prejudices and rustic manners, to which islanders are often subject" (H I.103).

28. Consider the relationship between England and the Netherlands (H III.327).

29. "The human mind is of a very imitative nature; nor is it possible for any set of men to converse often together, without acquiring a similitude of

manners, and communicating to each other their vices as well as virtues. The propensity to company and society is strong in all rational creatures; and the same disposition, which gives us this propensity, makes us enter deeply into each other's sentiments, and causes like passions to run, as it were, by contagion, through the whole club or knot of companions" (E 202).
30. See also Montesquieu, *The Spirit of the Laws*, XIX.27.
31. Montesquieu, *The Spirit of the Laws*, XX.1. Montesquieu sharpens his comments in the succeeding chapter (XX.2): "The spirit of commerce produces in men a certain feeling for exact justice, opposed on the one hand to banditry and on the other to those moral virtues that make it so that one does not always discuss one's own interests alone and that one can neglect them for those of others." Consider Hume own praise of feudal hospitality and courtesy (H I.150).
32. As Hume writes, "an acquaintance with the ancient periods of their government is chiefly useful by instructing them to cherish their present constitution, from a comparison or contrast with the condition of those distant times" (H II.525). See also, for example, H I.185; II.518–9; IV.354–5; IV.414.
33. Before the spread of commerce, "there was no medium between the severe, jealous Aristocracy, ruling over discontented subjects; and a turbulent, factious, tyrannical Democracy" (E 416).
34. Mossner, *The Life of David Hume*, p. 140, mentions that Hume found this essay frivolous.
35. Emblematic of the difference between Aristotle and Hume on the evaluation of luxury or an excessive love of wealth is their different views on charging interest on money lent. Aristotle condemns unqualifiedly as usurious what Hume would no doubt praise as legitimate interest rates. Cf. *The Politics*, 1058b1–4 with Hume's "Of Interest" (E 295–307). For a more complete comparison of ancient and modern evaluations of commerce along the lines outlined in the text, see Rahe, *Republics*, vol. 1, pp. 66–90 (Chapter III).
36. Adam Smith, *Theory of Moral Sentiments (Indianapolis: Liberty Fund, 1985)* pp. 181ff. (4.1).
37. *Federalist 10*, p. 52.
38. Alexis de Tocqueville, *The Old Regime and the Revolution*, translated by Alan S. Kahan, eds. Francois Furet and Francoise Melonio (Chicago: University of Chicago Press, 1998), Book 1, Chapter 3 for an elaboration of this point.

7 Religious Revolution and England's Humane Political Constitution

1. R. G. Collingwood, *The Idea of History* (Oxford: Oxford University Press, 1994), pp. 81–3, believes that Hume's restraint is a residue from ancient

or scholastic substantialism, by which Collingwood means a belief in a "static and permanent, an unvarying substratum underlying the course of historical changes and all human activities."
2. Consider Hume's retort to his relativist friend in "A Dialogue," appended to the end of EPM. After the friend questions the existence of a standard for moral judgment, Hume responds: "The Rhine flows north, the Rhone south; yet both spring from the same mountain, and are also actuated in their opposite directions, by the same principle of gravity. The different inclinations of the ground, on which they run, cause all the difference of their course" (EPM 333).
3. Alexis de Tocqueville, *Democracy in America*, Introduction pp. 3–6.
4. John W. Danford, *David Hume and the Problem of Reason*, p. 121.
5. Ibid., p. 130, "The critical first element is the rule of law, or what would today be called an independent judiciary and a science of jurisprudence which separates questions of justice from considerations of military loyalty."
6. By arresting the story of English political development before the vast sea change in religious opinion, Danford's treatment of Hume's theory of development may leave the impression that religious beliefs simply follow changes in the mode of production. This is a permanent temptation for Hume interpreters, given his view that the ethic of humanity follows the revolution in commerce. Other penetrating observers omit the waning of superstition from their account of the transition out of feudalism. See Eugene Miller, "Hume on Liberty in the Successive English Constitutions" in *Liberty in Hume's History of England* (New York: Springer, 1990), pp. 53–76 and David Miller, *Philosophy and Ideology in Hume's Political Thought* (Oxford: Oxford University Press, 1981), pp. 121–62.
7. Consider also the following: "If we consider the ancient state of Europe, we shall find, that the far greater part of the society were every where bereaved of their personal liberty, and lived entirely at the will of their masters" (H II.522).
8. Harold of Hastings, for instance, was raised by turbulent nobles because his father abandoned him for a pilgrimage to Jerusalem (I.139–40).
9. See Miller, "Hume on Liberty in the Successive English Constitutions," pp. 67–9.
10. Even after the Magna Carta restricted royal prerogative, Edward I "restored authority to the government," "maintained the laws against all the efforts of the turbulent barons," and "kept everyone in awe" (II.140, 119). Edward III and Henry IV fit in this category too.
11. Edward II, Edward's son, was one of the weakest and most unfortunate kings, and he paid for his weakness by being killed at the hands of the barons. Richard II and Henry VI fall into this category.
12. "The languishing state of commerce kept the inhabitants poor and contemptible; and the political institutions were calculated to render that poverty perpetual. The barons and gentry, living in rustic plenty and

hospitality, gave no encouragement to the arts, and had no demand for any of the more elaborate produce of manufactures: Every profession was held in contempt but that of arms: And if any merchant or manufacturer rose by industry and frugality to a degree of opulence, he found himself but the more exposed to injuries, from the envy and avidity of the military nobles" (H I.463–4).

13. See, for example, "Arbitrary power... is altogether ruinous and intolerable, when contracted into a small compass" (E 116); and "Submission to a petty prince, whose dominions extend not beyond a single city, is more grievous than obedience to a great monarch," Hume writes, because "the more the master is removed from us in place and rank, the greater liberty we enjoy" (E 383).
14. Consider Niccolò Machiavelli, *The Prince*, Translated by Harvey Mansfield (Chicago: University of Chicago Press, 1985), Chapter 9.
15. Danford, *David Hume and the Problem of Reason*, pp. 126–32.
16. These descriptions are taken from Hume's account of Henry III (1216–72). Robberies were common and "these crimes escaped with impunity, because the ministers of justice themselves were in a confederacy with the robbers" (II.70).
17. Edward was a "friend of law and justice" who established "more constant, standing, and durable laws than any made since"; "the regular order, maintained in his administration, gave the opportunity to the common law to refine itself, and brought the judges to a certainty in their determinations, and the lawyers to a precision in their pleadings." Learned observers, Hume observes, noted the "sudden improvement of English law during this reign" and that "law began now to be well established" (II.141–2).
18. Miller, "Hume on Liberty in the English Constitutions," p. 75.
19. As Hume writes in his summary of Edward III's reign (d. 1377), "the laity at this time seem to have been extremely prejudiced against the papal power, and even somewhat against their own clergy, because of their connexions with the Roman pontiff" (II.278).
20. Miller, "Hume on Liberty in the English Constitutions," p. 63.
21. Also Danford, *David Hume and the Problem of Reason*, p. 120; and Capaldi, "The Preservation of Liberty," in *Liberty in Hume's History of England*, p. 196.
22. Cf. Danford, *David Hume and the Problem of Reason*, p. 123.
23. I go further than Richard H. Popkin, "Hume: Philosophical Versus Prophetic Historian," in *The High Road*, pp. 237–8, who shows that Hume "rejected providential and prophetic history totally and in so doing set a pattern for purely secular history and the secular examination of man." My initial criticisms are based on the assumption that there are different species of secular history.
24. This is especially true of the charter, established by Henry III, that established the common's right to hunt and forage in forests (II.6).

25. This despite the fact that the Tudors greatly expanded the practice of extorting forced loans and beneficences, granted uneconomical monopolies, and imposed trade embargoes (IV.363–4).
26. The Tudors' rule resembles French monarchs' of Hume's day, see "Of Civil Liberty" (E 92–4).
27. Henry VII did intend on breaking up aristocratic estates by breaking up ancient entails and encouraging the nobility to break up their estates. This law was designed to alter the balance of power in England, and it had the indirect, perhaps unintended, effect of promoting commerce.
28. Consider esp. III.76–77.
29. Scholars attempting to account for the rise of civilization tend to emphasize economics and the institution of the rule of law at the expense of the withering of superstition. The topic of religion normally arises only as these scholars explain the decline of absolute monarchy. Consider Danford, *Hume and the Problem of Reason*, pp. 109–35; Craig Walton, "Hume's England as a Natural History of Morals" in *Liberty in Hume's History of England* (New York: Springer, 1990), p. 42; Eugene Miller, "Hume on Liberty" in *Liberty in Hume's History of England* (New York: Springer, 1990), pp. 80–1; Nicholas Capaldi, "The Preservation of Liberty" in *Liberty in Hume's History of England* (New York: Springer, 1990), p. 211. All the developments of civilization presuppose the withering of superstition; Hume's theory of development can be applied to areas outside of Christendom (e.g., Islamic countries) only if we understand that superstition must wither before a commitment to the rule of law will be established.
30. "Amidst the anxieties with which he was agitated, he was often tempted to break off all connexions with the court of Rome; and though he had been educated in a superstitious reverence to papal authority, it is likely, that his personal experience of the duplicity and selfish politics of Clement, had served much to open his eyes in that particular. He found his prerogative firmly established at home: He observed, that his people were in general much disgusted with clerical usurpations, and disposed to reduce the powers and privileges of the ecclesiastical order" (III.189). See also III.201.
31. Follow the progress of Henry's efforts to suppress the monasteries, III.161, 186, 227, 251.
32. "The authority of the king kept every one submissive and silent; and the new-assumed prerogative, the supremacy, with whose limits no one was fully acquainted, restrained even the most furious movements of theological rancour" (III.241).
33. "His own example, by encouraging speculation and dispute, was ill fitted to promote that peaceable submission of opinion, which he recommended" (III.311).
34. "So thoroughly were these principles imbibed by the people, during the reigns of Elizabeth and her predecessors, that opposition to them was

regarded as the most flagrant sedition, and not even rewarded by that public praise and approbation, which can alone support men under such dangers and difficulties, as attend the resistance to tyrannical authority" (IV.369).
35. Tocqueville, *The Old Regime*, pp. 155, 163–4 (II.9 and 10).
36. Hume's formulation of enthusiastic sensibilities as ready to sacrifice everything to "speculative and abstract principles" calls to mind his characterization of political parties from "abstract speculative principle," which "are known only to modern times" (E 60). Whig theory is a secular variation on enthusiastic religious principles, and Whig theorists resemble enthusiastic religionists in their political activity.
37. Under James I, Hume claims that new "dispositions" were "just beginning to exist and to appear in the parliament" (V.19), but those new dispositions began to exist under Elizabeth.
38. See, for example, IV.138ff. for an account of how Elizabeth used "royal power" against the "zeal for Protestantism."
39. In 1576, M. P. Peter Wentworth was jailed for a speech that defended the parliament's power to criticize royal policies. This remarkable speech contains "a rude sketch of those principles of liberty, which happily gained afterwards the ascendant in England" (IV.178).
40. Charles was cursed to govern in "a period when the precedents of many former reigns favoured strongly of arbitrary power, and the genius of the people ran violently towards liberty" (V.543). It is a "paradox in human affairs" that Charles was "led to a public and ignominious execution" less than one hundred years after Henry was "adored in his life-time." It is a paradox that Henry VIII's "memory is respected" while Charles I's name will be "ever after pursued by falsehood and by obloquy" (V.583).
41. Elizabeth awed the other European powers by equipping a fleet and organizing an army in a fortnight when the Spanish threatened to invade in 1588 (IV.378). The Netherlands, the other thoroughly Protestantized country, also experienced an almost immediate expansion of power.
42. Several gentlemen embraced the "universally diffused" spirit of liberty (V.179). The "generous train of nobility and gentry, who now attended the king in his distresses, breathed the spirit of liberty as well as of loyalty: And in the hopes alone of his submitting to a legal and limited government, were they willing in his defence to sacrifice their lives and fortunes" (V.394). For other statements about the lack of seriousness in the nobles and their attachment to modern principles of liberty and commerce, see V.132–3, 284, 290–1, 361, 387 with 437, 470, 476, although the nobles were also concerned about loyalty to the crown (V.378–9).
43. Tocqueville, *The Old Regime*, p. 153 (II.9): "In England, nobles and commoners together engaged in the same businesses, pursued the same professions, and what is still more important, married each other.... It has often been remarked that the English nobility has been more prudent, more able, more open than any other. What ought to be said is that there

has long been no nobility, strictly speaking, in England, if one takes the word in the old limited sense which it has kept everywhere else." See also p. 157.
44. Niccolo Machiavelli, *The Prince*, translated by Harvey C. Mansfield, Jr. (Chicago: University of Chicago, 1985), p. 30.
45. Ibid., p. 67.
46. Montesquieu, *The Spirit of the Laws*, p. 389 (Book 21, Chapter 20).
47. These quotations are drawn from Steven B. Smith, *Hegel's Critique of Liberalism* (Chicago: The University of Chicago Press, 1989), pp. 188–9.

8 Religious Belief and Hume's Philosophy of Common Life

1. Hume considers these questions several times, see T 95–8, 225; EHU 47–9.
2. Fr. Copelston's, *A History of Philosophy: Hobbes to Hume*, Volume V (Westminster: The Newman Press, 1964), p. 240, description is apt: "The characteristic feature of Berkeley's argument for God's existence is the use which he makes of his theory of 'ideas.' If sensible things are ideas, and if these ideas are not dependent simply on our minds, they must be referred to a mind other than our own. 'It is evident to everyone, that those things which are called the works of Nature, that is, the far greater parts of the ideas or sensations perceived by us, are not produced by, or dependent on the wills of men. There is, therefore, some spirit that causes them, since it is repugnant that they should subsist by themselves'" (PHK 1.107).
3. Thomas Reid, *An Inquiry into the Human Mind* (Chicago: University of Chicago Press, 1970), pp. 14–16 (Introduction; Section V).
4. See Michael Allen Gillepse, *The Theological Origins of Modernity* (The University Chicago Press, 2008), Chapters 1 and 6 for the importance of this idea of God in modern thought generally.
5. Hume writes an even more Berkeleyian characterization of this thought: It is "not the organs of sense, which, being agitated by external objects, produce sensations in the mind; but it is a particular volition of our omnipotent Maker, which excites such a sensation, in consequence of such a motion in the organ" (EHU 70–1).
6. This argument seems to be drawn from Berkeley. Consider, for instance, *PHK* 149, Berkeley's contention that "nothing can be more evident to anyone that is capable of the least reflection than the existence of God, or a spirit who is intimately present to our minds, producing in them all that variety of ideas or sensations which continually affect us, on whom we have absolute and entire dependence, in short 'in whom we live, and move, and have our being'."
7. See Roger Scruton, *A Short History of Modern Philosophy* (London: Routledge, 1981), p. 104.

8. Keith Yandell, "Hume on Religious Belief," in *Hume: A Re-Evaluation* (New York: Fordham University Press, 1976), p. 114, notes "an interesting parallel between Hume's treatment of belief in the external world and in causal connections, and his treatment of a minimally theistic belief."
9. "Matter...and spirit are at bottom equally unknown; and we cannot determine what qualities may inhere in the one or in the other" (E 591).
10. See also Locke, ECHU 4.3.6.
11. Those who see in Hume a species of ancient philosophic agnosticism believe that Hume's analysis stops at this point.
12. The immateriality and immortality of the soul are intimately connected, if not synonymous, in human nature (E 592); belief in the immaterial arises because people want to believe that there is something imperishable about their identity, and indulging this desire leads people beyond the border of this world toward immortality.
13. It is part of Hume's project of establishing the autonomy of morals. See, for instance, Frederick G. Whelan, *Order and Artifice in Hume's Political Philosophy* (Princeton: Princeton University Press, 1985), pp. 106–7, 308–9; J. C. A. Gaskin, "Hume on Religion," in *The Cambridge Companion to Hume*, edited by David Fate Norton (Cambridge: Cambridge University Press, 1993), pp. 332–5; and David Fate Norton, "Hume, Atheism, and the Autonomy of Morals" in *Hume's Philosophy of Religion* (Winston-Salem: Wake Forest University Press, 1986).
14. Livingston, *Philosophical Melancholy and Delirium*, p. 69, sees in these passages Hume's endorsement of "philosophical theism," a doctrine defined by the belief in "a perfect creator." Passages in NHR justify this conclusion. "No rational enquirer can, after serious reflection, suspend his belief a moment with regard to the primary principles of genuine Theism and Religion" (21). Theism is "conformable to sound reason" (53), coincides "with the principles of reason and true philosophy" (43), and gives rise to "rational worship or adoration" (43). "What a noble privilege is it of human reason to attain the knowledge of the supreme Being; and, from the visible works of nature, be enabled to infer so sublime a principle as its supreme Creator?" (75). See also NHR 24, 38, and 74. This argument from design was prominent in Hume's time, see Antony Flew, *Hume's Philosophy of Belief*, p. 214; and it is an enduring argument from St. Thomas Aquinas, *Summa Theologica*, Part I, Question 2, Article 3, the fifth way. Yandell, "Hume on Religious Belief," p. 116, raises the poignant problem to those who see Hume endorsing theism. This position faces "the obvious difficulty of making Hume more oblivious to the force of his powerful critique of that argument...than I at least would suppose possible for so astute a philosopher."
15. See also EHU 72–3 for a discussion of divine volition.
16. Hume originally included "Of Miracles" in the *Treatise*, but he refrained from including it because he feared it "would give too much Offence

even as the World is dispos'd at present" (Letter to Henry Home, December 2, 1737). R. M. Burns, *The Great Debate on Miracles* (East Brunswick, NJ: Associated University Presses, 1981) and M. A. Stewart, "Hume's Historical View of Miracles," in *Hume and Hume's Connexions*, edited by M. A. Stewart and J. P. Wright (University Park, Pennsylvania: Pennsylvania State University Press, 1994), pp. 171–200, demonstrate that the style and content of the essay were probably revised somewhat before its inclusion in the first *Enquiry*. So did Hume's attitude. Hume speaks of his "indifference about all the consequences that may follow" from its publication to his cousin Henry Home (Letters I.111). Hume also assessed the political environment differently, seeing it amenable to its publication. As he writes to James Oswald (October 2, 1747), "I do not see what consequences follow, in the present age, from the character of an infidel; especially if a man's conduct be in other respects irreproachable" (Letters I.106).

17. The most penetrating treatments of Hume as a philosopher of common life (Danford, *David Hume*; and Livingston, *Philosophical Melancholy and Hume's Philosophy of Common Life*) refrain from addressing his treatment of miracles within the context of his philosophy of common life.

18. John P. Wright, "Hume's Academic Scepticism," *Canadian Journal of Philosophy*, Vol. 16, No. 3 (September 1986), p. 430, "On Hume's view the discovery of such a hidden cause results from the supposition that there is an absolute necessity in nature, even where an established regularity fails to hold."

19. Michael P. Levine, *Hume and the Problem of Miracles: A Solution* (Dordrecht: Kluwer Academic Publishers, 1989), pp. 23–36; Leo Strauss, *Philosophy and Law*, translated by Eva Adler (Albany: SUNY, 1995), pp. 31–2; and C. S. Lewis, *Miracles* (New York: Macmillan, 1970), pp. 100–07.

20. The same distinction informs Gibbon's famous introduction to his treatment of Christianity in Chapter XV of *Decline and Fall of the Roman Empire*: "The theologian may indulge the pleasing task of describing Religion as she descended from Heaven, arrayed in her natural purity. A more melancholy duty is imposed on the historian. He must discover the inevitable mixture of error and corruption which she contracted on a long residence upon earth, among a weak and degenerate race of beings." Hume's passage seems to be more evidence that Hume's perspective assumes the untruthfulness of miracles taut court.

21. Consider I Corinthians 15:12: "If Christ has not been raised, our preaching is useless and so is your faith" (NIV).

22. See also Stephen P. Foster, "Hume at work in Gibbon's *Decline and Fall*." *The Modern Schoolman* 71 (March 1994), p. 234.

23. This episode illustrates three of Hume's four main "arguments" against the reliability of evidence on which belief in miracles could be founded: (1) Those attesting to miracles are too few, too unlearned, and too unreliable; (2) human beings are attracted to and motivated by "surprise and

wonder" associated with extraordinary events; and (3) miracles are observed chiefly among the "ignorant and barbarous nations" (EHU 116–9).

24. "No wonder, then, that mankind, being placed in such an absolute ignorance of causes, and being at the same time so anxious concerning their future fortune, should immediately acknowledge a dependence on invisible powers, possessed of sentiment and intelligence" (NHR 30).

25. Can Hume's emphasis on accident in the *History* be reconciled by his linking accident to superstitious religious beliefs? If accident always determined history, then superstitious beliefs would always be present, even in England. Superstitious religious beliefs had died in England by Hume's day, which either means that history is not dependent on accident (which would allow superstition to wither on the vine) or that people are ignorant of how much history is dependent on chance (which would allow it to whither due to what Hume would no doubt regard as a pleasing error).

26. "Barbarity, caprice; these qualities, however nominally disguised, we may universally observe, from the ruling character of the deity in popular religions. Even priests, instead of correcting these depraved ideas of mankind, have often been found ready to foster and encourage them" (NHR 73). Cf. Livingston, *Philosophical Melancholy and Delirium*, p. 71, "It is worth remarking that Hume did not employ the 'conspiracy of the priests' explanation of the cause of religious oppression so popular among freethinkers of his time." Livingston is correct in emphasizing the origin of priestly oppression in human passions, but Hume emphasizes that priests need not exploit these original passions. Human nature can be channeled in many different directions on these secondary matters. This is, for Hume, good news, because priests and others who claim immediate commerce with God have so corrupted natural sensibilities can also be effectively defrocked by Enlightenment philosophy.

27. See also Locke, ECHU 4.19.3–8.

28. John Earman, *Hume's Abject Failure* (New York: Oxford University Press, 2000), pp. 44–7, discusses the permutations that this phraseology underwent in the successive editions of EHU.

29. Lewis, *Miracles* (New York: MacMillan, 1960), p. 103. See also Earman, *Hume's Abject Failure*, pp. 3–4, who sees in Hume's argument the "kind of overreaching that gives philosophy a bad name." He continues: "Any epistemology that does not allow for the possibility that evidence, whether from eyewitness testimony or from some other source, can establish the credibility of a UFO landing, a walking on water, or a resurrection is inadequate." See also pp. 22–4, 31–2 and Michael P. Levine, *Hume and the Problem of Miracles: A Solution* (New York: Springer, 1989), pp. 23–36.

30. *Democracy in America*, pp. 283–5.

31. Ancient, feudal, and barbarous people lived in "continual alarm" (E 259) over war and rumors of war with neighbors, and Hume connects

the uncertain fortunes of war with the belief that gods "have an influence in every affair" (NHR 30).
32. These questions may ultimately be the reason for Griswold's odd plea for a more dialogic philosophy at the conclusion his monumental work *Adam Smith and the Virtues of Enlightenment*.
33. Strauss, *Philosophy and Law*, pp. 31–2.

9 Humanity and Theology in Hume's Religious Dialogues

1. See Will R. Jordan, "Religion in the Public Square: A Reconsideration of David Hume and Religious Establishment," *Review of Politics*, Vol. 64, No. 4 (2002), p. 693, who believes that Hume "accepts the fact that religious belief is an enduring part of human existence." Also John W. Danford, *David Hume and the Problem of Reason* (New Haven: Yale University Press, 1990), pp. 162–86 and Donald W. Livingston, *Philosophical Melancholy and Delirium* (Chicago: University of Chicago Press, 1998), p. 65. See NHR 75 for a passage that supports this point of view.
2. Ernest Campbell Mossner, *The Life of David Hume* (Oxford: Oxford University Press, 1954), pp. 286–9. I agree with Terence Penelhum, *Hume* (New York: Macmillan, 1975), p. 170, who finds the old title to be a more accurate title reflecting the essay's content.
3. "Divinity or Theology, as it proves the existence of a Deity, and the immortality of souls...has a foundation in *reason*, so far as it is supported by experience. But its best and most solid foundation is *faith* and divine revelation" (EHU 165).
4. The original title was abandoned for the current title in the mid-1750s, during a period of tumult in Scotland over Hume's writings. Mossner, *The Life of David Hume*, pp. 286–355. He also withheld publication of "Of Suicide" and "Of the Immortality of the Soul" and the *Dialogues* on the advice of friends. Hume's letter to William Strahan (8 June 1776) discusses the circumstances of his withholding publication.
5. Consider Mossner's observation about this section: "The two sections ["Of Miracles" and "Particular Providence"] are related in argument and designed to be considered together...although that has seldom been done by controversialists." Mossner, *The Life of David Hume*, p. 286.
6. Many scholars leave politics entirely out of this dialogue, which, as they read it, is concerned mostly with deconstructing the argument from design. See Penelhum, *Hume*, pp. 178–80.
7. Cf. Richard H. Popkin, "Hume: Philosophic Versus Prophetic Historian," in *The High Road to Pyrrhonism* (Indianapolis: Hackett Publishing Company, 1993), p. 245, suggests that Hume used the dialogue in Section XI because he "regarded his views here as more dangerous than [those] in the preceding chapter."

8. All citations in this section are to EHU unless otherwise noted.
9. Consider the discussion of tolerating polytheists in NHR 48–51.
10. Consider Hebrews 3:4, "For every house is built by someone, but God is the builder of everything." These statements have led one of the deepest Hume commentators to conclude that Hume "accepted, in some form, the argument from design." See Livingston, *Hume's Philosophy of Common Life*, p. 172.
11. So dazzled by Hume's arguments about design are scholars that they have too often failed to recognize the limited political import of the argument accorded by Hume. Hume realized that revealed doctrines are more associated with the heart of Christianity than the argument from design and the new title helps to draw attention to these revealed doctrines instead of the natural religion perspective. This pattern is repeated in the *Dialogues*. Consider, C. S. Lewis, *The Problem of Pain* (New York: Macmillan, 1977), Introduction.
12. This passage, and a similar one in the mouth of Cleanthes in the *Dialogues* (see below), is key for those who see Hume as an advocate of civil religion. See Jordan, "Religion in the Public Square," pp. 693–4. I disagree for two reasons. First, the statement favoring a civil religion is part of the action of the dialogue, not a statement of principle. As I will argue in the next paragraph, Hume moves from an endorsement of mercenary civil religion to a more confrontational philosophic pose as "Particular Providence" ends. Second, Hume's apparent psychology of civil religion, wherein people draw moral consequences from their faith, contradicts his statements elsewhere about the inefficacy of religion in affecting moral behavior and about the weak hold religion has on the moral imagination. See NHR 60, 71–2, 75.
13. Richard H. Popkin, *The History of Scepticism from Erasmus to Descartes*, Revised Edition (New York: Harper & Row, 1968).
14. Cf. Penelhum, *Hume*, p. 163, who argues that Hume acts to discredit "the tradition of representing Christian beliefs as extensions of scientific knowledge."
15. Penelhum, *Hume*, p. 171, regards the *Dialogues* to be "beyond any question the greatest work on philosophy of religion in the English language." Michael Morrisroe, Jr., "Characterization as Rhetorical Device in Hume's *Dialogues Concerning Natural Religion*," *Enlightenment Essays* (1) 1970: 95, goes further, calling it "the finest dialogue written in English." See also Mossner, "Hume and the Legacy of the *Dialogues*," in *David Hume: Bicentenary Papers*, edited by G. Morice (Edinburgh: Edinburgh University Press, 1977), p. 2. Hume was concerned to have William Strahan, his publisher, publish the book posthumously. Two months before his death, Hume wrote Strahan (June 8, 1776): "Some Years ago, I composed a piece, which would make a small Volume in Twelves. I call it *Dialogues on natural Religion*: some of my Friends flatter me, that it is the best think I ever wrote" (Letters II.323).

16. Keith E. Yandell, "Hume on Religious Belief," in *Hume: A Re-Evaluation* (New York: Fordham University Press, 1976), p. 111.
17. William Lad Sessions, *Reading Hume's Dialogues: A Veneration for True Religion* (Bloomington: Indiana University Press, 2002), marks a triumph for efforts to read the work as a dramatic whole, although scholarship has been moving in this direction since the mid-1970s. See also Penelhum, Hume, p. 180; John Bricke, "On the Interpretation of Hume's Dialogues" *International Journal for Philosophy of Religion* 6 (1975): p. 3; and A. G. Vink, "The Literary and Dramatic Character of Hume's *Dialogues Concerning Natural Religion,*" *Religious Studies* 22 (1986): pp. 388–90.
18. Cf. Danford, *David Hume and the Problem of Reason*, pp. 169–70, who sees Hume as opposing the excessive skepticism of Enlightenment science in the *Dialogues*.
19. Consider Popkin's "Hume and Kierkegaard," in *The High Road*, pp. 227–36.
20. Hume writes to Gilbert Elliot of Minto (March 10, 1751): "I cou'd wish that Cleanthes' Argument coud be so analys'd, as to be render'd quite formal & regular. The Propensity of the Mind toward it, unless that Propensity were as strong & universal as that to believe in our Senses & Experience, will, I am afraid, be esteem'd a suspicious Foundation. Tis here I wish for your Assistance. We must endeavour to prove that this Propensity is somewhat different from our Inclination to find our own Figures in the Clouds, our Face in the Moon, our Passions & Sentiments even in inanimate Matter. Such an Inclination may, & ought to be controul'd, & can never be a legitimate Ground for Assent" (Letters I.155). See also the postscript to this letter. Hume never seems to have surmounted this weighty objection.
21. Such is the view of R. J. Butler, "Natural Belief and the Enigma of Hume," *Archiv fuer Geschichte der Philosophie* (1960); James Noxon, "Hume's Agnosticism," *The Philosophical Review* 78 (1964): p. 251; and Yandell, "Hume on Religious Belief," pp. 117–20.
22. J. C. A. Gaskin, "Hume's Critique of Religion," *Journal of the History of Philosophy* 14 (1976), p. 303 and "God, Hume, and Natural Belief," *Philosophy* (1974).
23. See also Bricke, "On the Interpretation," p. 12.
24. There is a similar philosophic observation in "The Sceptic," in which the philosophical observation is confuted by natural desires that exist in the here and now (see E 173–5). The most compelling Christian reply to the problem posed by Cleanthes is found in Augustine, *City of God*, I.8.
25. Mossner, "Hume and the Legacy of the *Dialogues,*" in Morice, *David Hume: Bicentenary Papers* (Austin: Univeristy of Texas Press, 1977), p. 6, estimates that Philo's speeches occupy two-thirds of the text.
26. There is a long history of scholarship noting the tentativeness, ambiguity, and implausibility of Philo's confession and I align myself with this conclusion. See Graham Priest, "Hume's Final Argument." *History*

of *Philosophy Quarterly* 2 (1985), pp. 349–52; and Sessions, *Reading Hume's Dialogues*, pp. 188–205.
27. J. C. A. Gaskin, "Hume's Critique of Religion" in *David Hume: Critical Assessments*, Edited by Stanley Tweyman (London; New York: Routledge, 1995), p. 63, comments reflect my view: "Belief in god in the sense of the term which Philo allows at the end of the *Dialogues* would carry no duty, invite no action, allow no inference, and involve no devotion." See also William H. Austin, "Philo's Reversal." *Philosophical Topics* 13 (1985), pp. 106–7.
28. Cf. Danford, *David Hume and the Problem of Reason*, p. 184, who underplays or denies Cleanthes' role in provoking Demea.
29. Noxon, "Hume's Agnosticism," pp. 258–9.
30. See also Penelhum, *Hume*, p. 169, "If, therefore, it could be shown that religious beliefs can not be supported by arguments which are simple extensions of mental habits which are based on inescapable elements in human nature, it would follow that human nature without religion is a real possibility."
31. "What those principles are, which give rise to the original belief, and what those accidents and causes are, which direct its operations, is the subject of our present enquiry" (NHR 21).
32. Cf. Pascal, *Pensees*, # 139: "Thus life flows away. Men look for repose through combat against certain obstacles; but when these have been overcome, rest becomes insufferable because of the tedium it engenders. They must escape from this and beg for excitement. No condition is happy without noise and amusement, but every condition is so when one enjoys some kind of distraction" with E 270.
33. Rene Descartes, *Selected Philosophical Writings* (Cambridge: Cambridge University Press, 1988), p. 47 (Part 6): "I am sure there is no one, even among its practitioners, who would not admit that all we know in medicine is almost nothing in comparison with what remains to be known, and that we might free ourselves from innumerable diseases, both of the body and of the mind, and perhaps even from the infirmity of old age, if we had sufficient knowledge of their causes and of all the remedies that nature has provided."
34. Hume may see his own death as a heroic forerunner to the way death will be thought of as the ethic of humanity spreads, see "My Own Life" (E xl–xli) and Adam Smith's letter to William Strahan (9 November 1776) about it (E xliii–xlix).
35. Hume uses a similar phrase only when he describes the Roman constitution as the product of "an extraordinary concurrence of circumstances" (E 259), although they were not an a-religious people. When viewed against the canvas of human history, it is the humane revolution that appears "romantic and incredible" (EPM 256). England's "most perfect and accurate system of liberty that was ever found compatible

with government" developed because an incredible confluence of chance events (H II.525), and it was clearly a rather extraordinary occurrence. Consider also E 94, 259, 416 for indications that the humane revolution in politics is historically extraordinary.

36. Especially EPM 270, where Hume writes that Christian virtues "serve no manner of purpose."

10 Toward a More Philosophical Philosophy of Common Life

1. Leo Strauss, *"What Is Political Philosophy?"* (Chicago: University of Chicago Press, 1988), p. 23.

INDEX

Aristotle
  middle class polity, 115, 117–19, 231n35
  relation to common sense, 14–18, 37, 45, 76, 205, 222n10
  substance and form, 14–18

Berkeley, George
  Christian apologetics, 158–62
  "fundamental principle" of modern philosophy, 33–5, 159–60
  Hume's critique of, 162
  miracles, 160–2

Descartes, Rene
  death, 195
  modern metaphysics, 2–3, 19, 23, 30, 173

Hobbes, Thomas
  modern metaphysics, 20–1, 23, 46, 169, 176
  state of nature, 108, 172

Hume, David
  abstract, speculative principles, 75–9, 135–6
  active sovereignty, 30–1, 75–95, 163–4
  causation, 38–9, 40
  commerce and humanity, 192–7
  common life (also common sense), 56–8, 155–8, 175–6
  common life philosophy, problems in, 125, 127–8, 135–7, 150–3, 156–7, 171–2, 192–7, 201–6

  critique of ancient metaphysics, 13, 31–2
  critique of modern metaphysics, 13, 32
  critique of selfish system of morals, 44–9
  critique of social contract theory, 87–91
  Dialogues concerning Natural Religion, 173, 182–92
  enthusiasm, 142–3, 144–5
  history and nature, 58, 60–3, 64, 68–9, 123–53
  human nature, 53–6, 123–7
  imagination as complex faculty, 41–4, 51
  judgment (also standard of taste), 51–3, 60–3, 63–71, 126, 157
  miracles, 164, 165–9, 177
  mixed blessings, 73–4, 147–50, 199–200
  mixed kind of life, 71–4, 127, 136, 200
  natural assumptions, 39–41, 71, 126, 150–3, 163, 165
  natural mechanism of progress, 130–3, 135
  natural theology, 164–5, 171, 179–80, 184–6
  nature, 59–63
  paradoxes in, 41–4, 51–2, 53–6, 71–4
  personal identity, 35–8, 41, 163–4
  primary and secondary qualities, 31–5, 39–40

Hume, David—*Continued*
  psychology of religion, 167–71,
    178–82, 186–92
  standard of taste (*see* judgment)
  superstition, 129–30, 133–5

Locke, John on
  aspiration for orthodoxy, 81, 86,
    94, 221n8
  critique of ancient metaphysics,
    13–14, 19–20, 22
  inconsistent reliance on natural
    assumptions, 24–7, 41, 213n15
  primary and secondary qualities,
    20–4, 33
  social contract theory, 9–10, 78, 86,
    87–91

Machiavelli, Niccolo
  Hume's critique of (and adherence
    to), 148–9, 194

Montesquieu, Charles-Louis de
    Secondat
  modern commerce, compared to
    ancient mores, 101–3, 112,
    114, 148

Nietzsche, Friedrich, 28, 98, 114,
    173, 202

Pascal, Blaise
  psychology of religion, compared
    to Hume's, 159, 171–2, 182,
    202–3
  spirit of finesse, 1–3

Tocqueville, Alexis de
  aristocracy and democracy distinction
    compared to Hume, 100, 127–8,
    137, 142, 145, 153, 201
  psychology of religion, compared
    to Hume's, 171–2